IMAGES
of America

NEW HARMONY
INDIANA

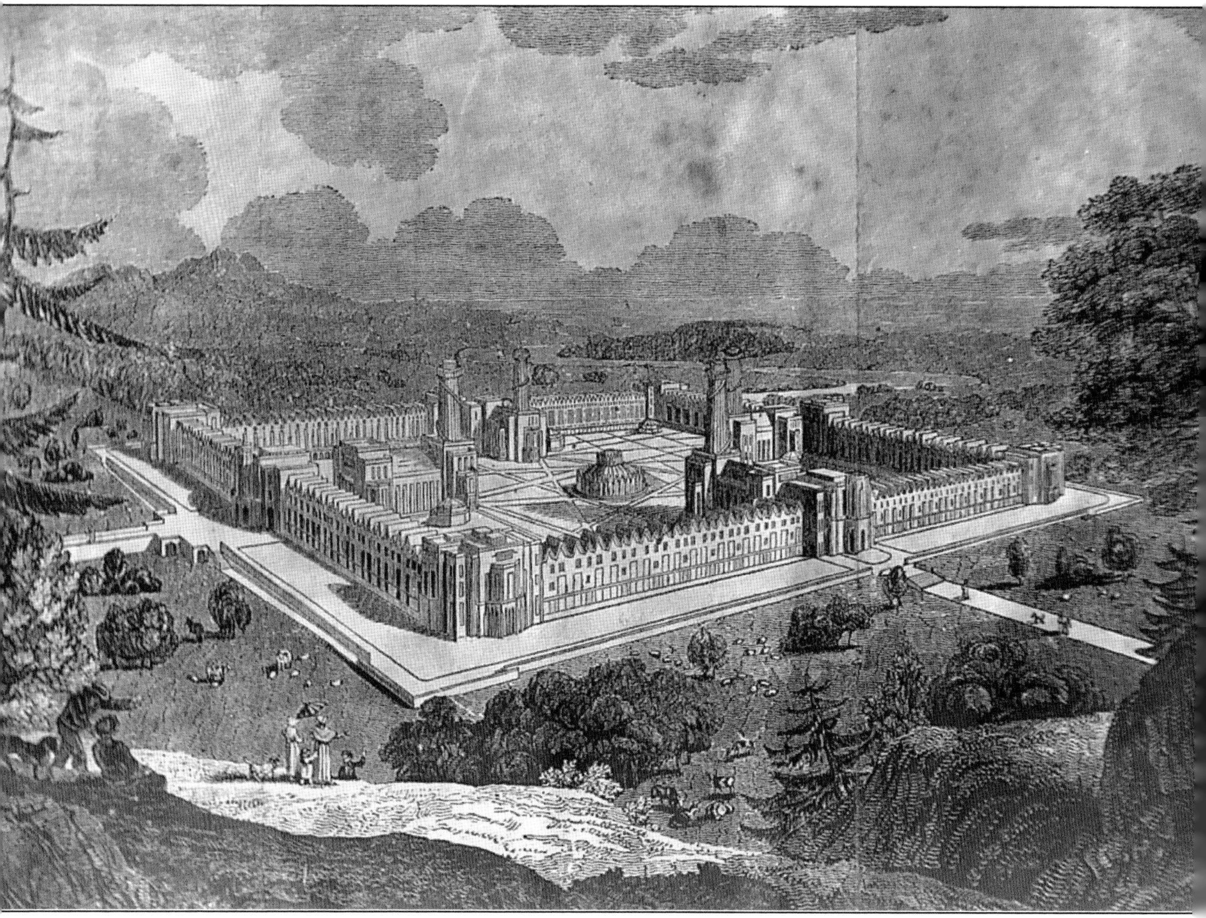

Robert Owen, founder of the second utopian experiment in New Harmony, proposed building a new, self-contained "village for mutual cooperation" south of town. He toured the eastern United States with a drawing and a model of the plan, hoping to attract support for his ideas. Each generation of New Harmony citizens has dreamed of and planned for a better future. (Photograph from the collection of Historic New Harmony.)

IMAGES
of America

NEW HARMONY
INDIANA

Connie A. Weinzapfel, Darrel E. Bigham, and Susan R. Branigin

ARCADIA
PUBLISHING

ISBN 978-0-7385-0344-8

Published by Arcadia Publishing
Charleston, South Carolina

Printed in the United States of America

Library of Congress Catalog Card Number: 2007923203

For all general information contact Arcadia Publishing at:
Telephone 843-853-2070
Fax 843-853-0044
E-mail sales@arcadiapublishing.com
For customer service and orders:
Toll-Free 1-888-313-2665

Visit us on the Internet at www.arcadiapublishing.com

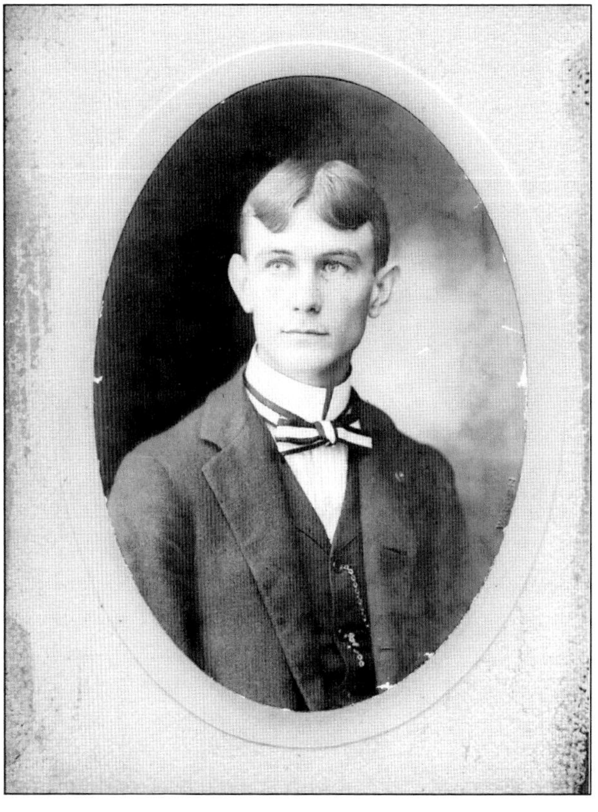

Seen here is an 1890 portrait of Homer Fauntleroy from the collection of New Harmony State Historic Site.

Contents

ACKNOWLEDGMENTS

In the card catalogue of New Harmony's Workingmen's Institute, under the category of photographers, 16 names from the town and environs are mentioned. The earliest dated name is "Thomas Cox, 1850," and at the end of the list are W.F. Lichtenberger and Homer Fauntleroy. This book is a compilation of photographs taken by these two men who documented the late 19th and early 20th centuries in this remarkable town. Represented here is a time of transition in New Harmony. Strong civic leadership is evident, as the town overcomes flood and fire and takes on major public works in preparation for the centennial of 1914.

William Frederick Lichtenberger (1849–1924) was a businessman in New Harmony, where he first owned a furniture store, then succeeded his brother Clarence in the family's dry goods business. He was also known as a fine artist, painting in oil and watercolor, and working with photography. He exhibited his works at the New Harmony Workingmen's Institute, of which he was a life-long member. So honored was he that that venerable institution closed on the day of his funeral, Saturday, June 21, 1924, from 9 a.m. to 1 p.m., in his memory.

Homer Fauntleroy (1866–1952) was descended of a very early New Harmony family. He was manager of the local Cumberland Telephone Company but resigned on August 1, 1909, to pursue his first love, photography. A 1935 *New Harmony Times* story describes how Homer salvaged old photographs and glass negatives from the demolition of the Nash Building in New Harmony, which formerly had been a photography studio. He maintained a portfolio of over 300 prints that he would use to illustrate the history of the town. He was an early preservationist, along with his sister, Mary Emily. He documented much of the town from 1896 until his death, focusing not only on the original Harmonist structures, but also on Victorian homes, the downtown business district, and municipal buildings. Fauntleroy captured daily life and special events, both familial and public.

The entire collection of glass negatives was assembled by New Harmony amateur historian, Donald Blair (1909–1992) and given to the University of Southern Indiana in October 1985. Historic New Harmony wishes to thank Gina Walker of the University of Southern Indiana Special Collections/University Archives for assistance with this project. All images in this book, unless otherwise noted, are from the Blair Collection. We also wish to thank Sherry Graves and Nancy Manchette from the Workingmen's Institute for their research assistance.

This book is a companion to Historic New Harmony's special exhibits for the year 2000, *New Harmony at the Millennium: The Past and the Future on View*. It is the hope of this editor that the citizens of New Harmony will draw inspiration from these images, and begin today to consider their own role in the history of this place, as we approach New Harmony's bicentennial.

INTRODUCTION

Approaching its centennial in 1914, New Harmony was a small market town that shared many of the features of its counterparts in the lower Wabash and Ohio valleys. But New Harmony was not exactly like other places. Resources, location, economic patterns, leadership, culture, and fate made the fabric and texture of New Harmony different. It was also distinctive because of the features in its earliest years—buildings, town plan, names of streets, descendants of the utopians, and cultural inheritance. About 230 Harmonists, for instance, lay in repose in the cemetery at the western edge of the town. "No place in the country has a more interesting history," wrote W.P. Leonard, Posey County's first historian, in 1882. New Harmony, he insisted, was "probably more widely known than any other town of its size in the country . . . solely due to the relations which the Rappites and Owens bore towards it."

The town's origins were distinctive. Founded in 1814 by one set of German utopians who left ten years later, it was the site of a second community, established in 1824 by the British industrialist and utopian, Robert Owen. Owen attracted a number of intellectuals whose legacies extended far beyond his short-lived experiment. His children also played an important part in the town's development and in regional and national history.

According to the federal census of 1910, New Harmony was the second largest town in Posey County, with 1,229 residents. Most were natives of Indiana. Of those not born in the state, most were from Illinois or Kentucky. Only 30 were foreign-born. Slightly less than one in eight had one or two foreign-born parents. None was African-American. The town was demographically and culturally homogeneous.

According to the 1913 history of Posey County, written by John C. Leffel, the town had two banks, a flour mill, three grain elevators, and "extensive mercantile establishments representing every branch of trade." There were two weekly newspapers, the *Times* and the *Register*, both Democratic. A spur of the Illinois Central connected it by rail at Stewartsville to Evansville on the south and on the north to Chicago. Roads were unpaved, and only a handful of residents owned automobiles or trucks. The town operated an electric light plant.

Census records reveal a town dependent on agriculture and simple manufacturing, and yet also a town with great occupational diversity. Half of the residents listed an occupation. By far the most frequently registered was laborer (95). About one quarter were unskilled laborers. There were 65 dealers, merchants, and proprietors. New Harmony had six physicians, a dentist, three clergymen, two librarians, two veterinarians, two attorneys, and four actors. Some occupations reflected recent technological or organizational innovations, such as workers at the "theatorium," electricians, and clerical and sales positions. One of the town's proprietors ran an automobile garage. One of the most prosperous residents was an Irish immigrant, Frank Lawless, who operated a plumbing, heating, and sheet metal business. He was in his fourth term as town board president.

Posey County was one of Indiana's leading agricultural counties. Although one in seven in the town worked directly in agriculture, about six in ten were employed in occupations other than farming and manufacturing, and of these, commerce was dominant. A close second was domestic servants, all female. Most worked in their homes as seamstresses or washwomen. Women represented one quarter of all workers. The rising number of female workers (many of them married) and the expansion of clerical and sales positions—which represented the highest proportion of the 1910 work force—clearly indicated the effects of modernization on the town.

In many respects social relations in New Harmony resembled those in other small towns. The people of New Harmony lived almost exclusively in small single-family dwellings. The census of 1910 identified 343 homes—and only 347 families. Only about one in three rented their homes, and among homeowners a whopping 81% owned their homes free and clear. All but 55 families were nuclear—husband, wife, and children. About three in four had male heads of family, and the average family had about 3.5 members. All of this was in stark contrast to urban family life in 1910.

New Harmony had four churches. The oldest was St. Stephen's Episcopal (1842), but the largest congregation was the Methodist Episcopal. The newest were Roman Catholic and German Evangelical. The town also had a number of fraternal and benevolent societies with the oldest, the Odd Fellows, formed in 1851. The Posey County Agricultural Society had hosted annual county fairs just east of the town since 1859.

Given the paucity of automobiles, the poor condition of roads, and the absence of a bridge over the Wabash, most residents of New Harmony spent little time outside of their community, except if they had business at the county seat, 15 miles to the south. They might also take a steamboat excursion down the Wabash or the train to Evansville.

New Harmony had had public schools since the 1850s, but the concept of public education came to New Harmony with Robert Owen and partner William Maclure. On the eve of its centennial, New Harmony erected a two-story school building that incorporated the doorway from the Harmonist church. It had a state-commissioned high school. Recently passed state laws regarding uniformity of term and curriculum clearly shaped schooling in the town, as did requirements that students remain in school to age 14. According to the 1910 census, the town had 17 teachers, typically single women in their twenties, and a male school principal. Horace Pestalozzi Owen, president of the New Harmony Banking Company and the only male descendant of the Owen family living in New Harmony, had been president of the school board for 25 years.

Schooling contributed to a high literacy rate, as did the two weekly newspapers. Only 25 residents could not read or write. Especially vital was the Workingmen's Institute, the only surviving library of the 160 supported under the will of William Maclure and a visible link to the Owen community. Horace Owen was its president. Nora Fretageot, widow of a descendant of the Owenite era, was librarian. Due to the generosity of longtime resident and self-made man Dr. Edward Murphy and his wife, between 1890 and 1910, the Institute secured a new building and an endowment. In addition to manuscripts and nearly 17,500 books, it had an art and science museum and a lecture series. In 1913, three years after Murphy's death, the Institute purchased the lot adjoining it to the east for a community auditorium.

The Workingmen's Institute was one reason New Harmony had a high quality of cultural life. The town was also home to Martin Golden and his theatrical family, and the 1910 census listed three actors in yet another family. The town had had a men's literary society since 1865, and had had a women's literary society—the Minerva Society—since 1859. It boasted a recently-opened "theatorium." Local "Corn King" Alfred Ribeyre, who owned 7,000 acres, also contributed to the enhancement of civic life. Annual Independence Day ceremonies, like the county fair, brought residents together in civic events that reinvigorated community spirit.

Like all small towns in Indiana, New Harmony's culture also was shaped by an intense partisanship in politics and a *laissez-faire* approach to government. The town, founded in 1814 and chartered in 1850, was reincorporated in 1881. Governed by town trustees, it had low taxes and few services. It did not have a public water or sewer system, but some of its streets were macadamized, with concrete curbs. It did have an electric plant and provided some fire protection for its citizens. There were two parks—Murphy and Maclure—the result of local philanthropy. There had been a post office since the town's establishment. The postmaster was Morris B. Pote, age 68 in 1910. Pote was a second-generation American who had marched with Sherman in Georgia and the Carolinas.

In three years, though, the federal government would influence New Harmony in many ways as the country became involved in a world war that began in the town's centennial year. The war signified larger factors that were shaping small towns in the early 20th century. New Harmony's population, for instance, had declined by almost 10% since 1900, and would fall another 10% by 1920. All rural communities near emerging metropolises—in this case, Evansville—faced a similar fate as jobs and the quality of life associated with urban areas beckoned. State and federal government decisions, whether about schools or rural roads, also shaped the town. And mass culture and consumerism, accelerated in the 1920s, would greatly affect life in small towns.

The economies of places like New Harmony were also being shaped by corporate and technological innovations, all external in nature. Large, highly-structured businesses were by 1914 the dominant force in the economy, and the economy was also being driven by advancements in electricity and the internal combustion engine. Rural life reflected this. Between 1900 and 1920, for instance, the number of Posey County farms dropped 10%, the average size of a farm grew by about the same proportion, and the percentage of farms operated by owners declined 25%. Not surprisingly, Posey County's population also fell.

But in 1914 there remained something about New Harmony that made it different—utopian in its origins, thoroughly American in its market capitalism and democratic values, and, as one-time state geologist and native son Edward T. Cox described it, "romantically situated in a rich, beautifully cultivated valley, surrounded by a semi-circular range of undulating hills."

Darrel E. Bigham
University of Southern Indiana

One

Agriculture and the Wabash

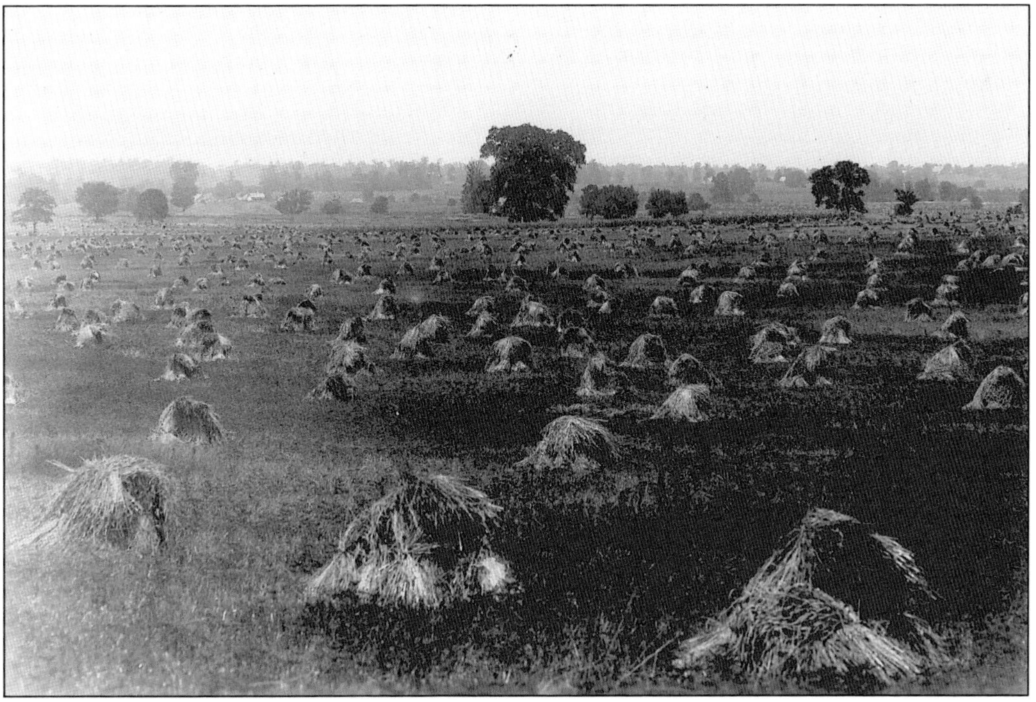

The abundance of natural resources—fertile soil, abundant stone, clay, and timber—on the banks of the Wabash River drew the Harmonists to the site where they built their town. This harvest scene highlights the reliable yearly bounty produced by the rich Posey County land. This 1895 field belonged to J.D. Owen. (Photographer: William Frederick Lichtenberger.)

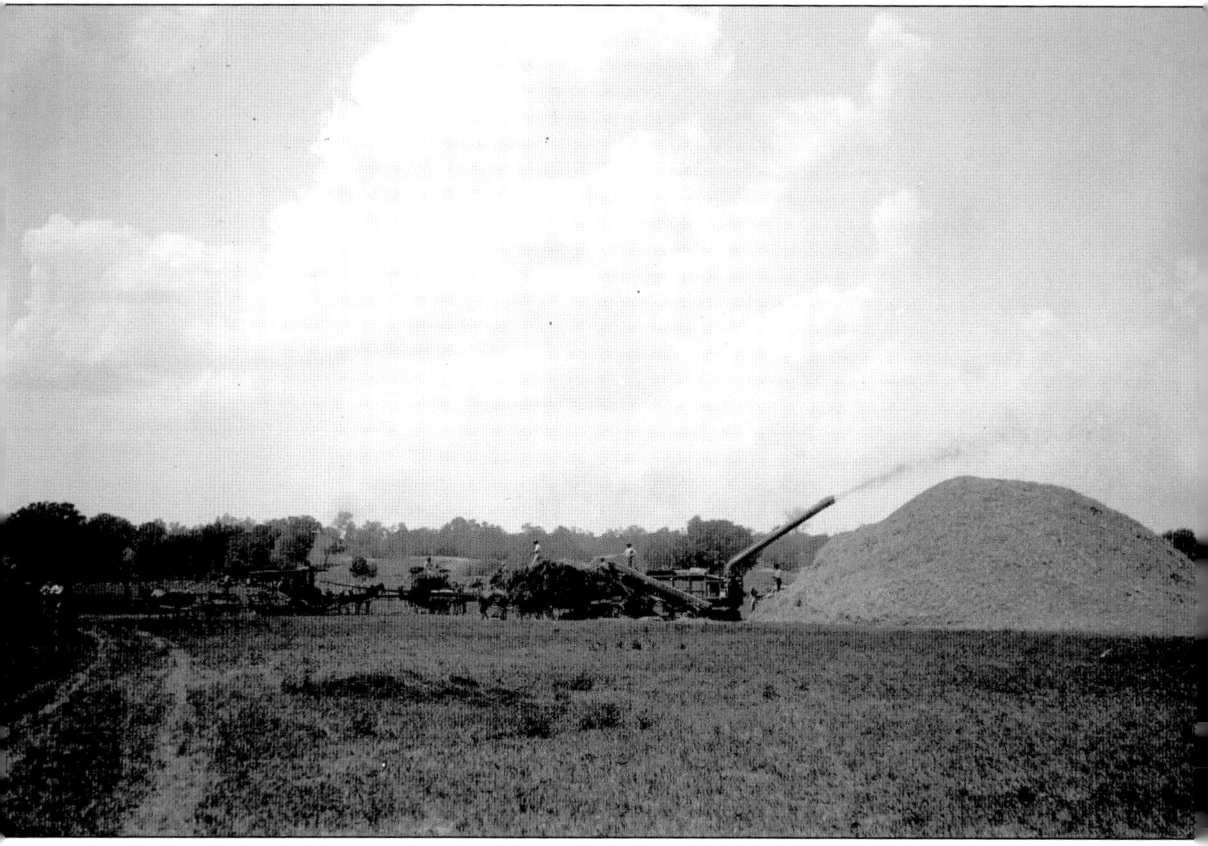

Using Elmer Kemmerling's machine, threshing takes place July 19, 1906, at the Burk Farm for Elmer E. Elliott. (Photographer: Homer Fauntleroy.)

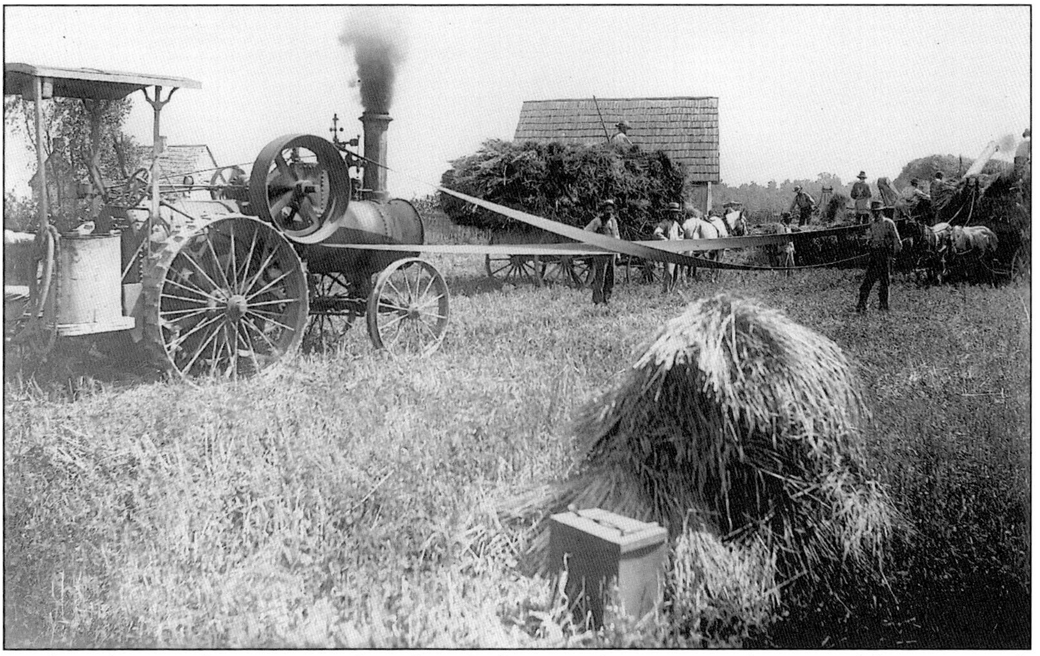

In this photograph, a group of unidentified men takes part in the annual harvest ritual. Mechanization greatly improved the lives of farm workers, seen here using a steam engine to thresh wheat. (Photographer: William Frederick Lichtenberger.)

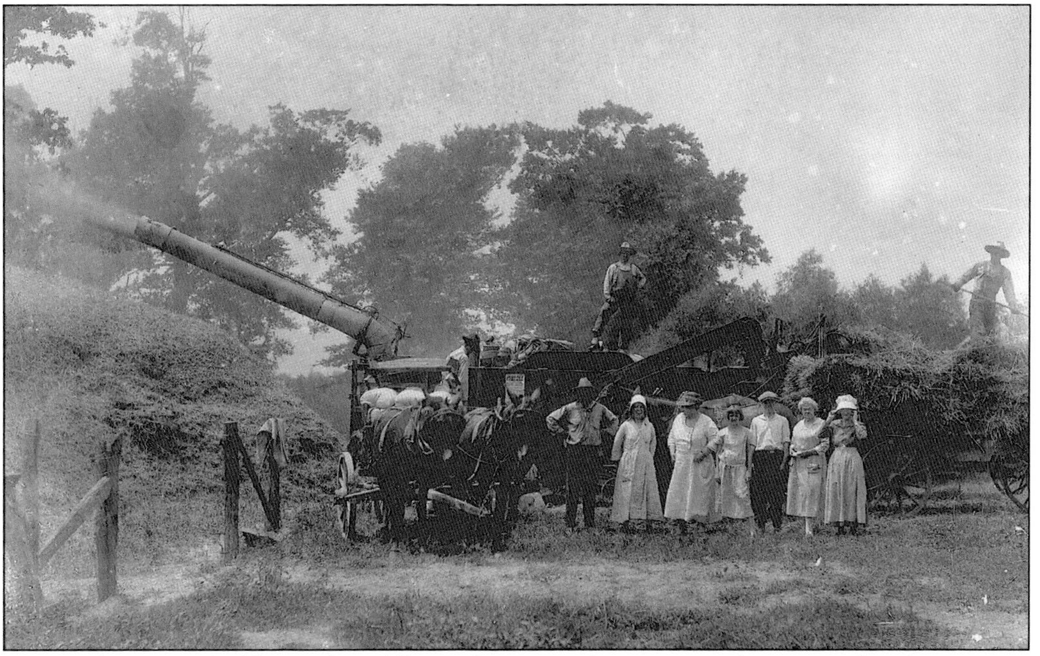

A mixed group of older and middle-aged men and women is shown in this farm scene. (Photographer: William Frederick Lichtenberger.)

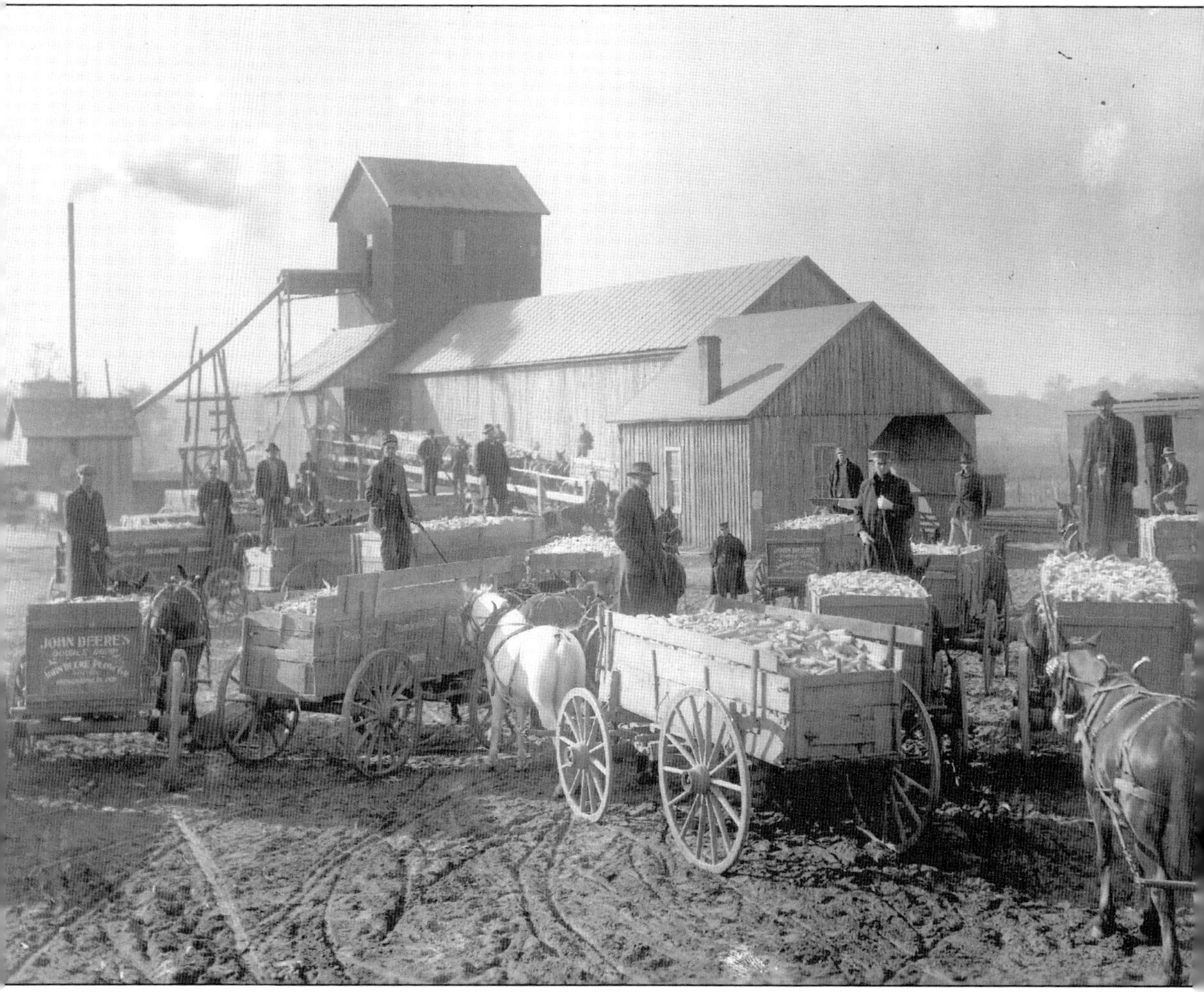

Horse-drawn wagons full of corn gather around the lot at the grain elevator near the New Harmony depot. Note that at least two of the wagons are painted with the following advertisement: "John Deere's Double Dump, John Deere Plow Co., Indianapolis, Ind." (Photographer: William Frederick Lichtenberger.)

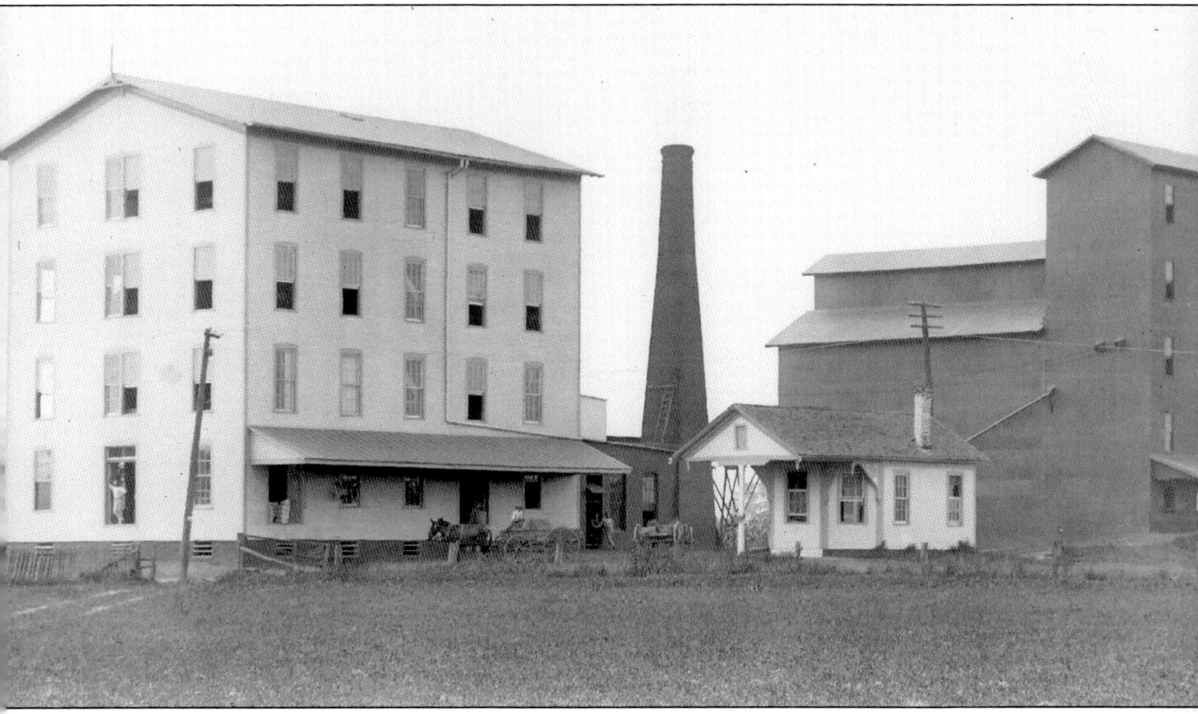

This July 19, 1906 photograph shows the Corbin Milling Company, on New Harmony's east side. (Photographer: Homer Fauntleroy.)

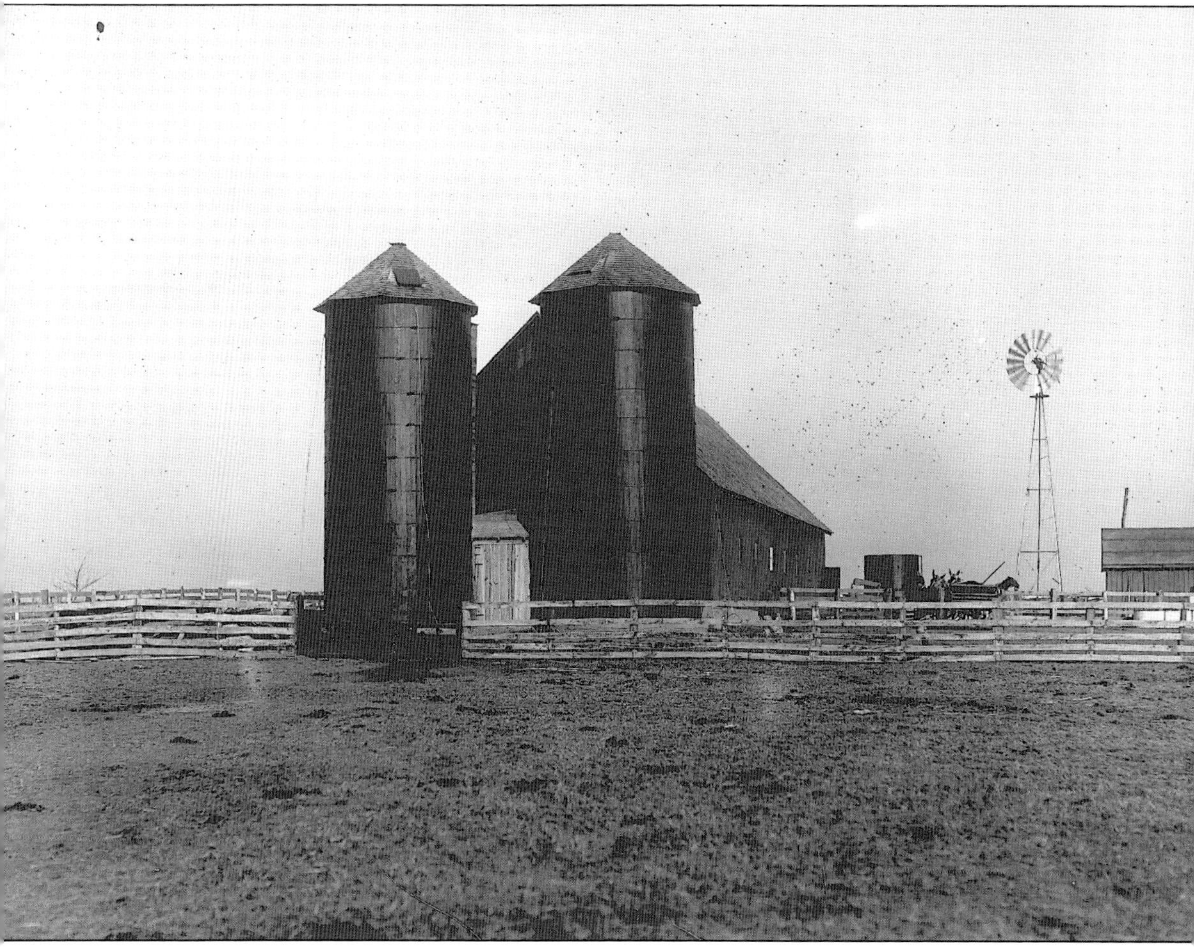

These silos were on the farm of E. Steaphen.

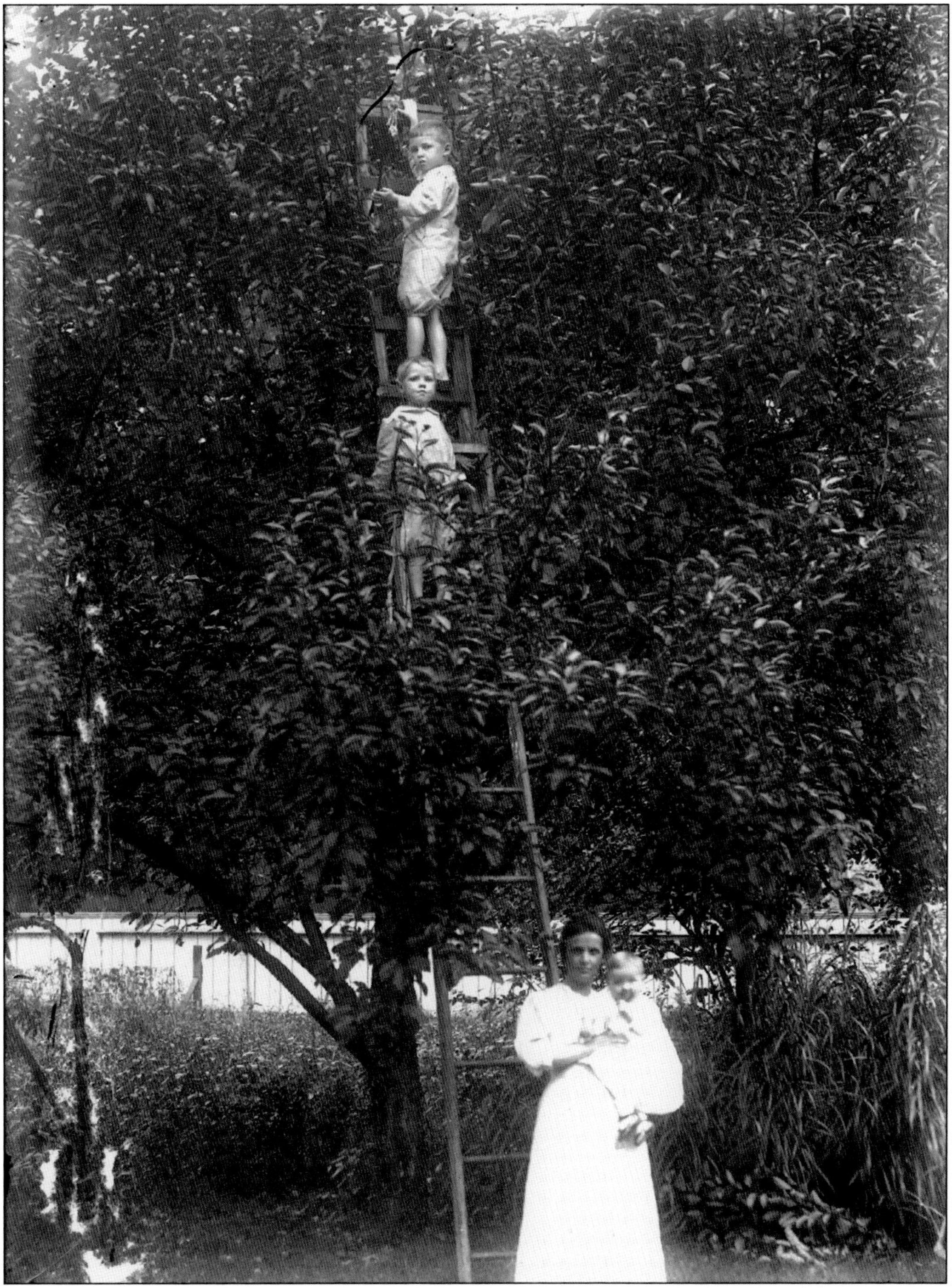

New Harmony resident Emma Freret and three youngsters pick cherries. (Photographer: Homer Fauntleroy.)

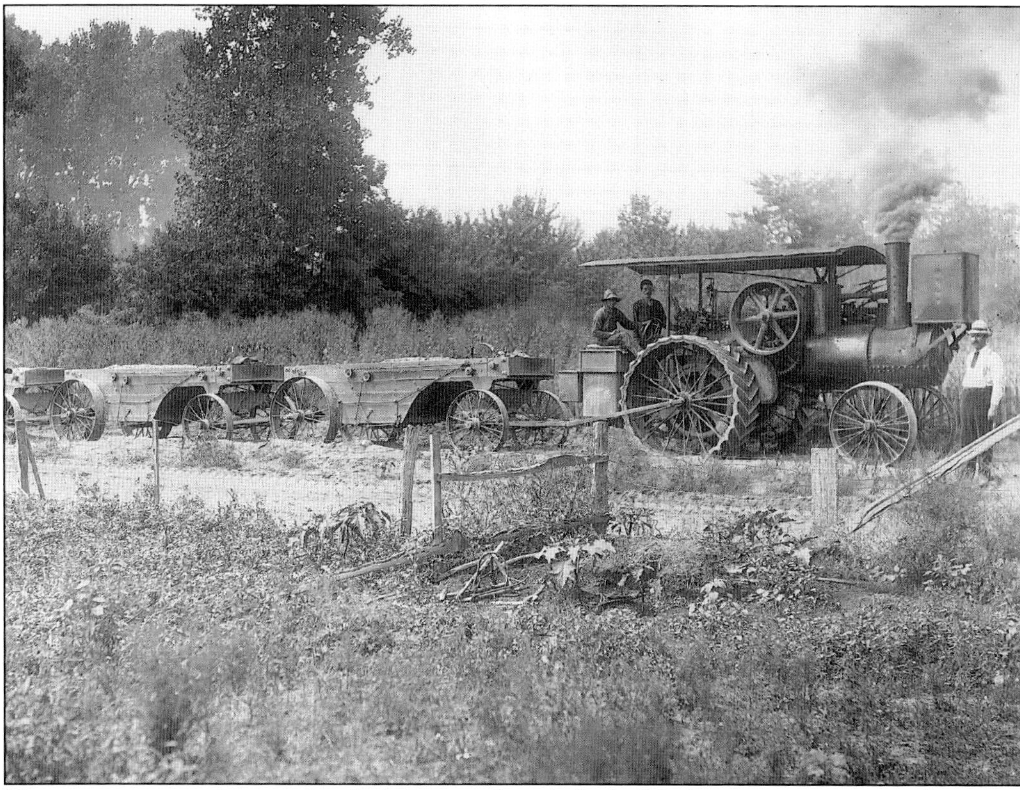

Here a steam traction engine is being used to help build the new country roads around New Harmony. Its three dump wagons are full of gravel. (Photographer: William Frederick Lichtenberger.)

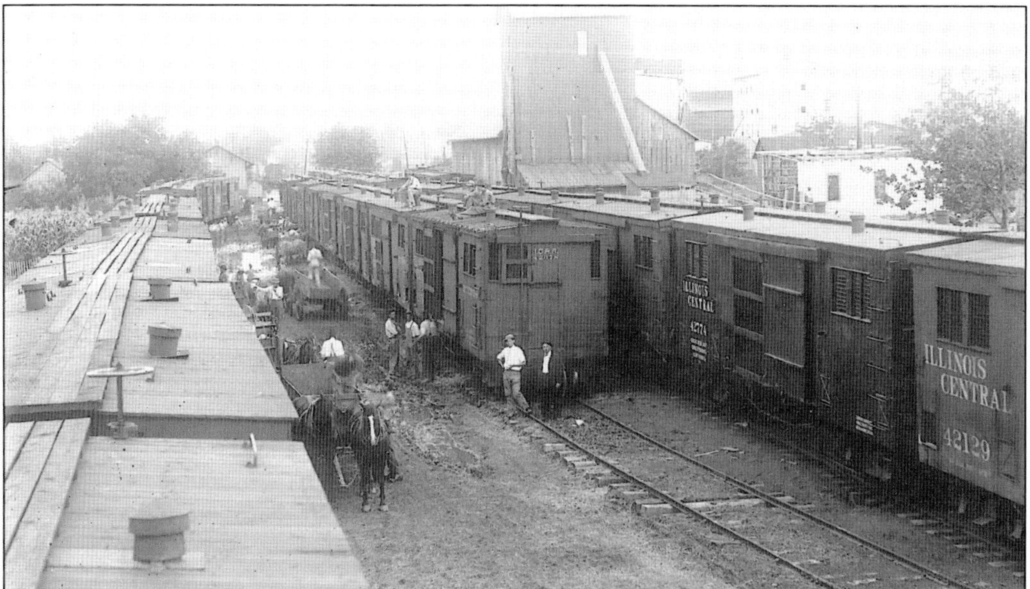

Shown here is one of the Illinois Central trains that passed through New Harmony. Note the depot building, upper left.

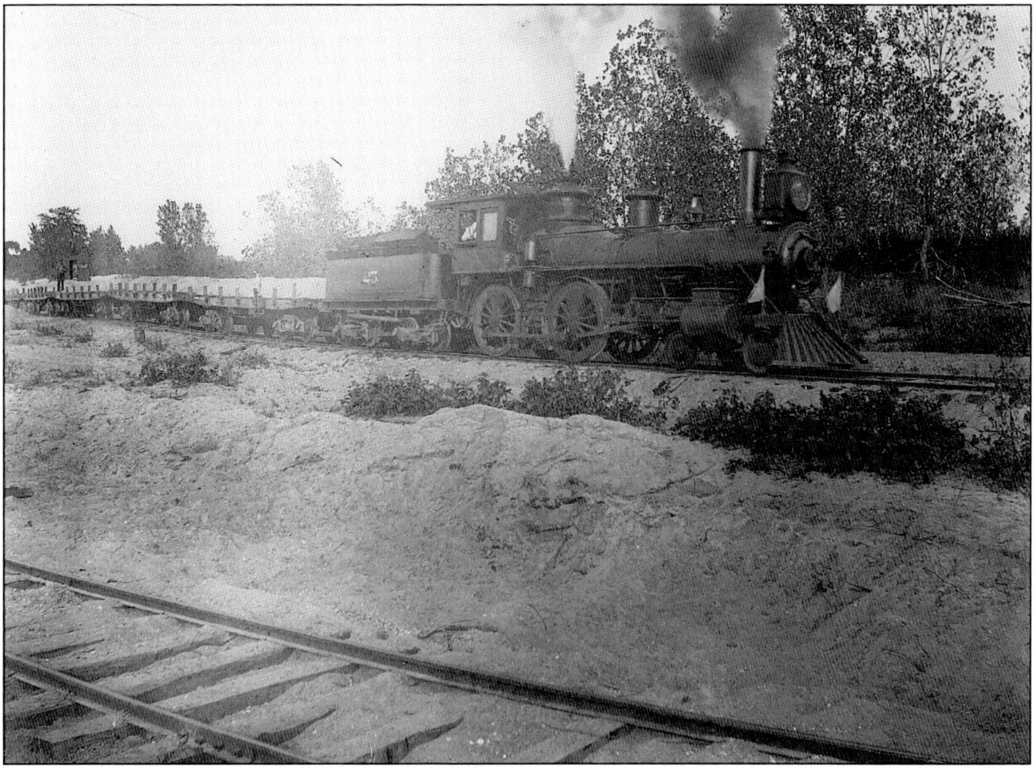

This train appears to be hauling gravel on its many cars. (Photographer: William Frederick Lichtenberger.)

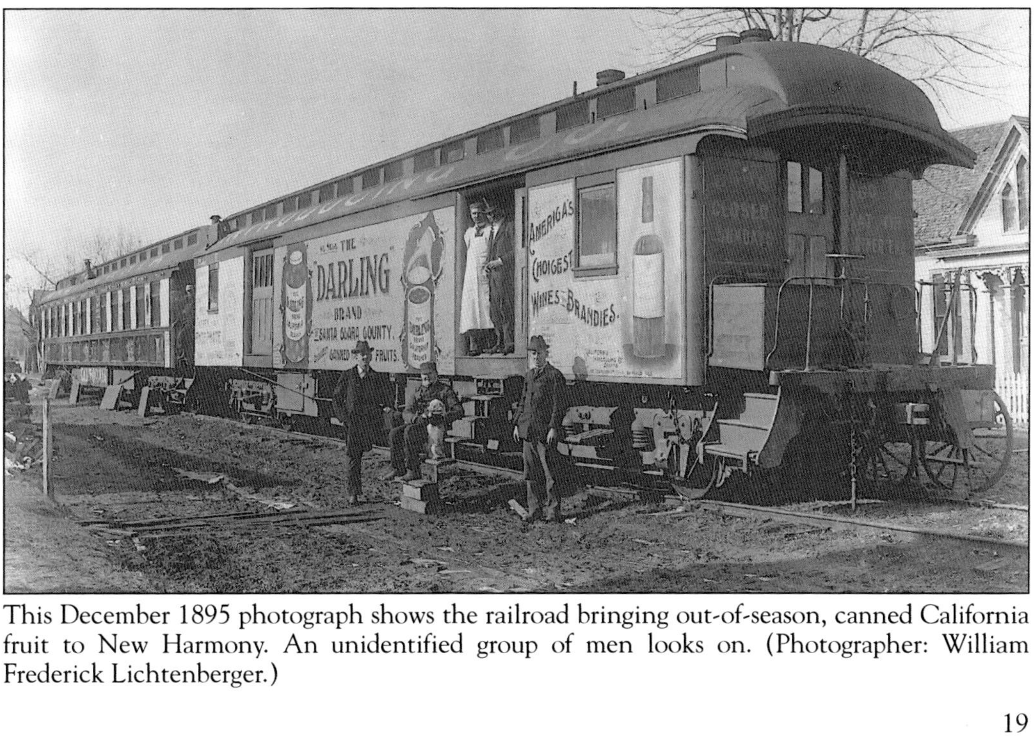

This December 1895 photograph shows the railroad bringing out-of-season, canned California fruit to New Harmony. An unidentified group of men looks on. (Photographer: William Frederick Lichtenberger.)

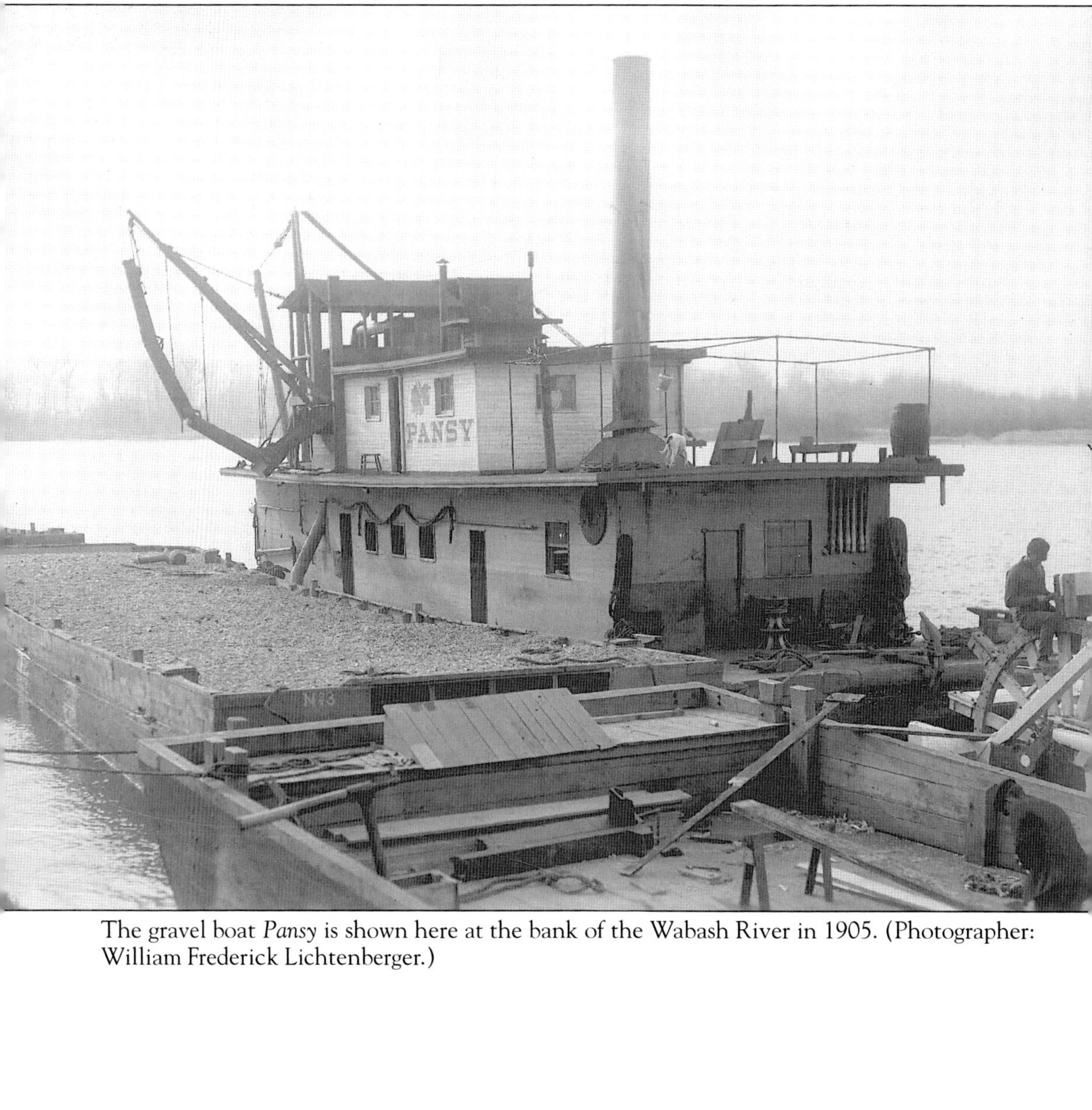

The gravel boat *Pansy* is shown here at the bank of the Wabash River in 1905. (Photographer: William Frederick Lichtenberger.)

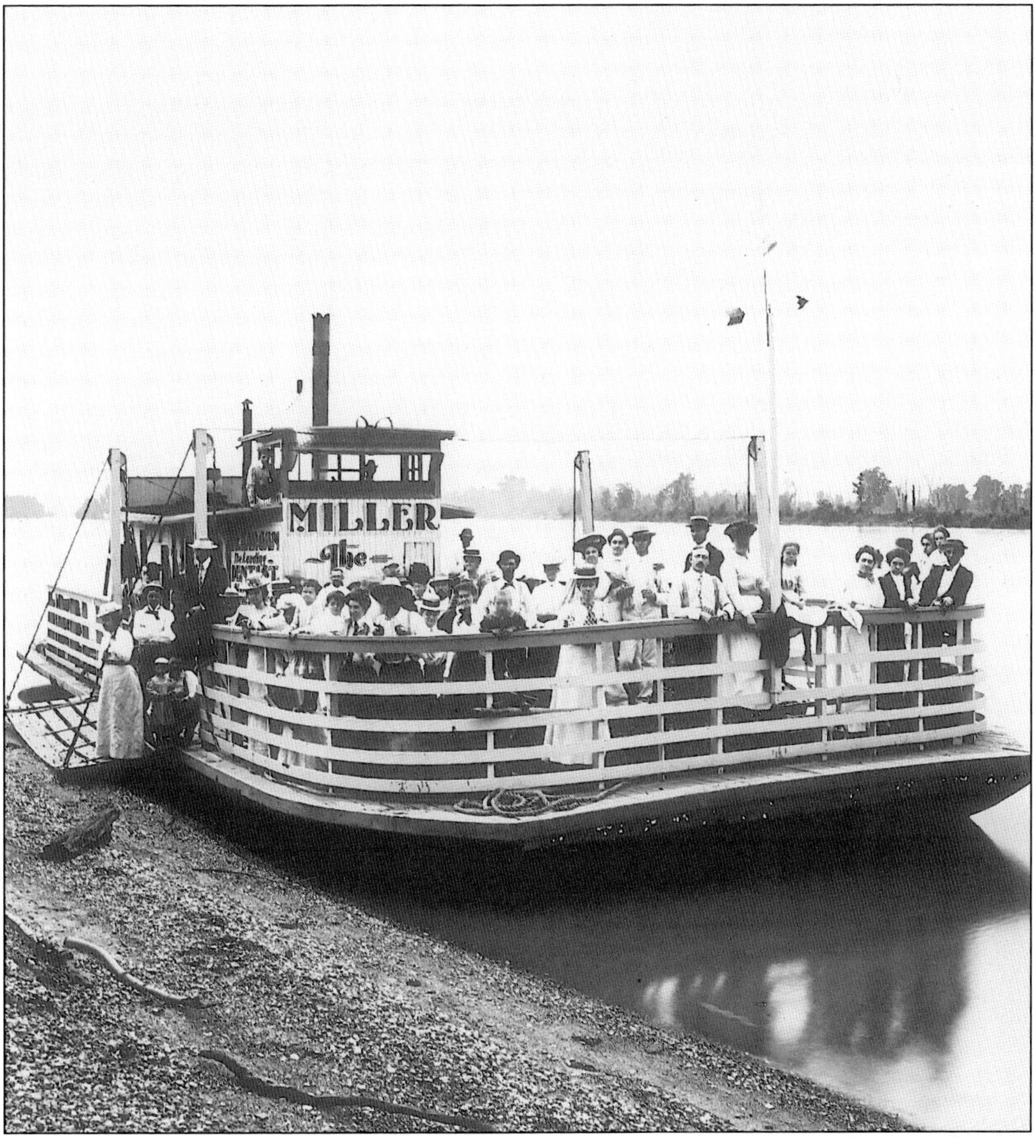

Here a group of passengers takes a ride on the Wabash River ferry boat, *Miller*, on July 4, 1900. Note the sign reading "The Leading Dentist." (Photographer: William Frederick Lichtenberger.)

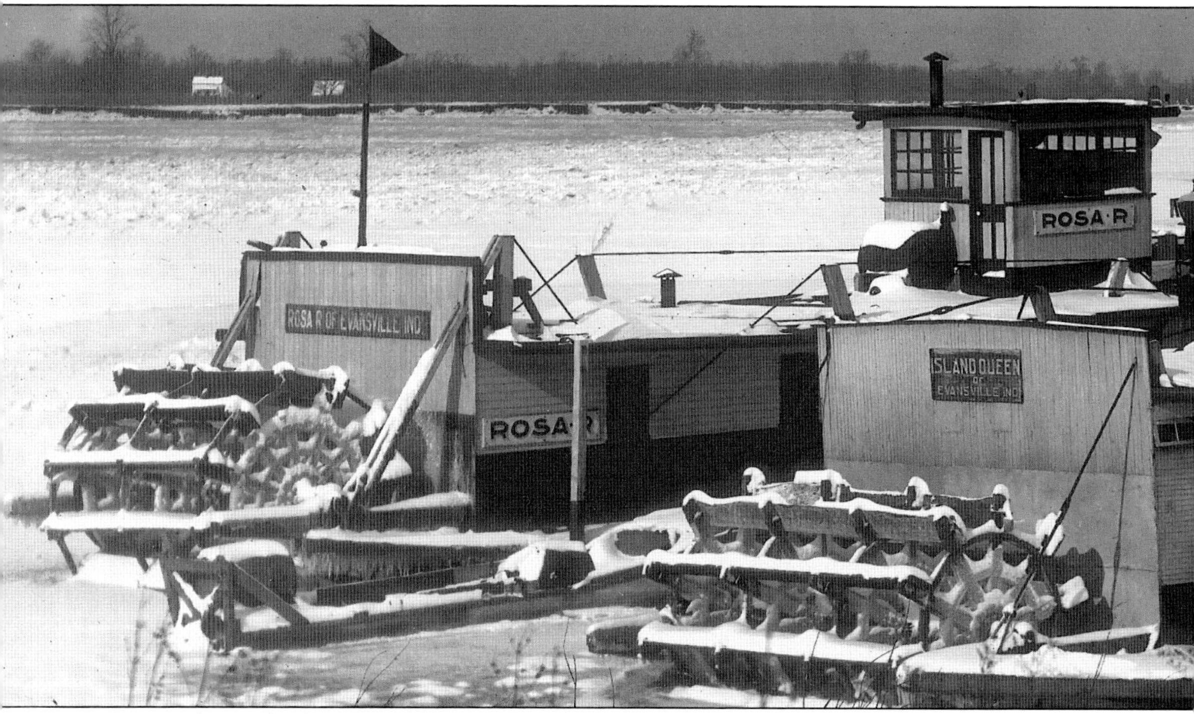

Ice on the Wabash River in January 1912 traps the *Rosa R.* of Evansville, the *Island Queen* of Evansville, and Wabash Survey Quarter Boat #3, of the U.S. Engineering Department of

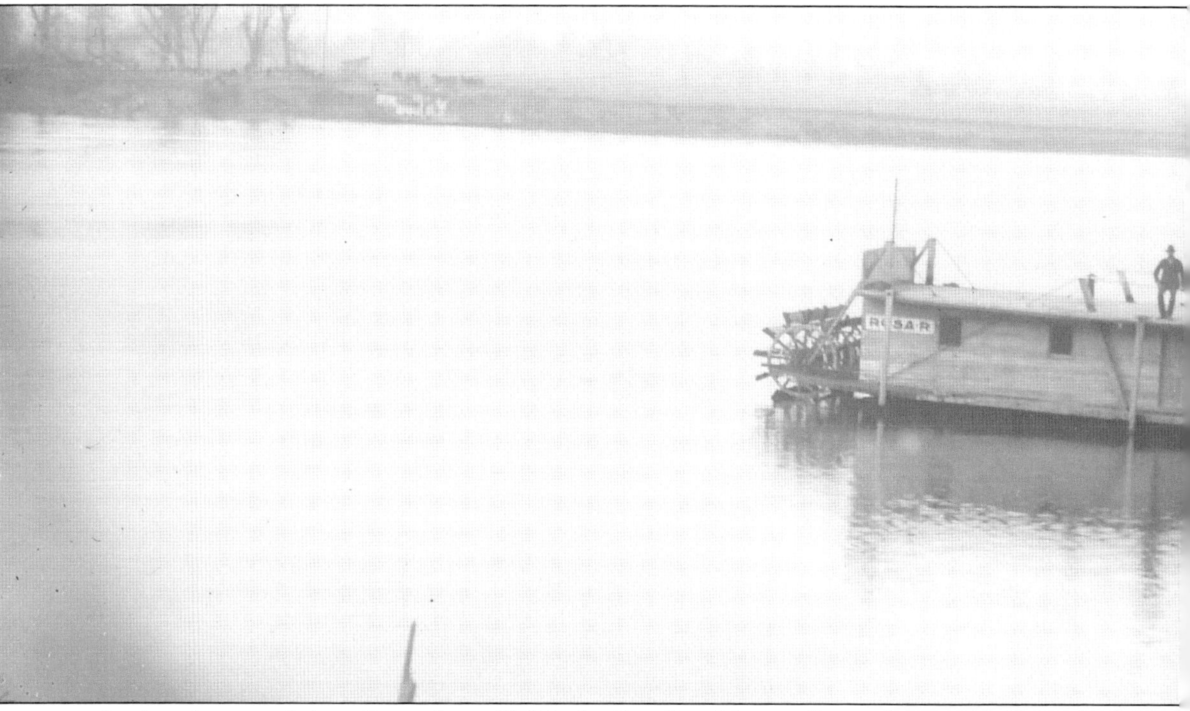

In this photograph from December of 1908, the *Rosa R.* of Evansville can be seen in the Wabash River, while the old hull of *The Laura* is being overhauled on the riverbank. (Photographer:

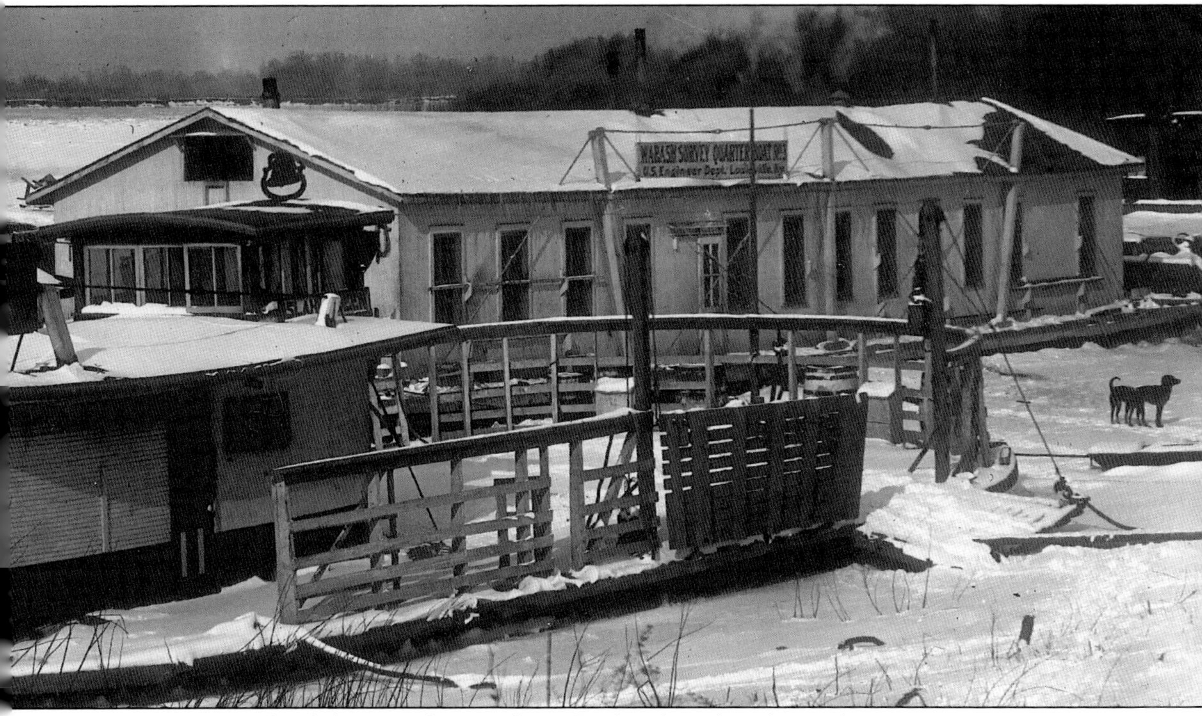

Louisville, Kentucky. (Photographer: William Frederick Lichtenberger.)

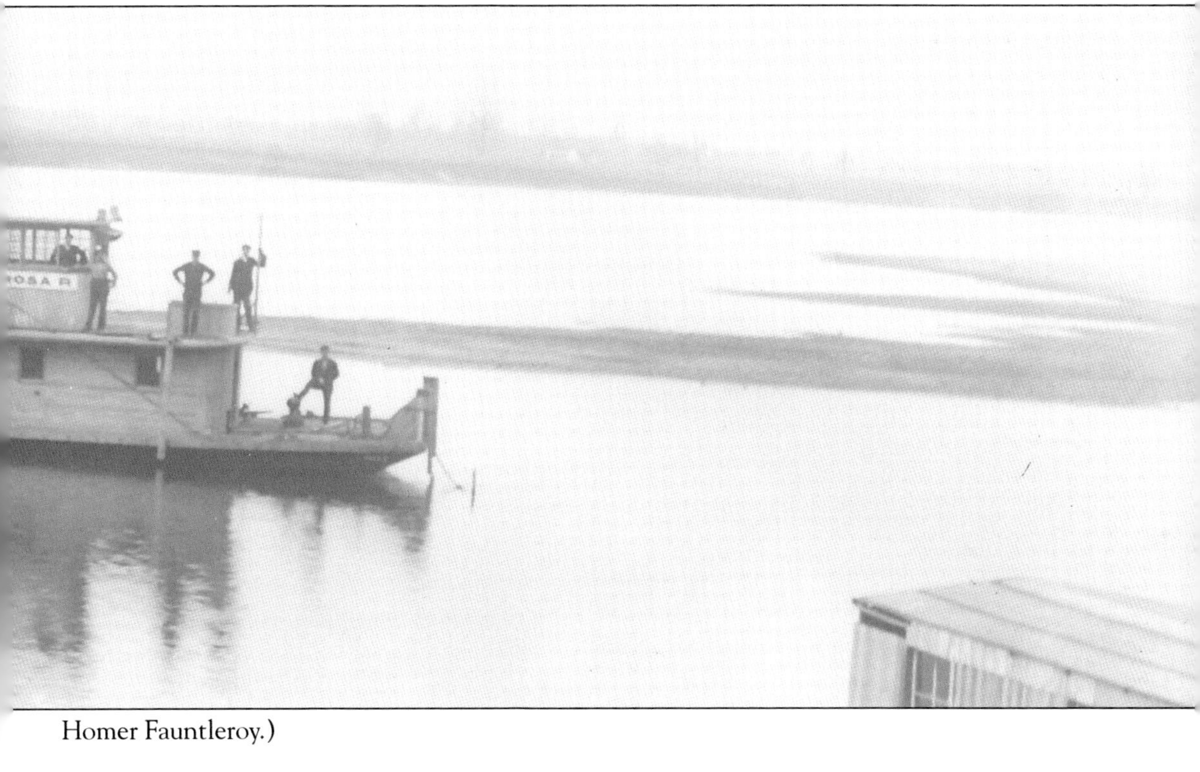

Homer Fauntleroy.)

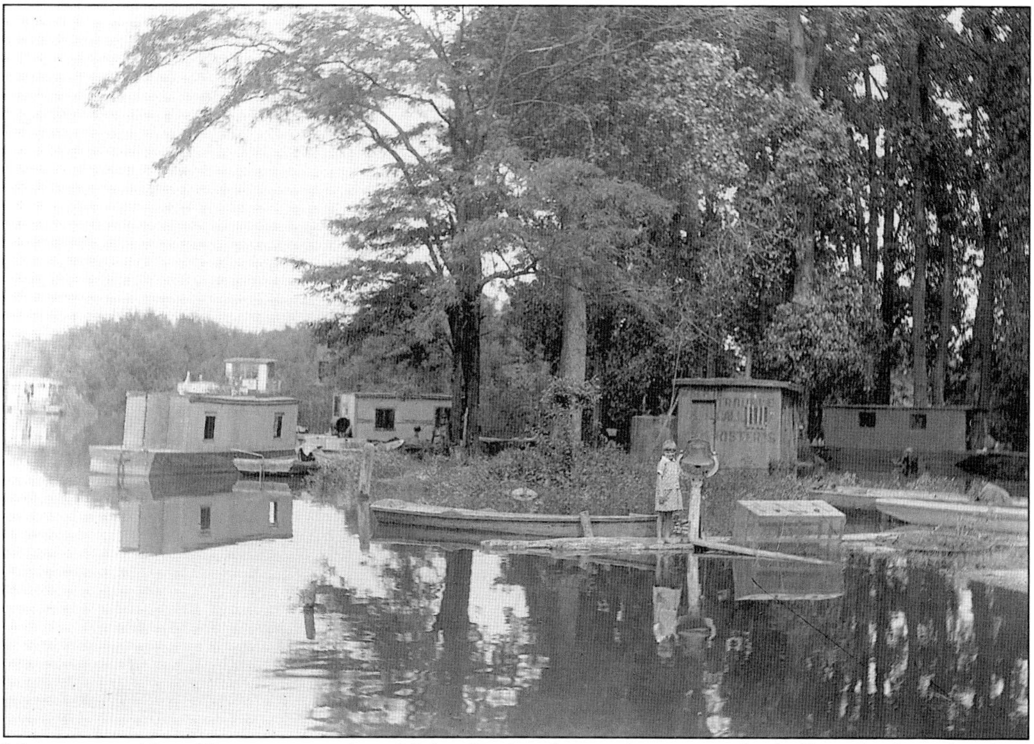

Here, young New Harmony resident Helen Richards stands next to the bell at the ferry landing during high water—15 feet, 6 inches—on the Wabash River in September, 1926. (Photographer: Homer Fauntleroy.)

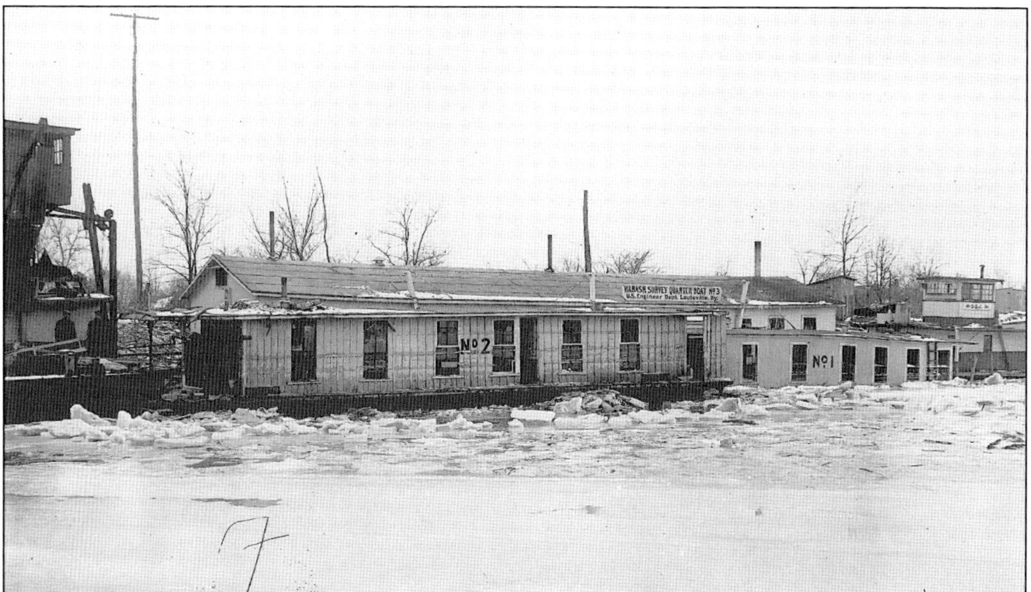

The Wabash River Survey Quarterboats #1, #2, and #3, as well as the *Rosa R.*, are locked in the river's icy grip. (Photographer: Homer Fauntleroy.)

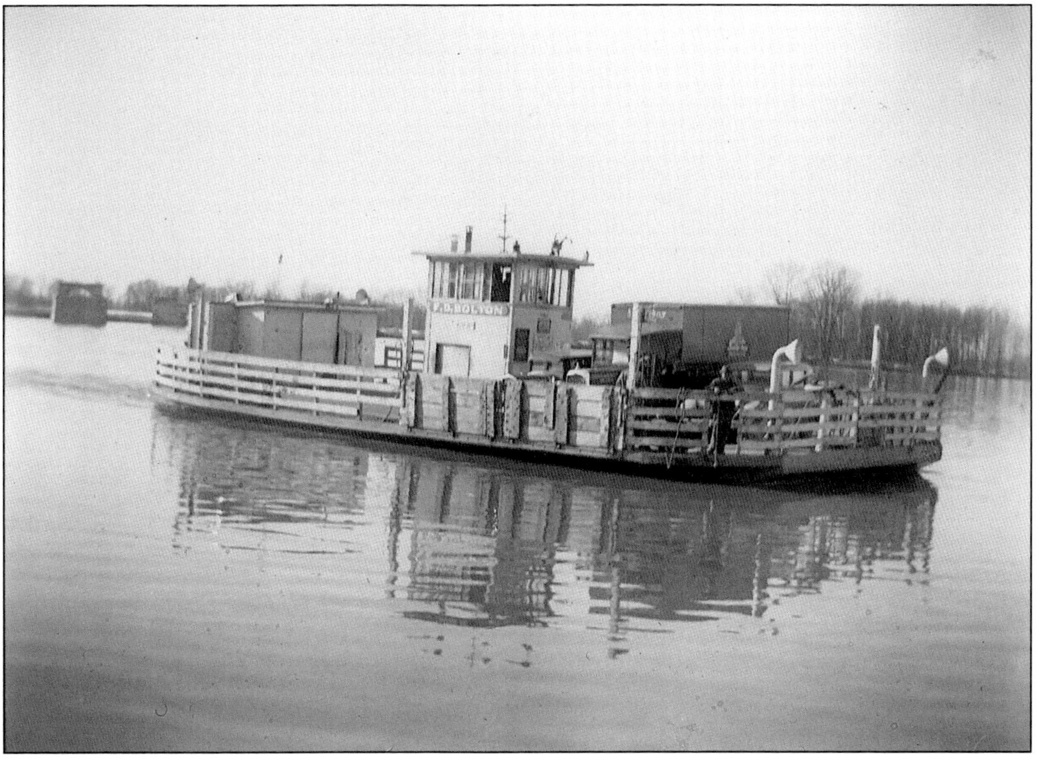

This photograph shows the New Harmony ferryboat, the *F.D. Bolton*.

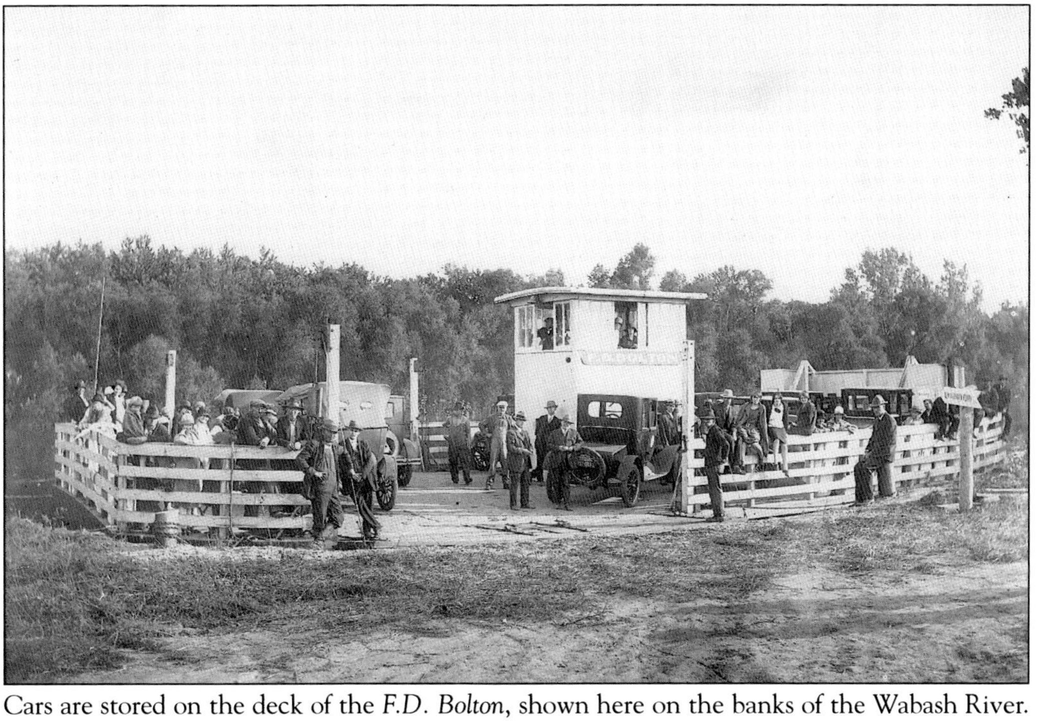

Cars are stored on the deck of the *F.D. Bolton*, shown here on the banks of the Wabash River. (Photographer: William Frederick Lichtenberger.)

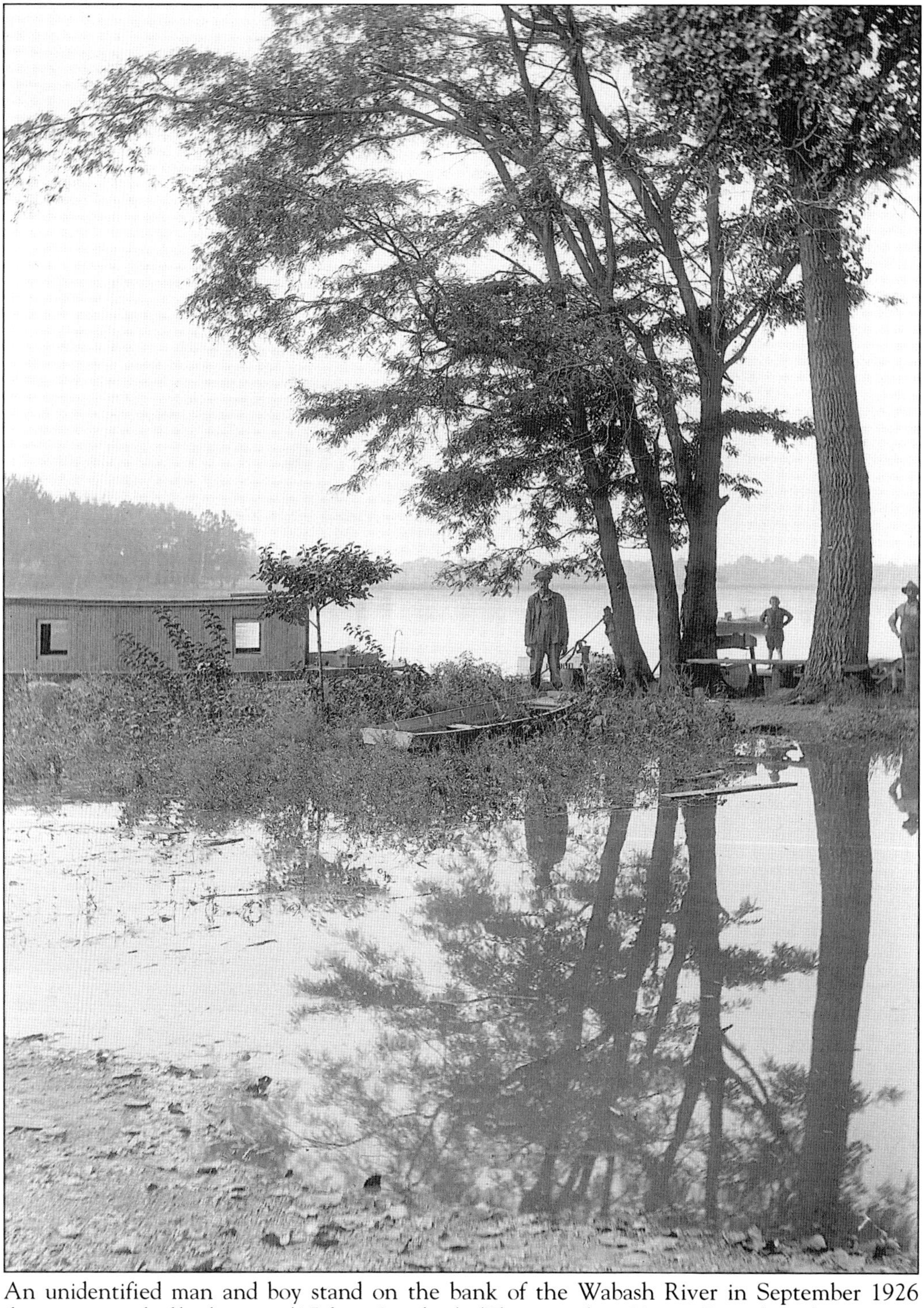

An unidentified man and boy stand on the bank of the Wabash River in September 1926 during a period of high water (15 feet, 6 inches). (Photographer: Homer Fauntleroy.)

Two

MERCANTILE AND DOWNTOWN

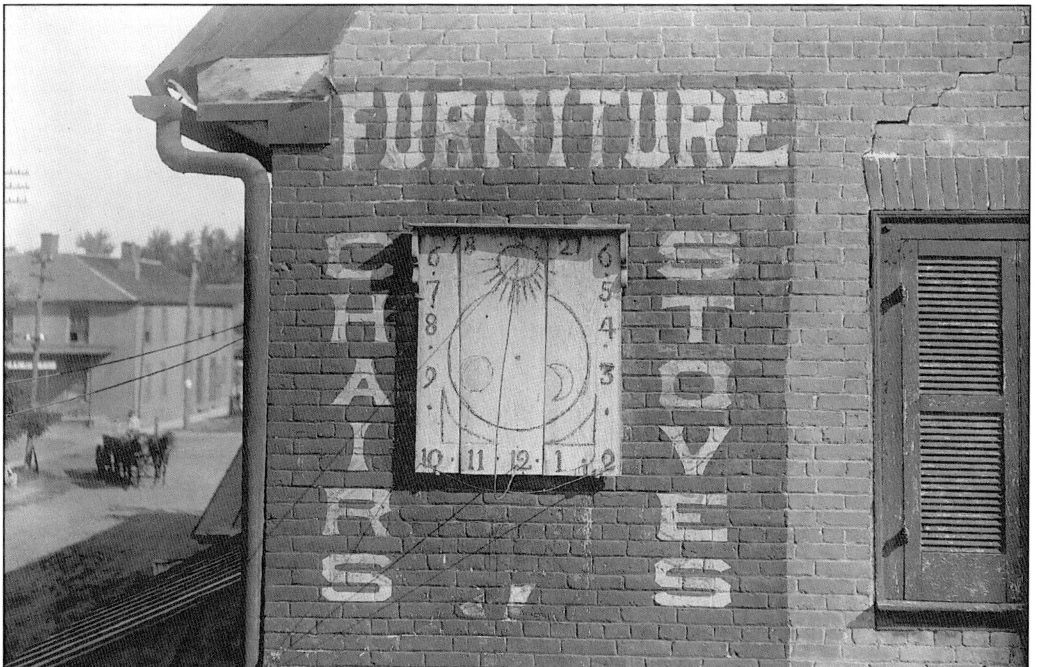

The Harmonist sundial, placed on the south side of Community House No. 2 in 1821, reads 8:40 a.m. on this day in 1907. The photograph poignantly illustrates the conversion of Harmonist community structures to modern commercial uses. (Photographer: Homer Fauntleroy.)

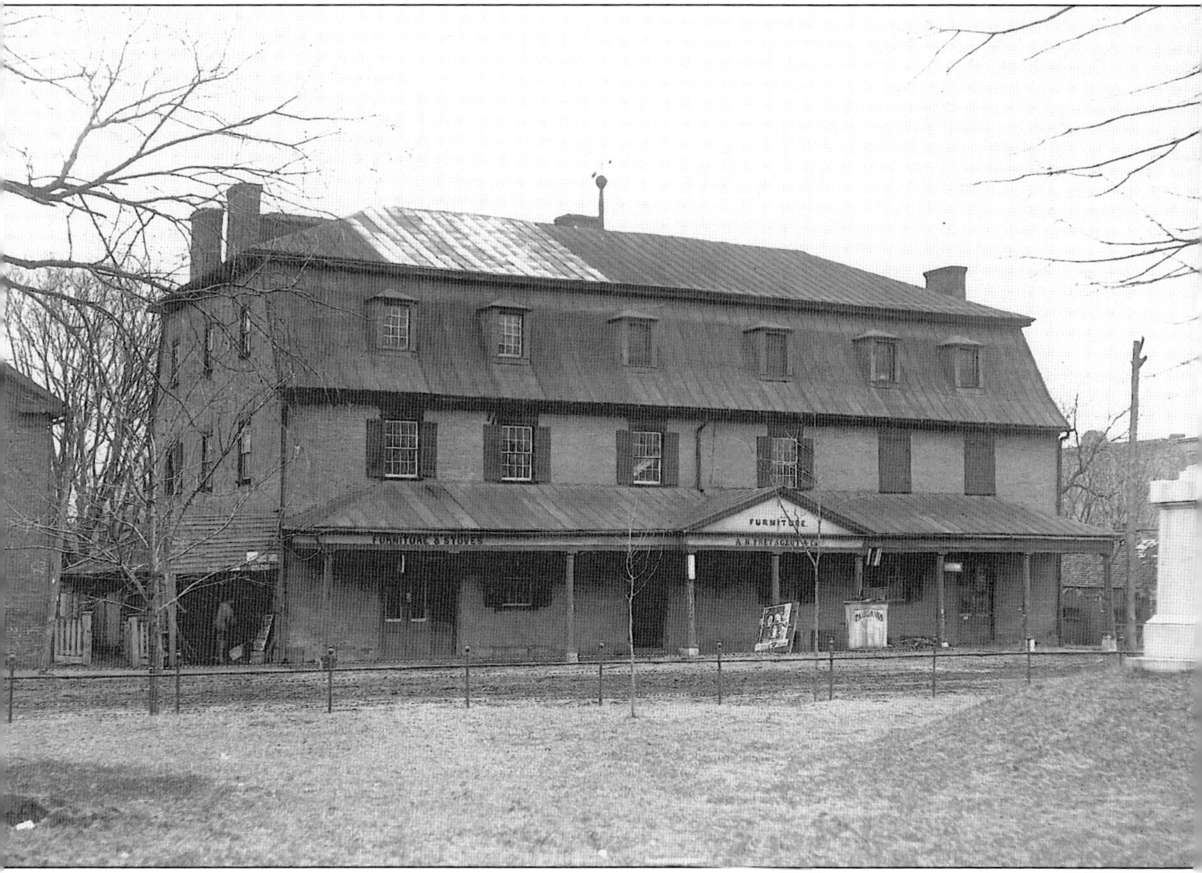

The former Harmonist Community House No.2, shown here in March of 1906, was known at that time as the Fretageot Building. Thomas Say's monument is visible on the grounds of the Maclure home in the right foreground. (Photographer: Homer Fauntleroy.)

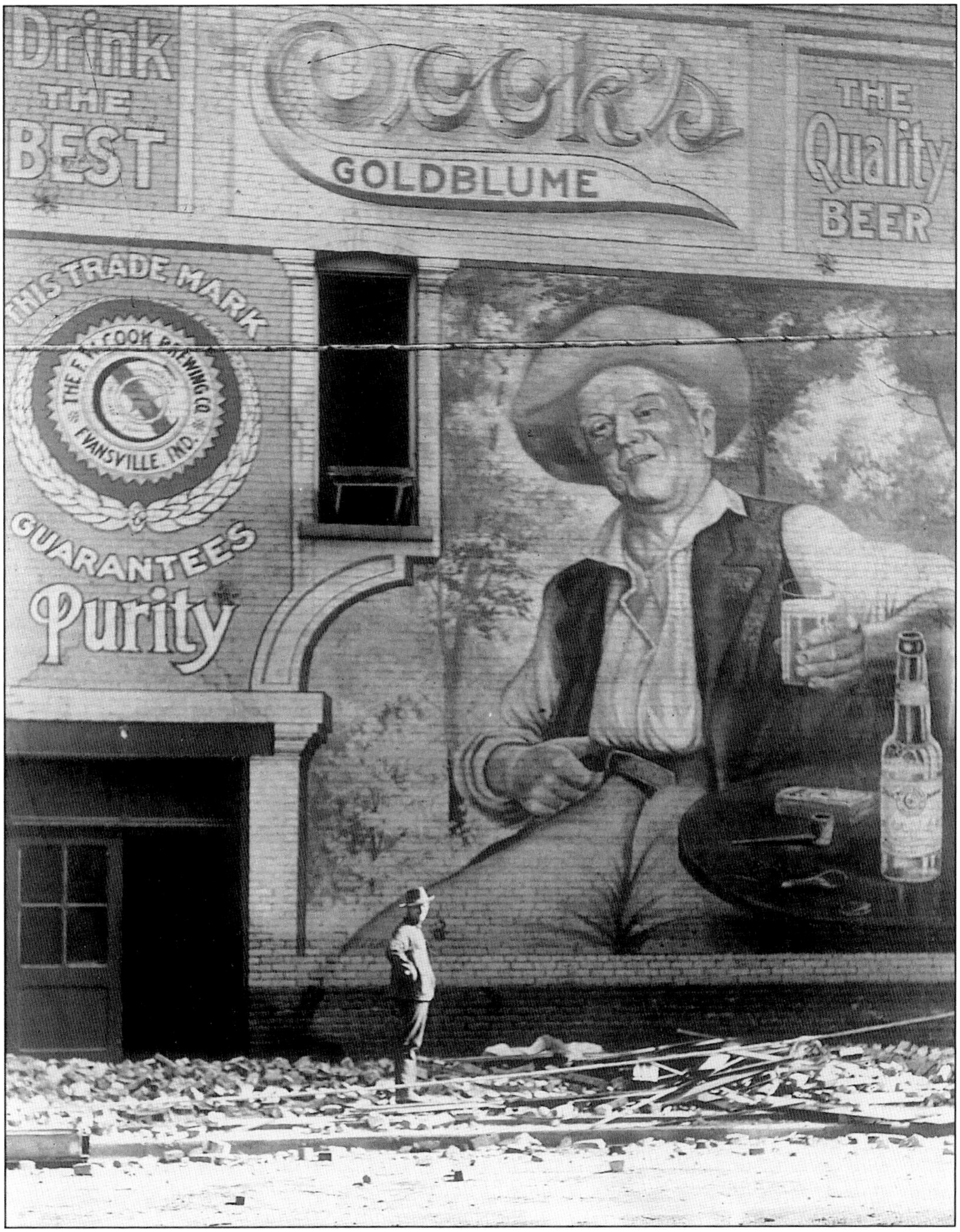

This April 1921 photograph shows a large, painted advertisement for Cook's Beer, located on the side of the building that stood at the southeast corner of Church and Main Streets. The building was being demolished to make way for the new bank building, which was constructed on that lot. (Photographer: Homer Fauntleroy.)

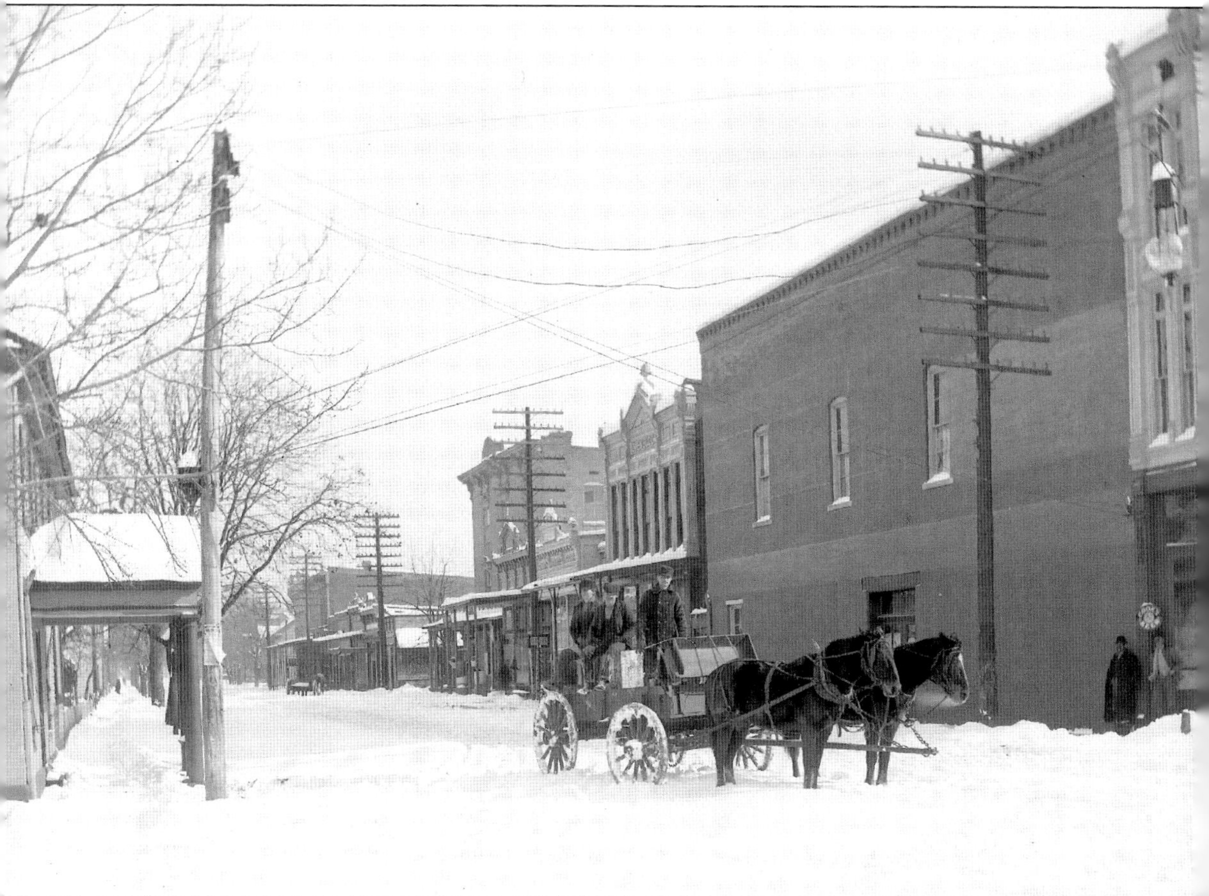

An unusual 18-inch snow fall covers New Harmony in this January 26, 1904 photograph, taken on Church Street looking east from Main Street. Unidentified residents enjoy the winter scene. This photograph shows the north face of the H.C. Husband and Co. store, before the Cook's Beer advertisement was painted on it. Note the round "Cook's Beer" sign near the door. (Photographer: Homer Fauntleroy.)

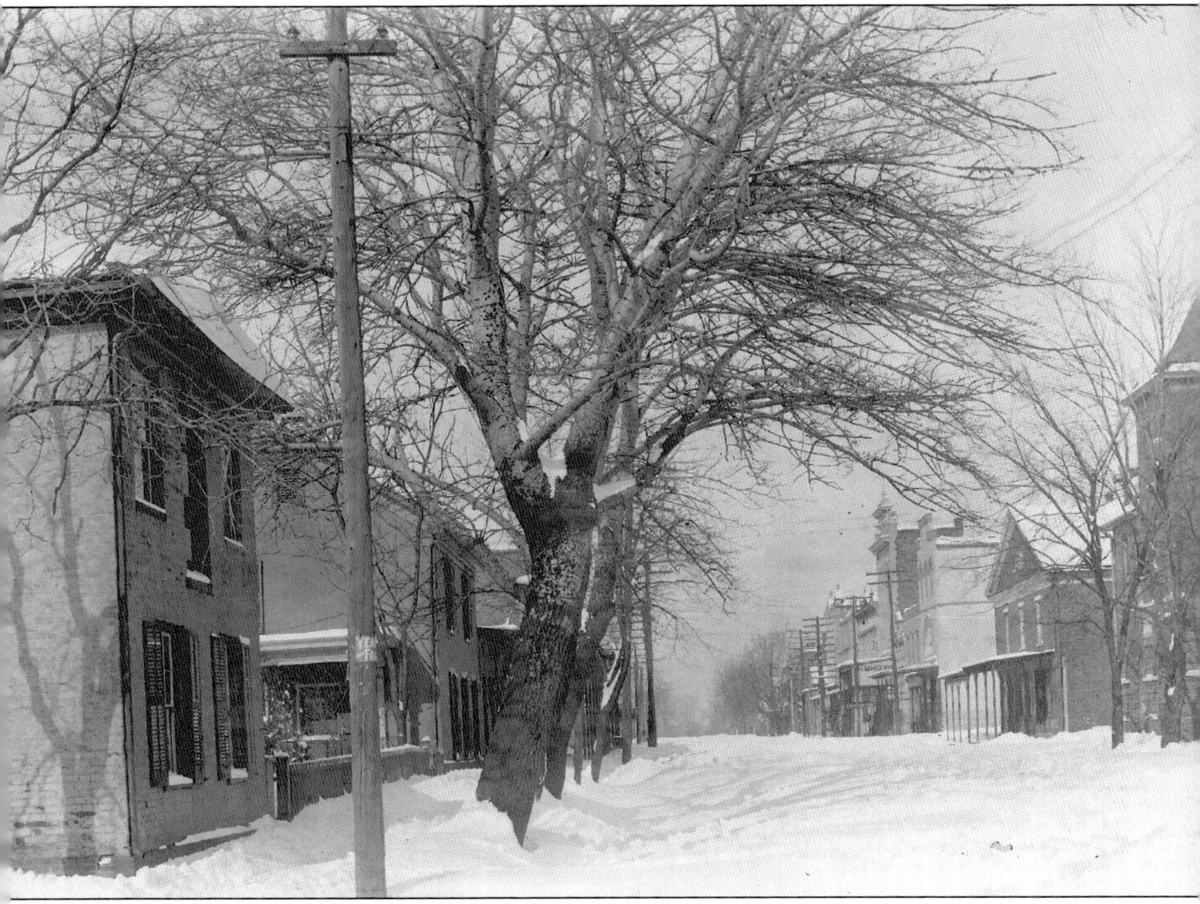

This January 25, 1904 photograph shows Main Street in New Harmony, covered with 18 inches of snow. (Photographer: Homer Fauntleroy.)

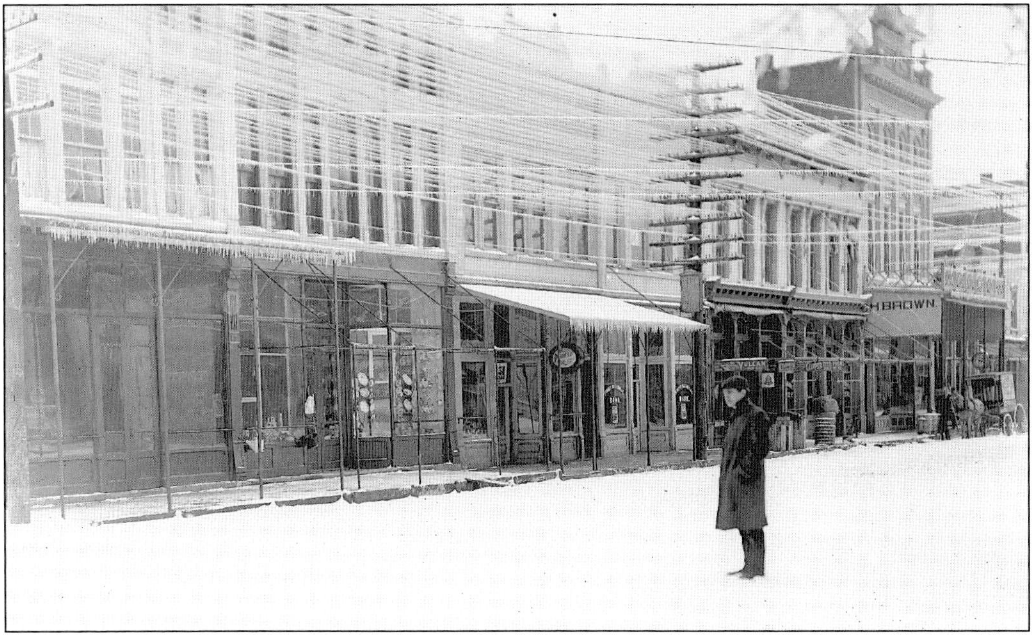

Shown in this 1905 Main Street winter scene are those buildings that stood (and in most cases still stand) on the east side of Main Street. (Photographer: Homer Fauntleroy.)

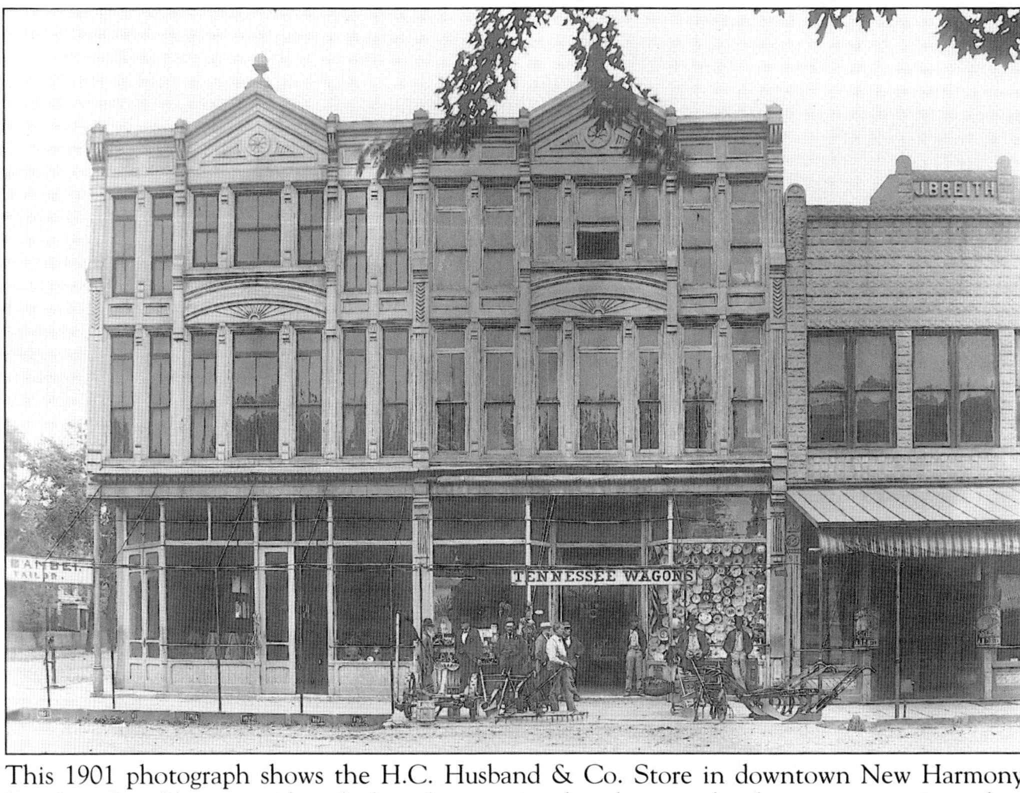

This 1901 photograph shows the H.C. Husband & Co. Store in downtown New Harmony. Resident Joe Ghump is identified as the man in the photograph who is not wearing a hat. (Photographer: Homer Fauntleroy.)

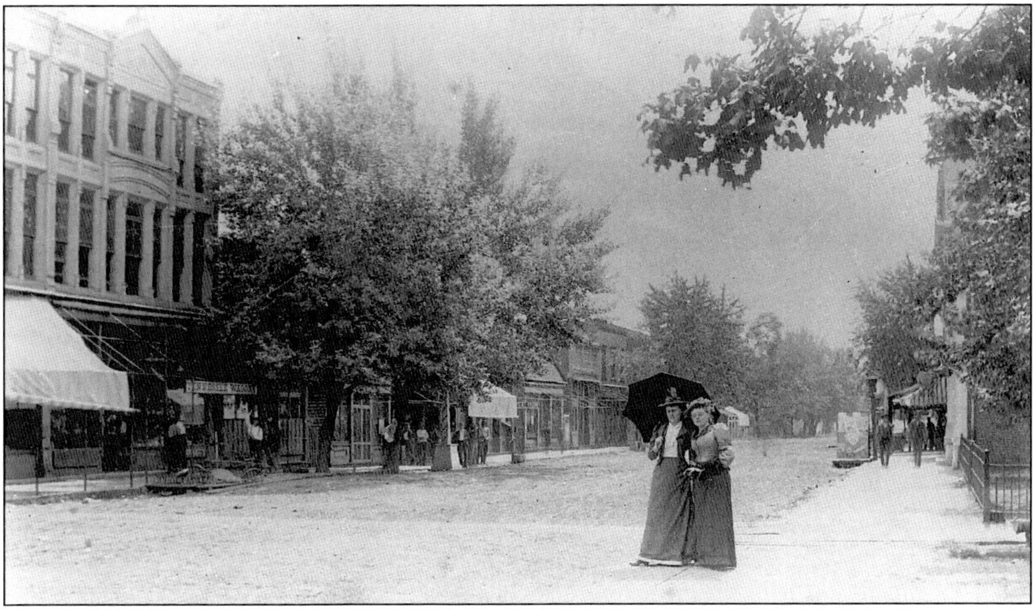

Posed in this 1893 photograph are Matilda Lichtenberger and Grace Thomas. (Photographer: William Frederick Lichtenberger.)

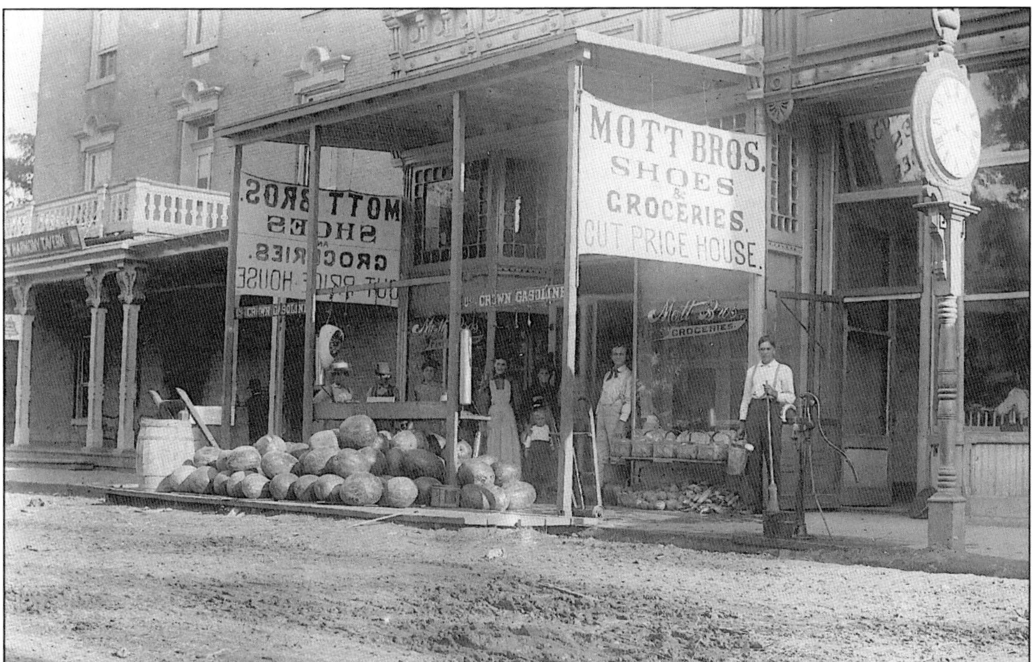

This summer 1897 photograph shows Motts Brothers' Store on Church Street. The Tavern stands to the east of the Motts' store. (Photographer: Homer Fauntleroy.)

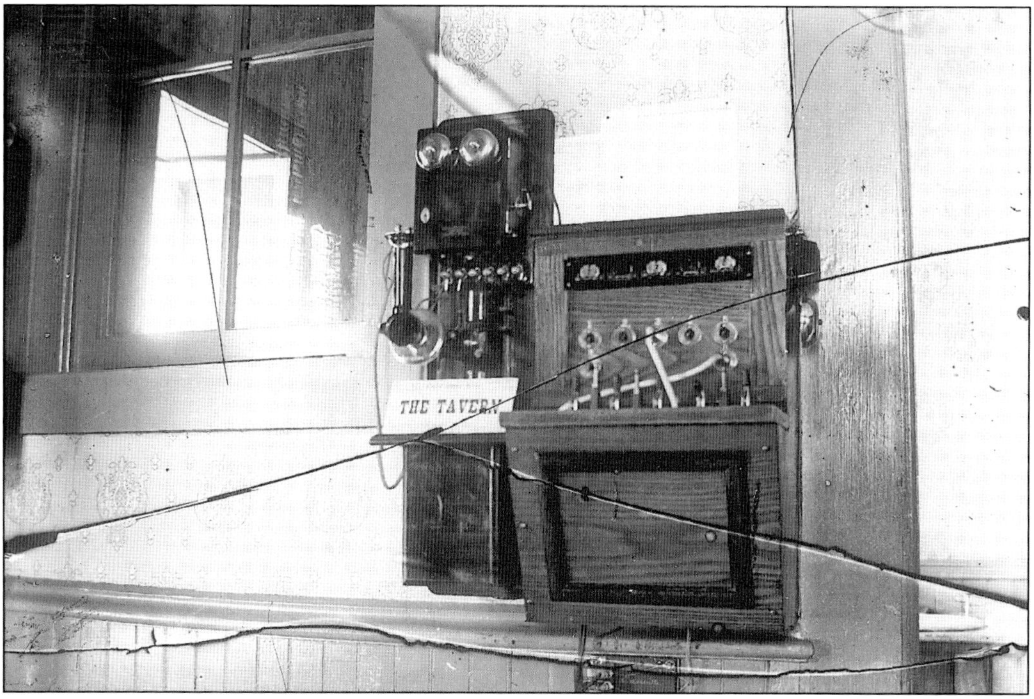

This photograph, taken in 1897, shows the Tavern's telephone in New Harmony after its installation. The first New Harmony telephone subscriber was Corbin Milling Company. Two toll lines came into New Harmony, one from Princeton, Indiana, and one from Evansville. These lines were then connected to individual booths in Dransfield Drug Store. The lines were moved to the office of the Tavern, and a three-drop switchboard was installed there so that Corbin Milling Company's line could be connected to either the Evansville or Princeton toll lines. (Photographer: Homer Fauntleroy.)

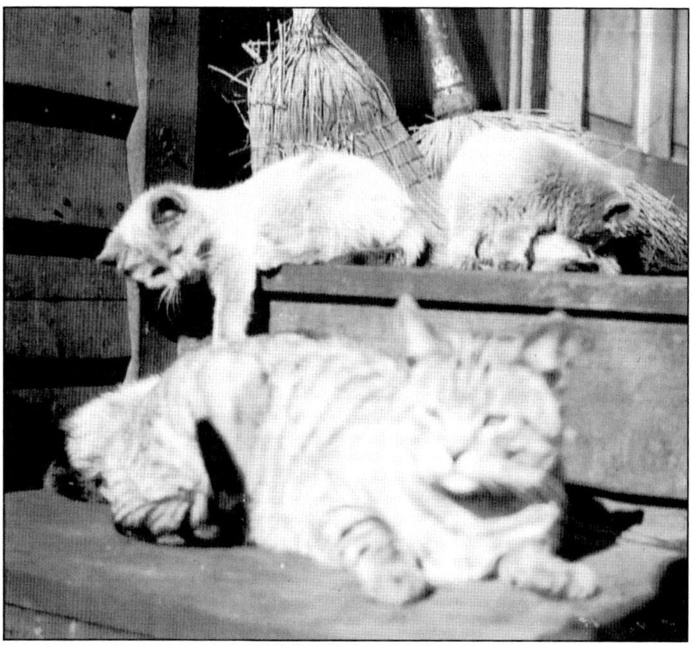

The archival record for this December 12, 1895 photograph reads as follows: "Cats on Tavern back porch. Three of Mattie's kittens and Nervy lying down." (Photographer: Homer Fauntleroy.)

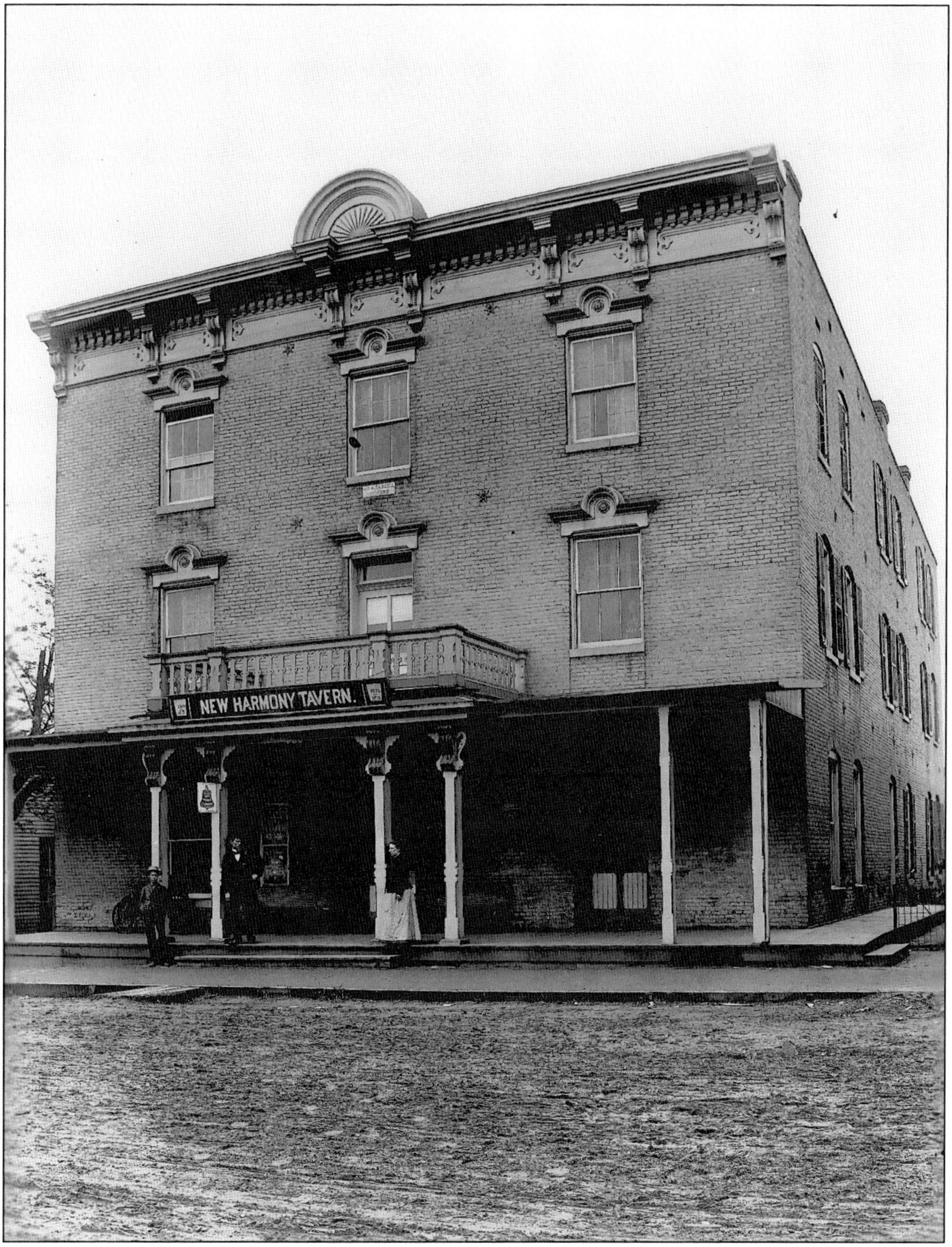

This photograph shows Harmonist Community House #3, on Church Street. It was later known as the Tavern.

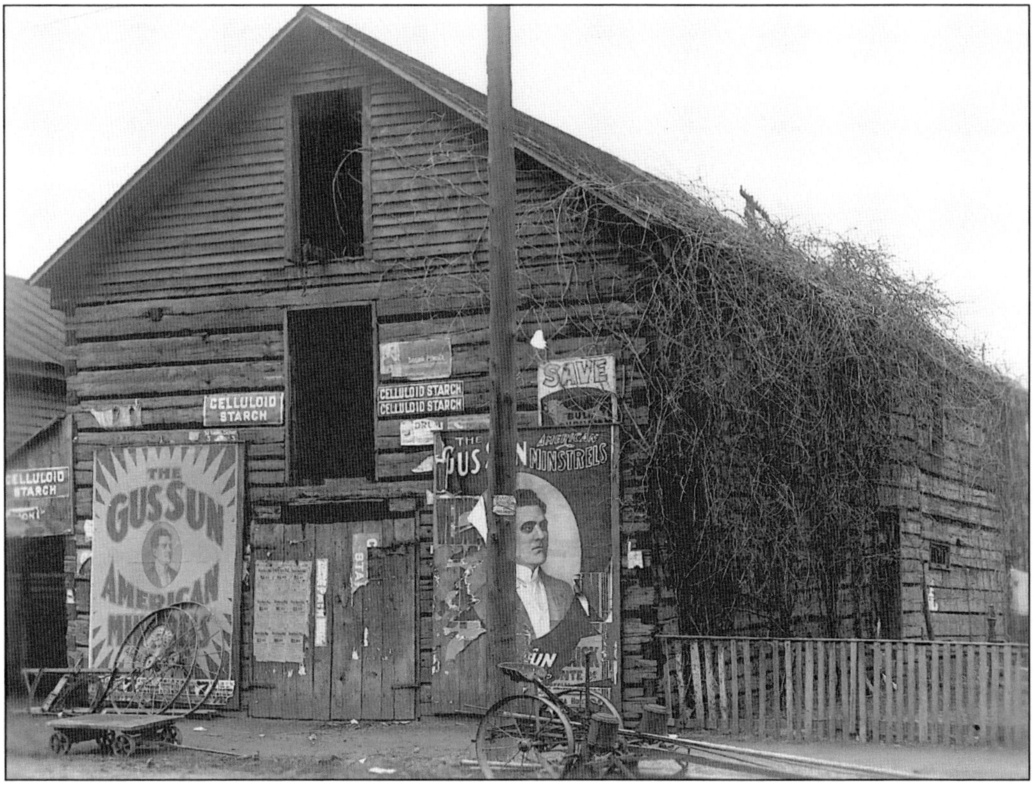

This old log building, the Harmonist castor oil factory, stood on Tavern Street across from the Gypsy Girl Livery Stable. It is shown here on March 8, 1906. (Photographer: Homer Fauntleroy.)

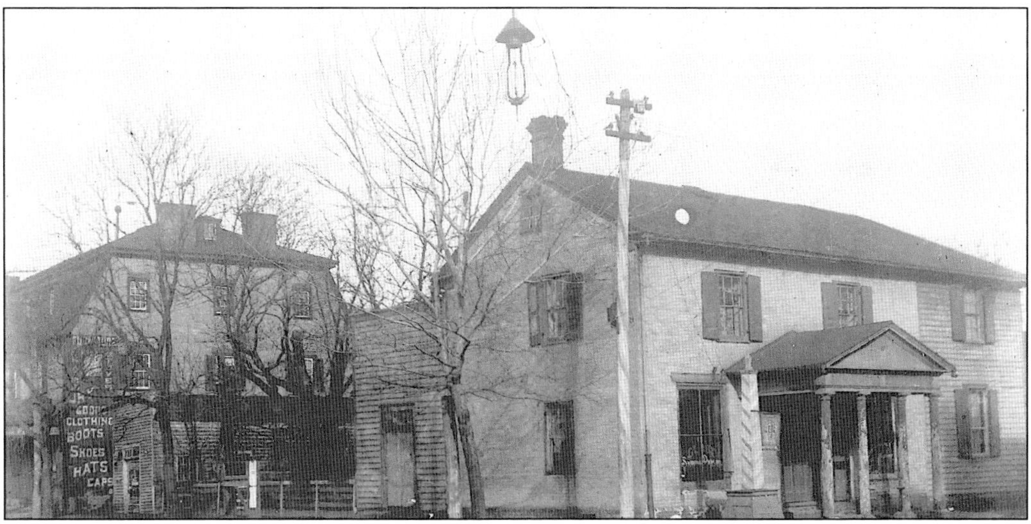

The northeast corner of Church and Main Streets was at one time known as "Sampson's Corner." This Harmonist brick structure has frame additions attached to its east and north sides, and it appears that a barber shop was operated out of the west side of the house. Other points of interest in the photograph include the carbon light over the intersection of the streets, and the sign in the window that reads "The Globe_____ Parlor."

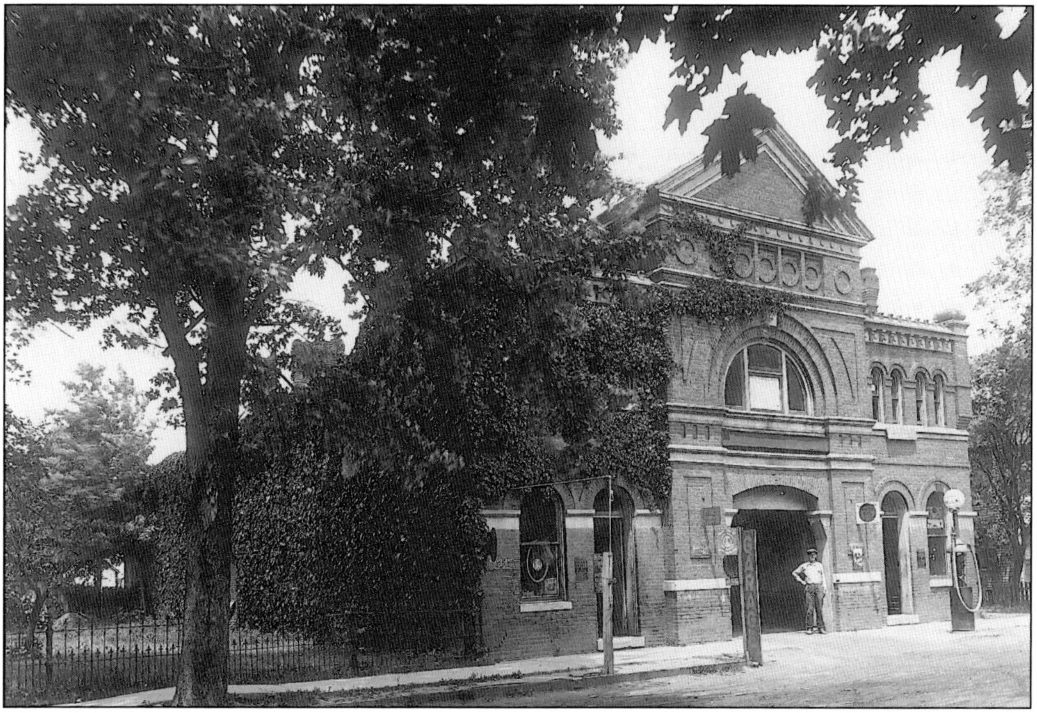

The New Harmony Opera House was originally built by the Harmonists on Church Street as Community House No. 4. New Harmony businessman Eugene Thrall constructed the Romanesque Revival façade in 1888. In 1913, the Opera House began its 50-year term as a garage. Here, it is shown as Wardelmann's Garage. (Photographer: Homer Fauntleroy.)

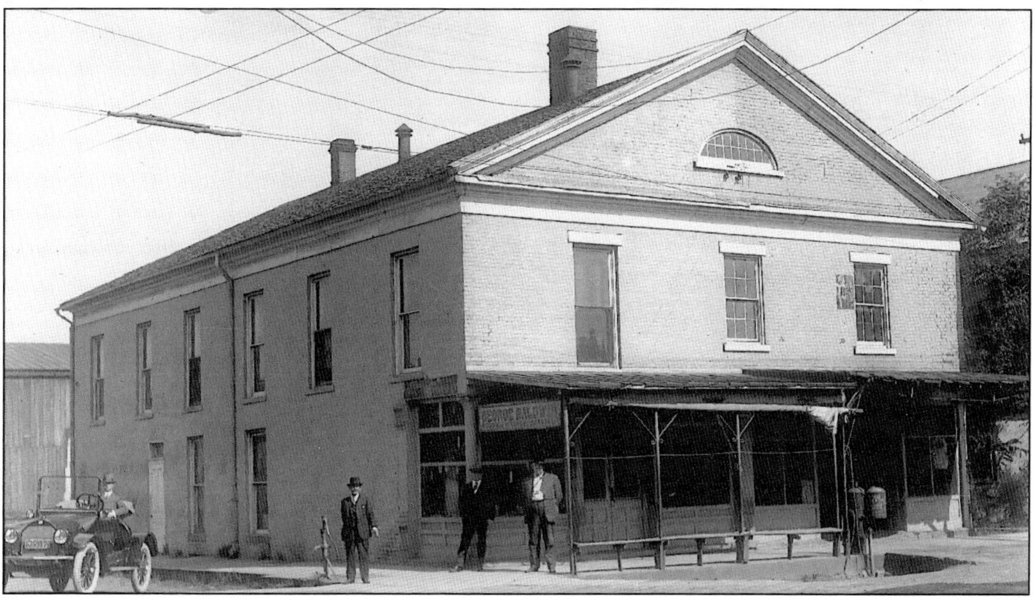

The building in this photograph, located at the southeast corner of Main and Tavern Streets in New Harmony, is George Baldwin's harness shop. This site was later chosen as the location for the new International Order of Oddfellows (IOOF) building (currently the grocery). (Photographer: William Frederick Lichtenberger.)

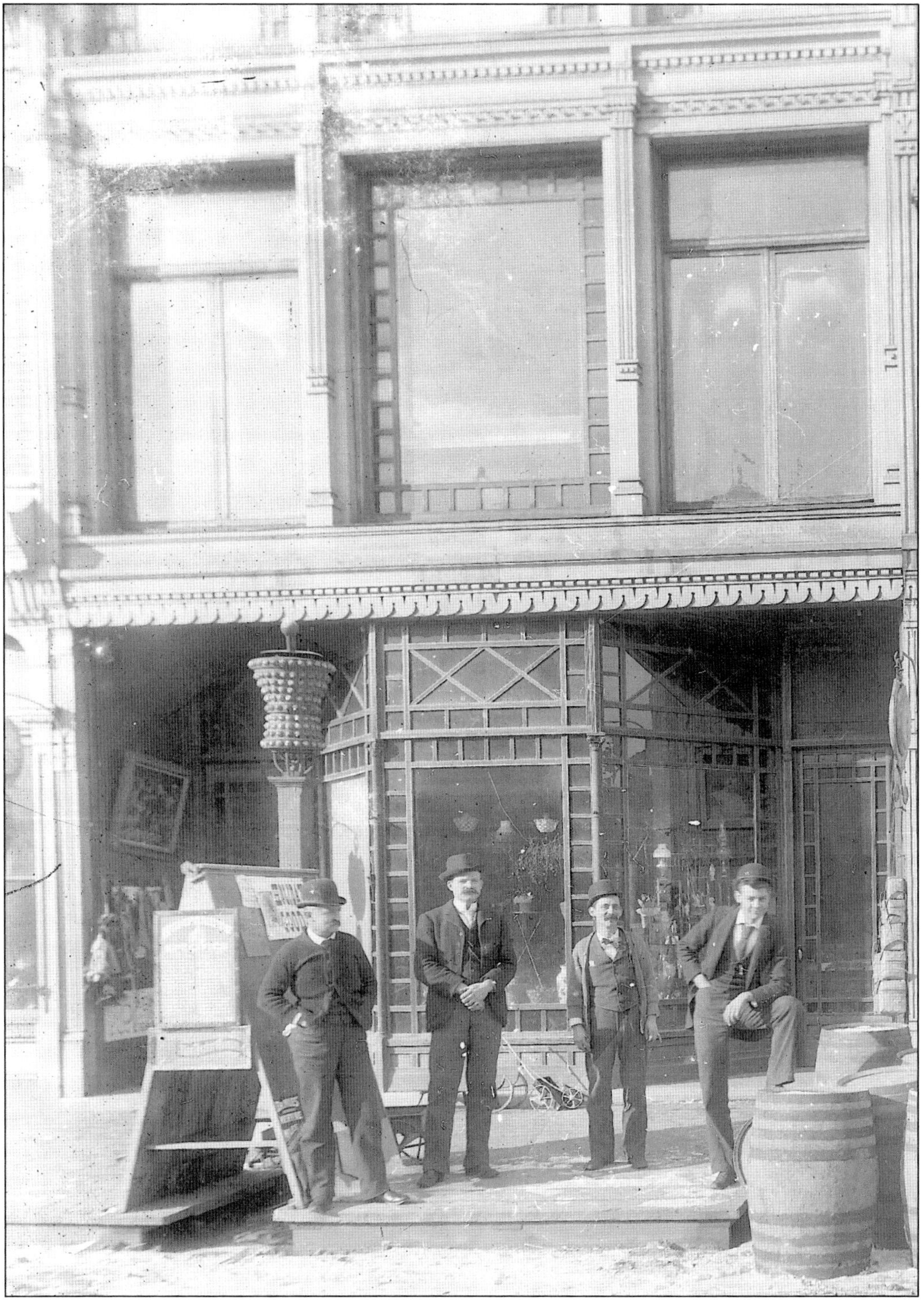

This photograph captures a group of unidentified men, perhaps local merchants, posing in front of the Mumford Building in downtown New Harmony. (Photographer: William Frederick Lichtenberger.)

Three

Culture and Leisure

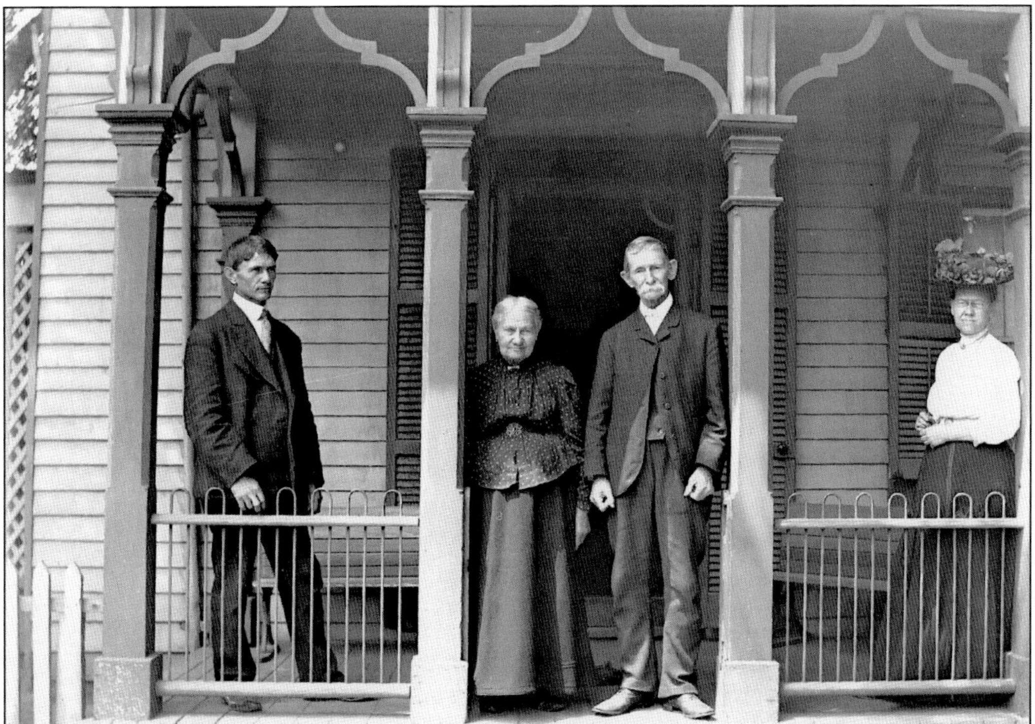

Photographer Homer Fauntleroy and his sister Mary Emily pose with their parents, Rachel and William Henry Fauntleroy, on the front porch on June 15, 1906. (Photographer: Homer Fauntleroy.)

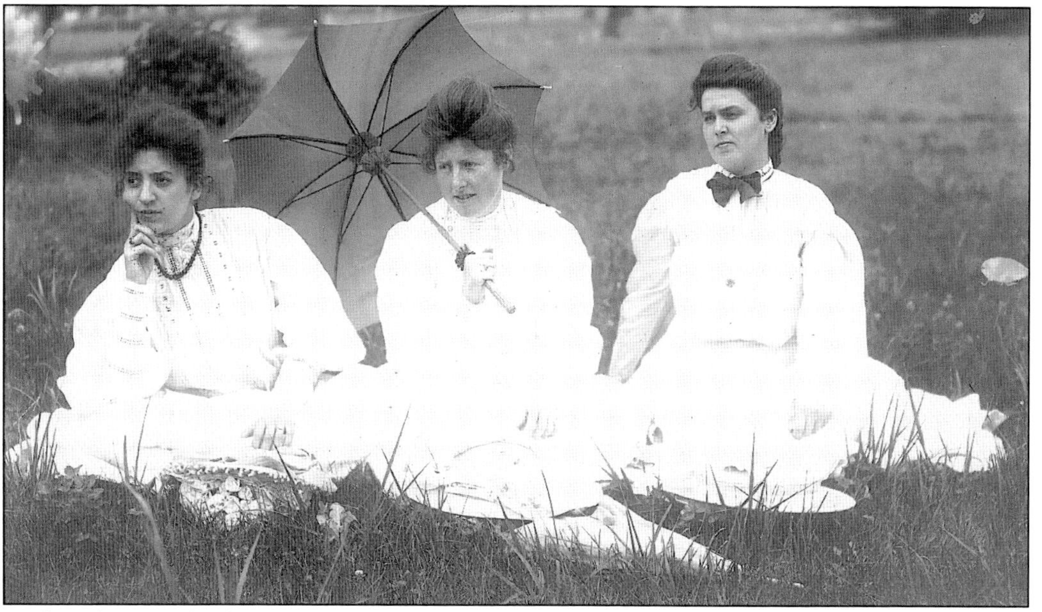

In this photograph, three girls identified as "Barbara, Agnes, and Nellie" enjoy an afternoon at one of New Harmony's parks. (Photographer: William Frederick Lichtenberger.)

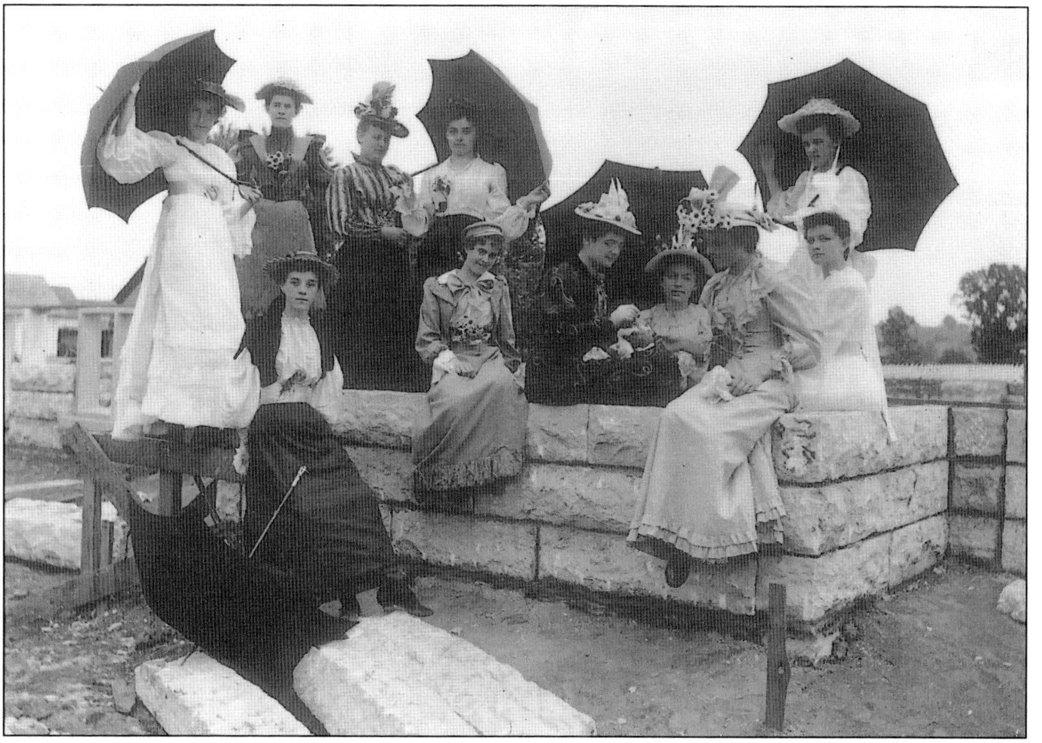

These well-dressed New Harmony ladies rest atop and around the foundation stones of the Workingmen's Institute, which is shown under construction in 1894.

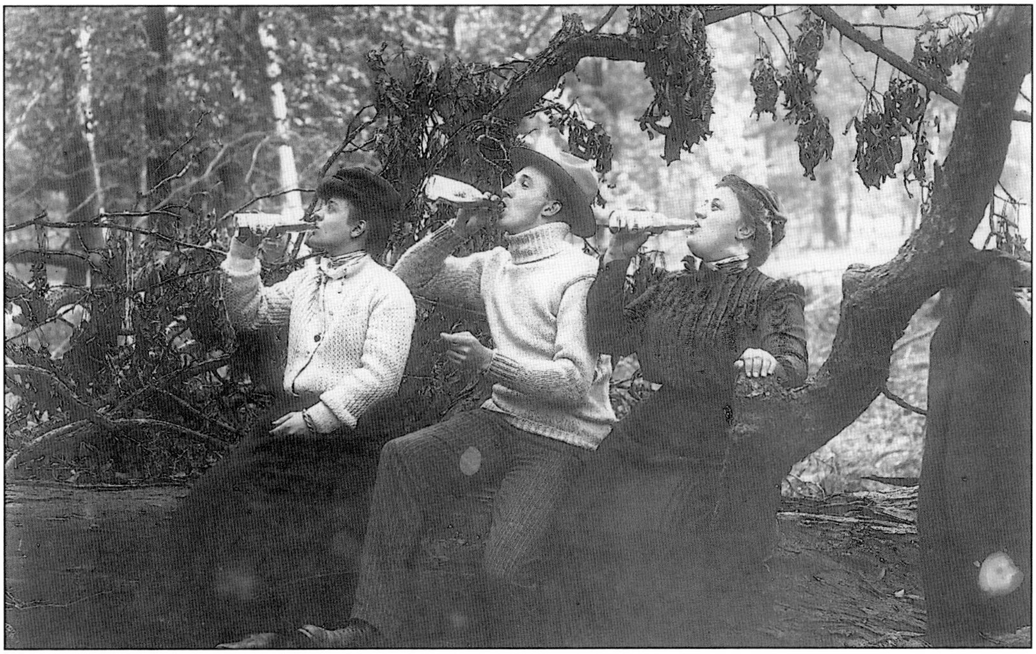

This group of friends enjoys some liquid refreshment! (Photographer: William Frederick Lichtenberger.)

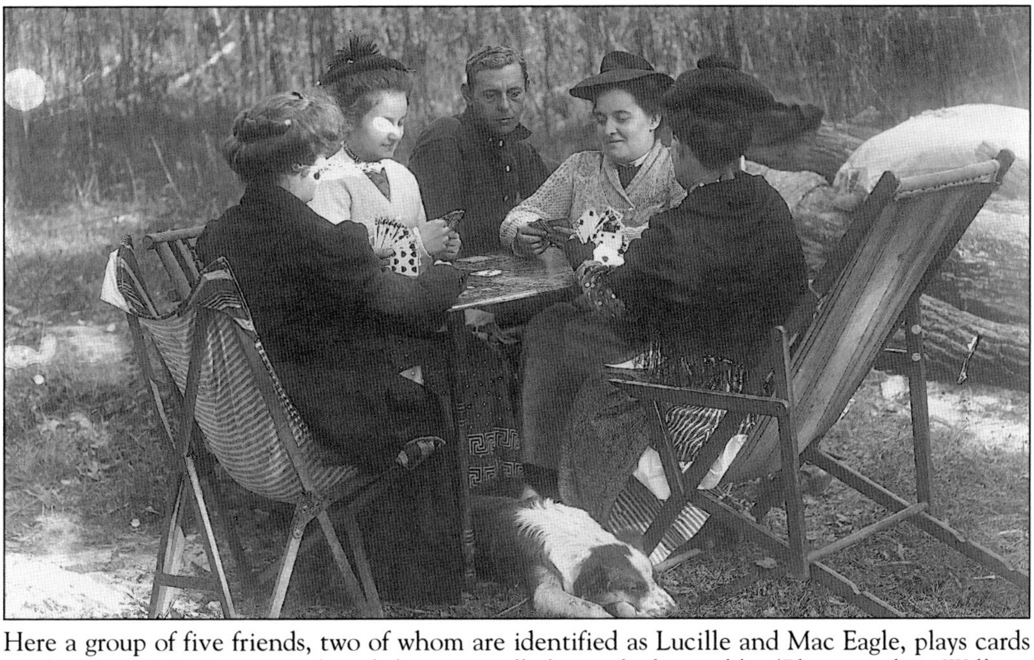

Here a group of five friends, two of whom are identified as Lucille and Mac Eagle, plays cards outdoors in 1909. A canine friend sleeps soundly beneath their table. (Photographer: William Frederick Lichtenberger.)

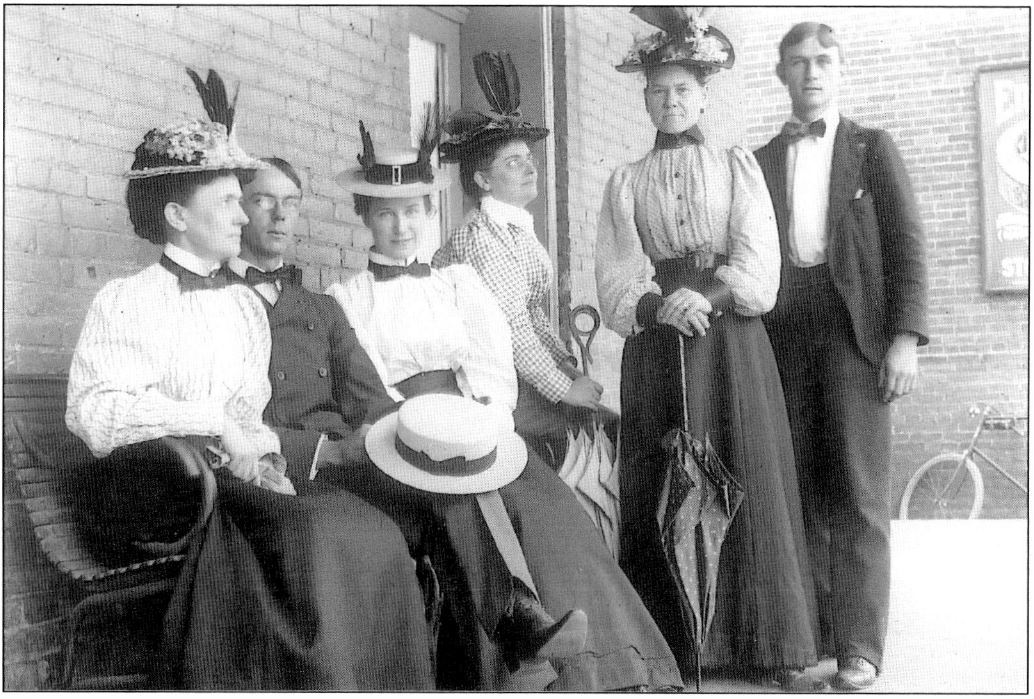

Assembled on the porch of the Tavern on August 13, 1897, are, from left to right: Eloise Mumford, William Mumford, Sallie Law, Maggie Roseman, Mary Emily Fauntleroy, and Homer Fauntleroy. (Photographer: Homer Fauntleroy.)

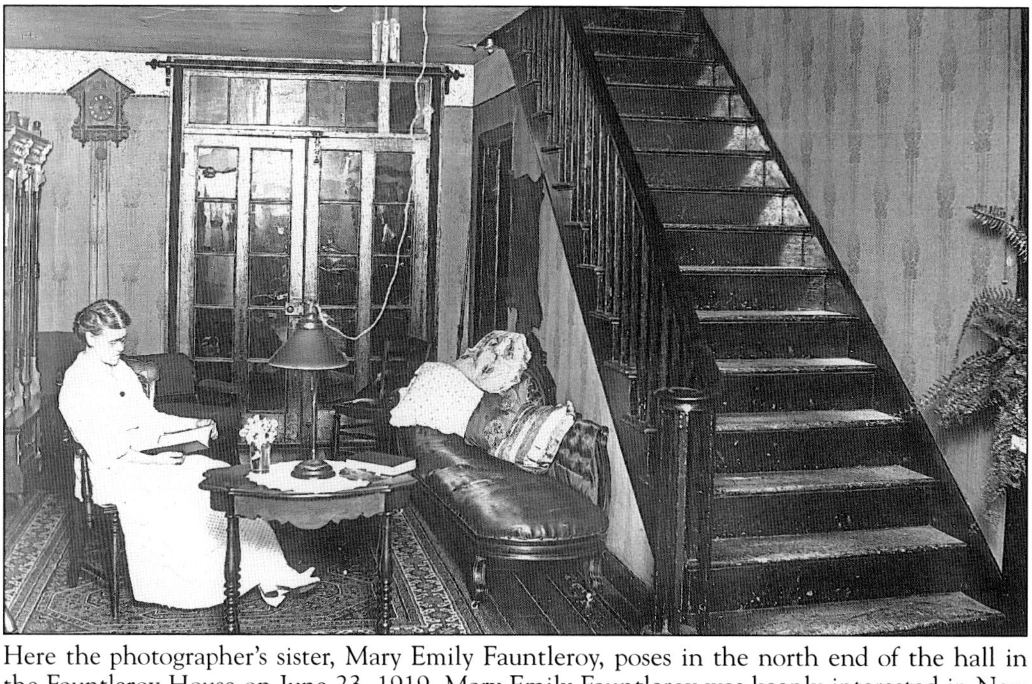

Here the photographer's sister, Mary Emily Fauntleroy, poses in the north end of the hall in the Fauntleroy House on June 23, 1919. Mary Emily Fauntleroy was keenly interested in New Harmony history, and was a pivotal figure in the preservation of such buildings as the Fauntleroy Home and Community House No. 2. (Photographer: Homer Fauntleroy.)

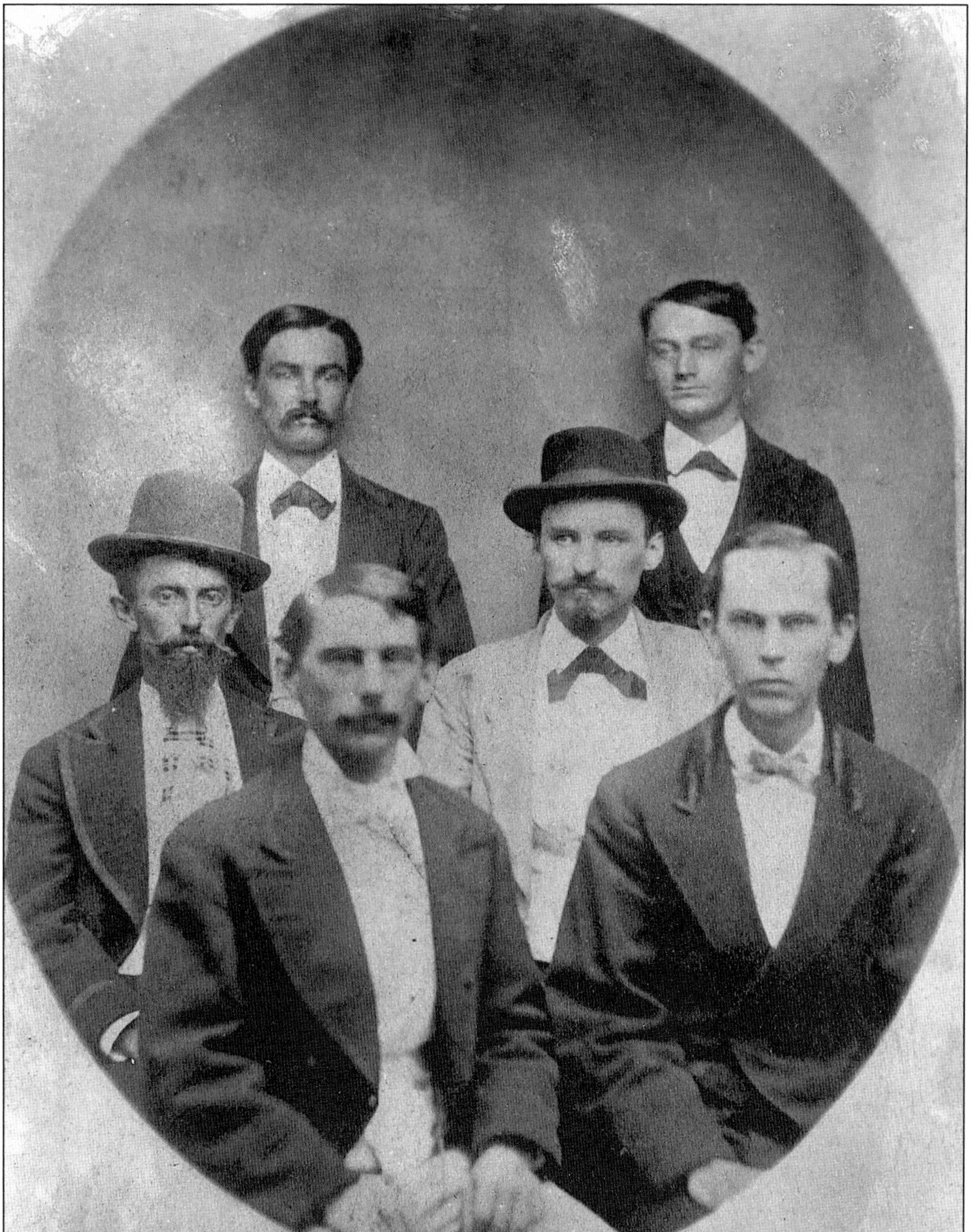

Gathered together are members of the New Harmony Literary Society, organized in 1865. Pictured are Arthur Dransfield, Will Miller, George Wheatcroft, Clarence Lichtenberger, Will Owen, and George Goble.

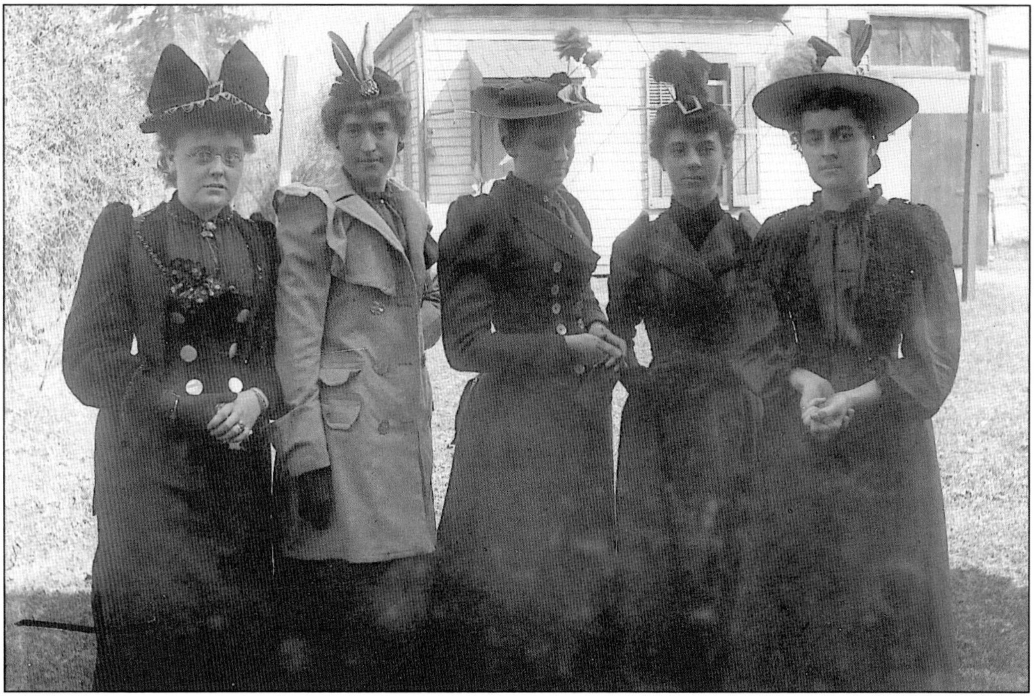

Five unidentified ladies gather together, dressed in their Sunday finery, on March 12, 1893. (Photographer: William Frederick Lichtenberger.)

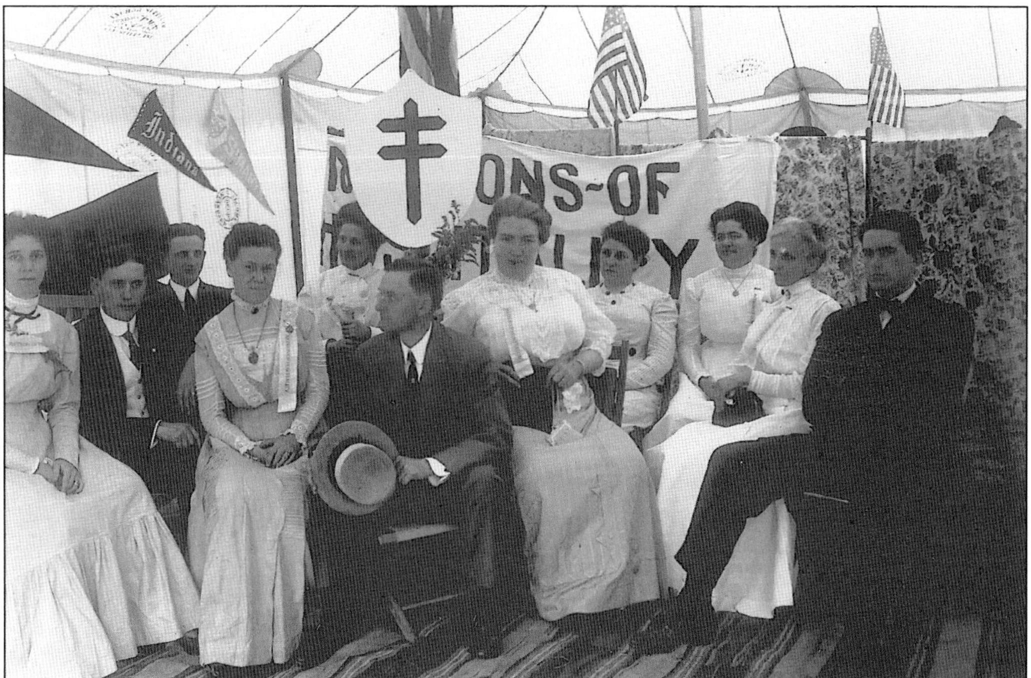

These unidentified individuals are located in the "Welcome Tent" at the fair in September 1910. The partially obscured banner reads "Matrons of Hospitality," as do the ribbons the ladies are wearing. (Photographer: William Frederick Lichtenberger.)

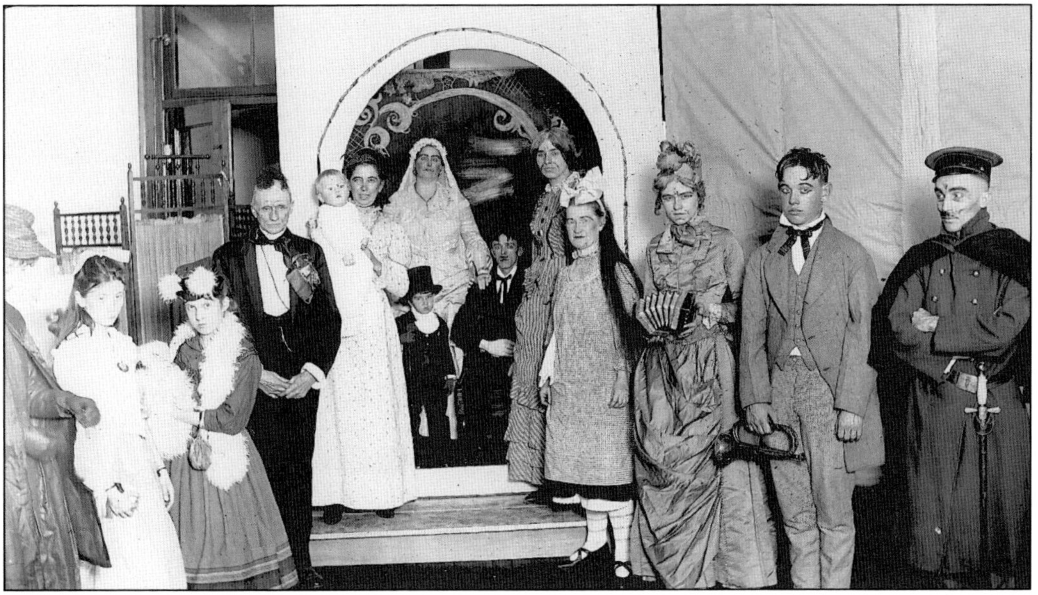

This photograph captures a group of costumed young people at the New Harmony School on December 12, 1919.

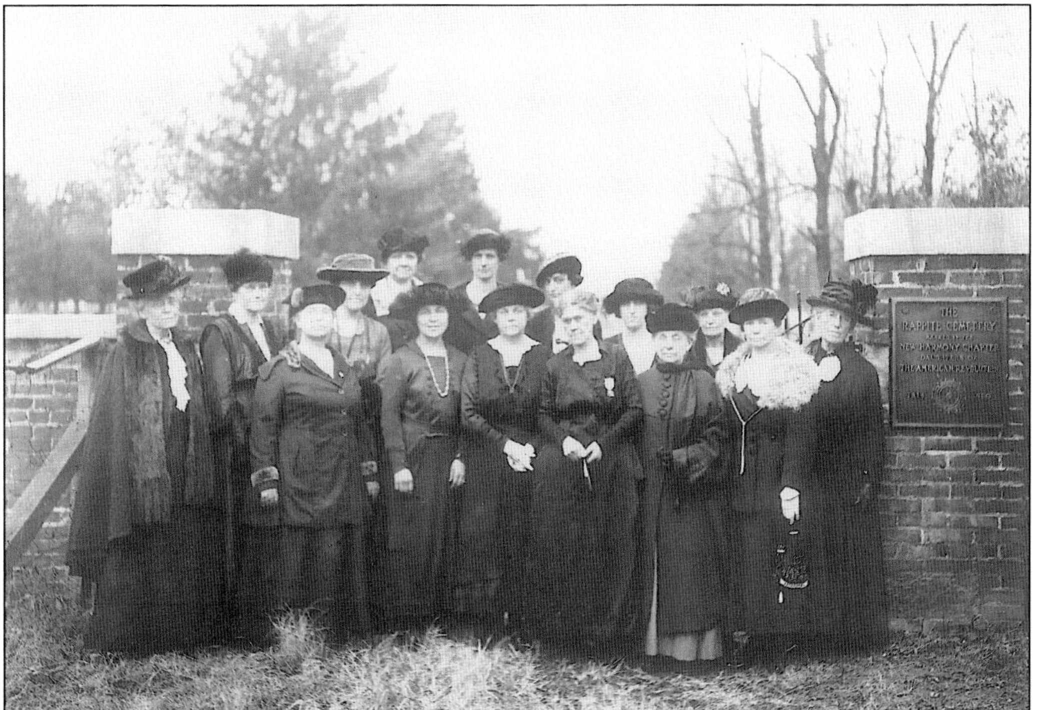

This group of mostly unidentified women, probably members of the local chapter of the Daughters of the American Revolution, gathers at the entrance to the Harmonist Cemetery, to dedicate the bronze plaque at right. Mary Emily Fauntleroy is fourth from the right in the front row. The photograph was taken *c.* 1922.

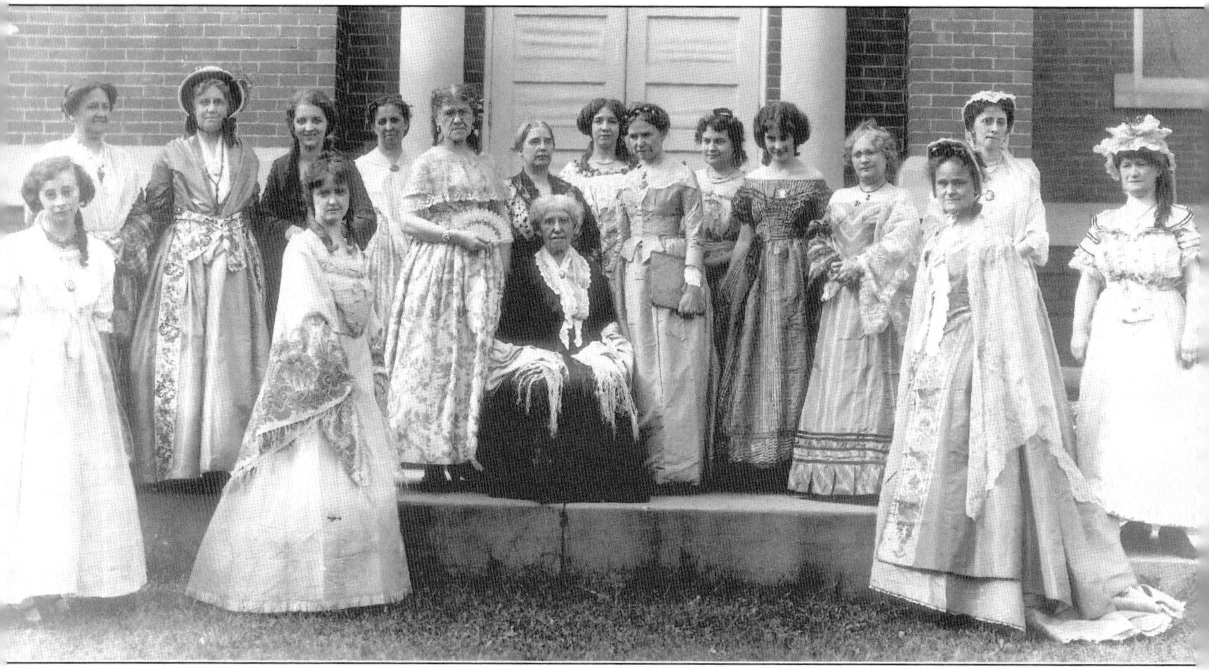

These unidentified ladies, members of the Daughters of the Minerva Society, gather in front of Murphy Auditorium on October 20, 1922. The back of the photograph identifies their attire as "Owen Period clothing."

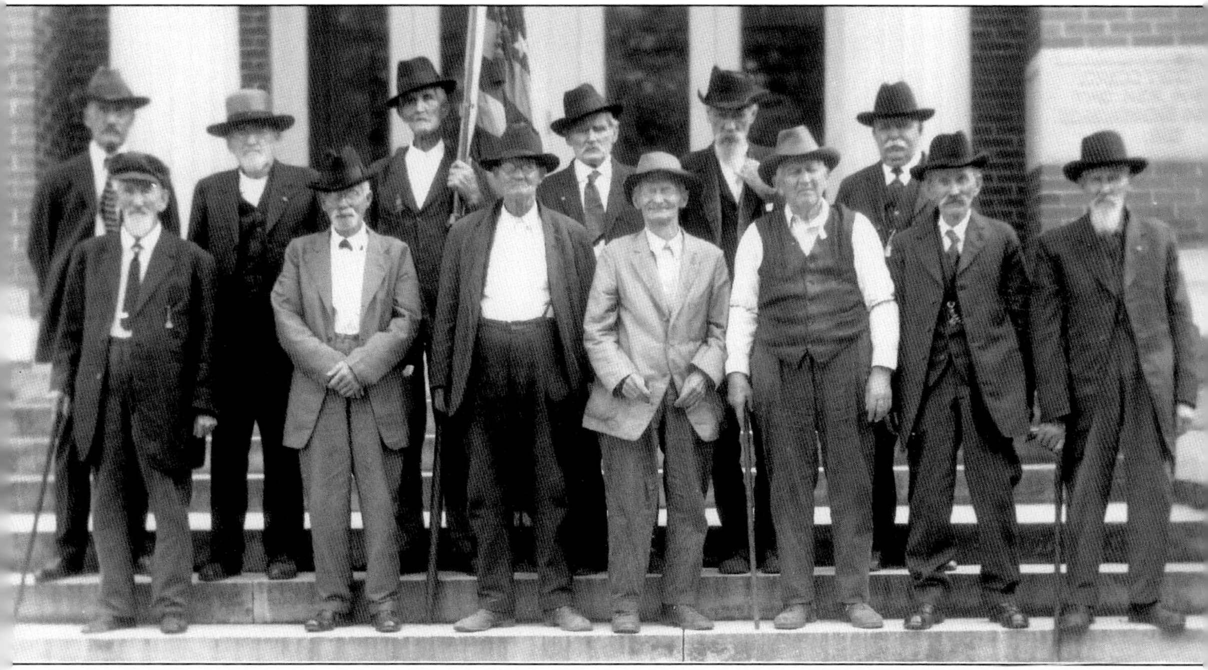

This group of men, one of whom is holding an American flag, stands on the steps of Murphy Auditorium in 1913. They are, from left to right: (front row) James Chaffin, M.B. Pote, George Wilson, William Hartmann, John Jackson, Mr. Kern, and Joe Angleton. (back row) Bill Ford, John Sanders, Charles Johnson, John Eaton, John Woods, and Jack Robinson. (Photographer: William Frederick Lichtenberger.)

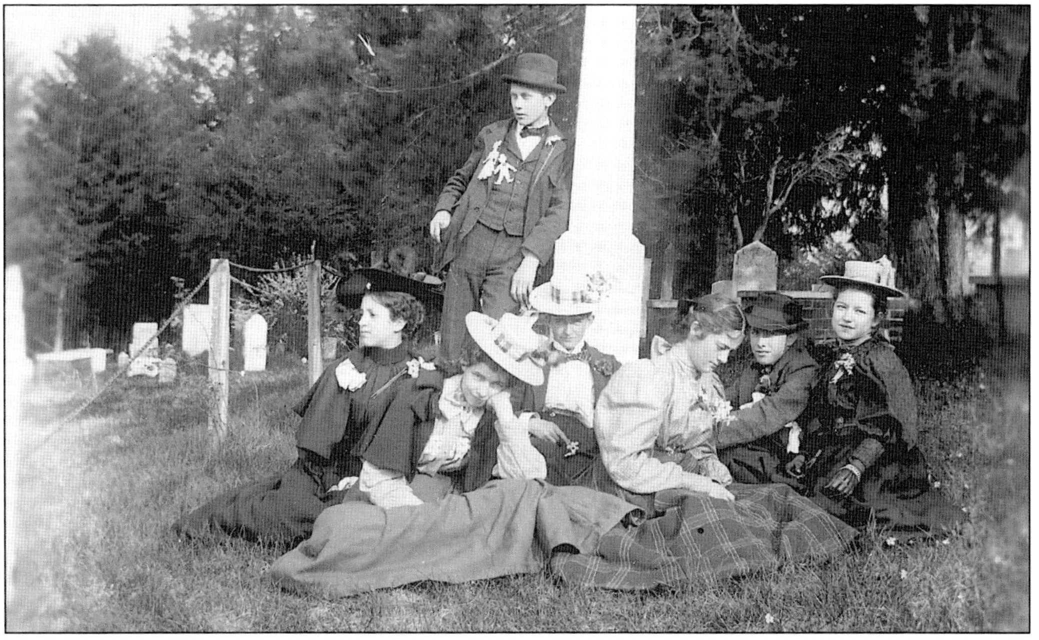

These unidentified individuals gather at the Rudd Viets grave marker in Maple Hill Cemetery.

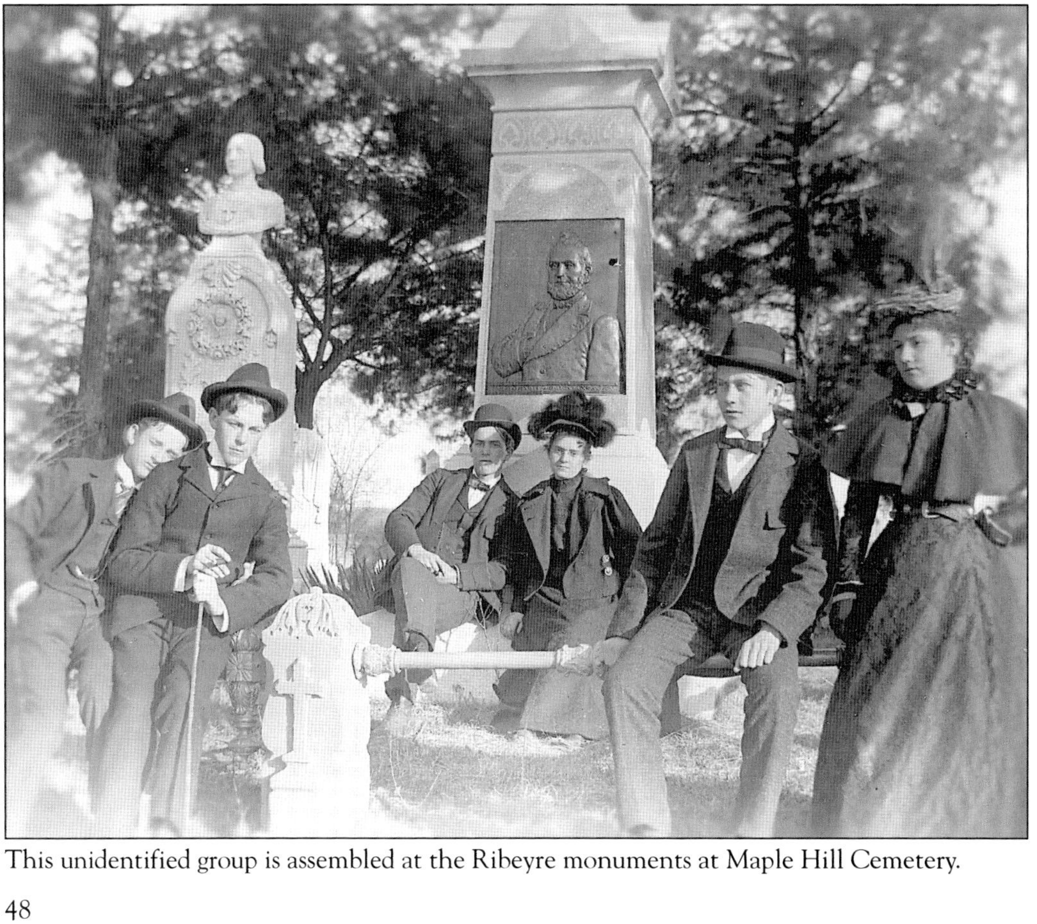

This unidentified group is assembled at the Ribeyre monuments at Maple Hill Cemetery.

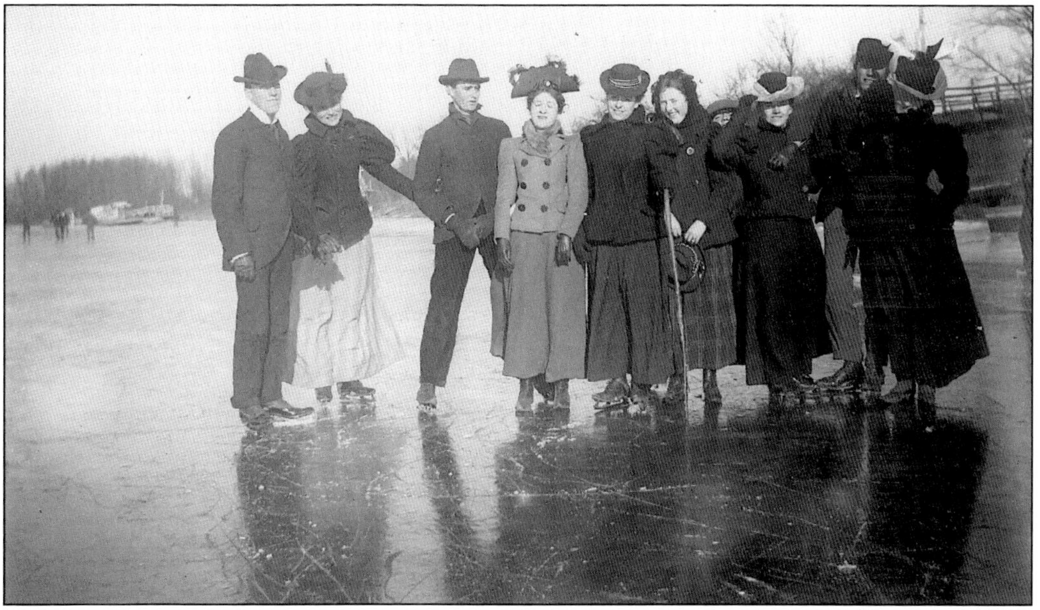

This group of friends ice skates on the Wabash River on December 11, 1898. They are, from left to right: Fred Tretheway and his wife, Minnette Richards; Nibs (Billie) Bennett; Nellie Hargraves; Nellie Mott; Agnes Alsop; Neva Walz; Frank Mott; and Nathalie Newsome. Standing behind the group is Homer Stallings. (Photographer: Homer Fauntleroy.)

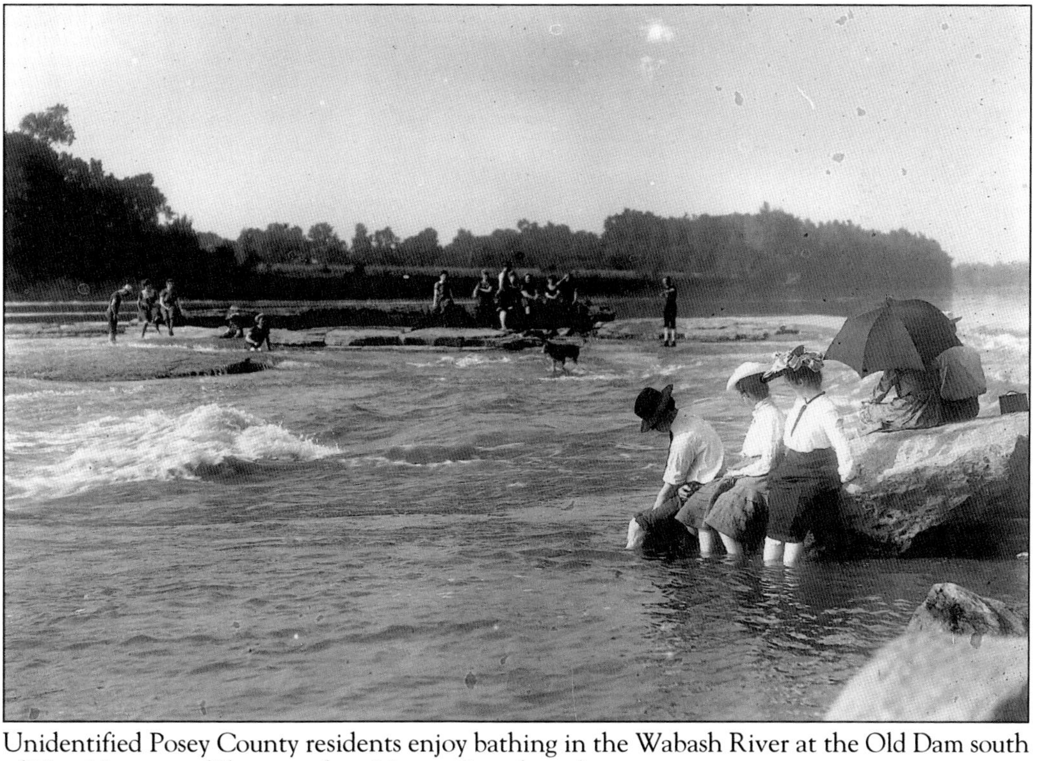

Unidentified Posey County residents enjoy bathing in the Wabash River at the Old Dam south of New Harmony. (Photographer: Homer Fauntleroy.)

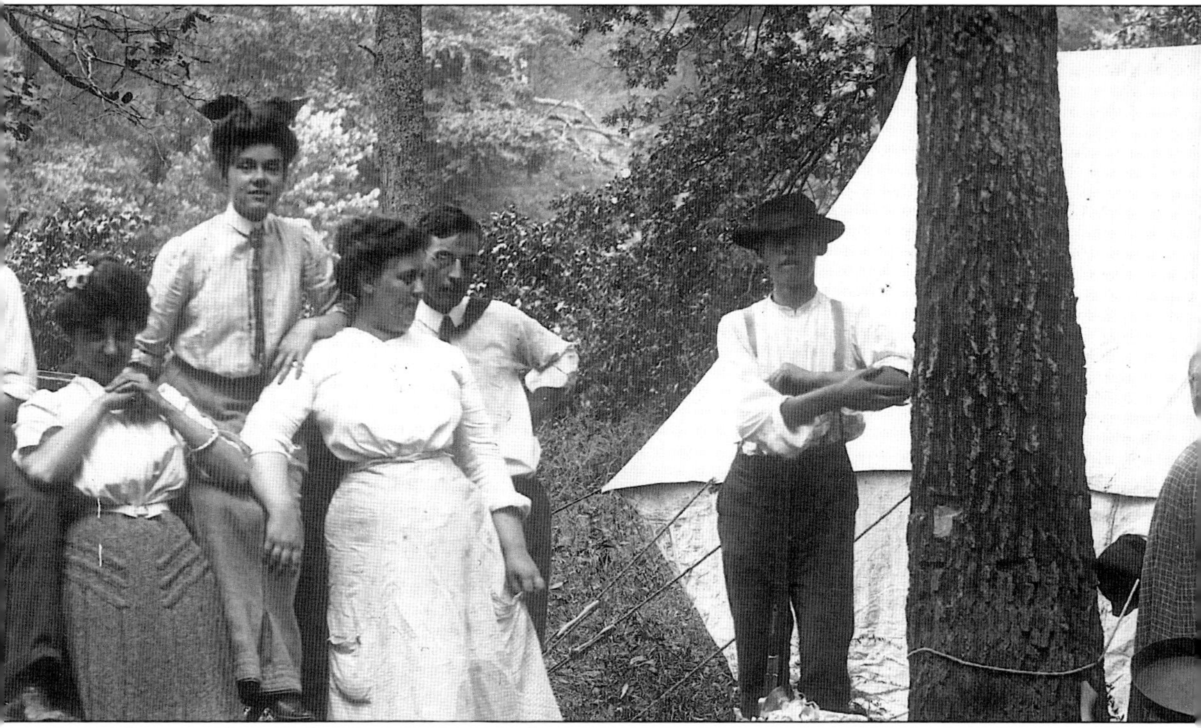

These unidentified Posey County residents enjoy a camp site at Foot's Pond. (Photographer:

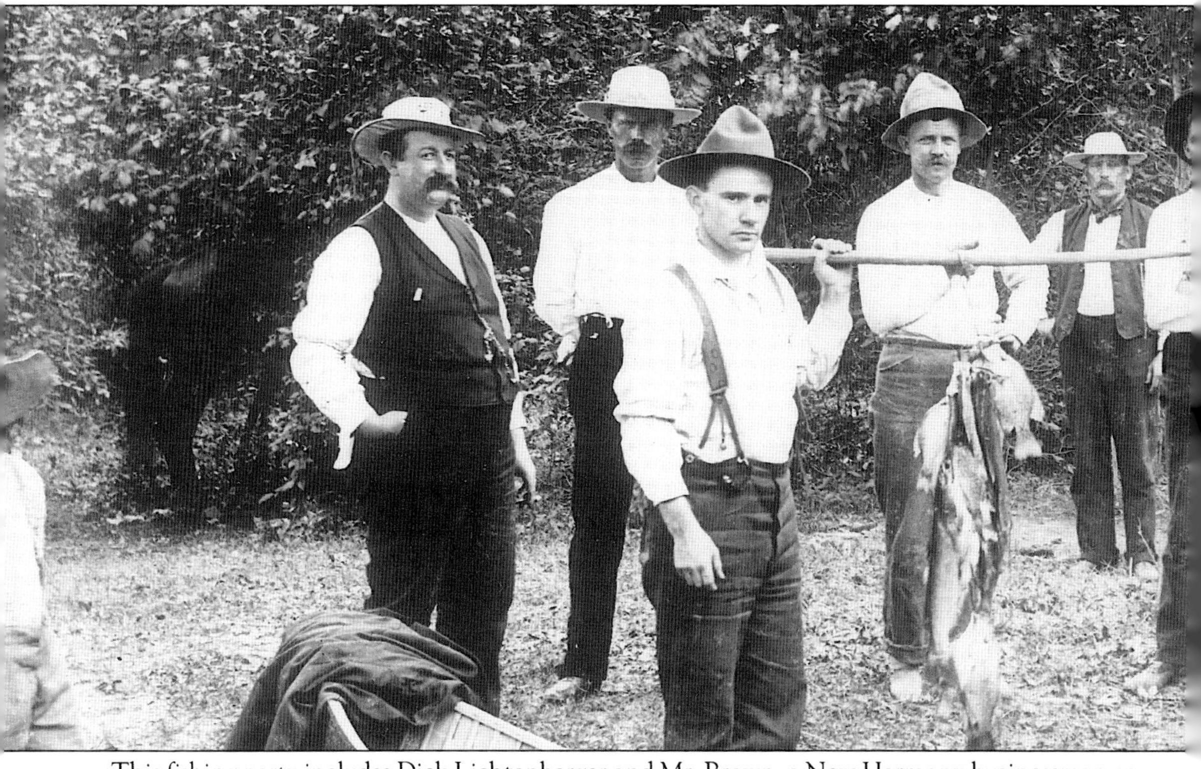

This fishing party includes Dick Lichtenberger and Mr. Brown, a New Harmony businessman,as

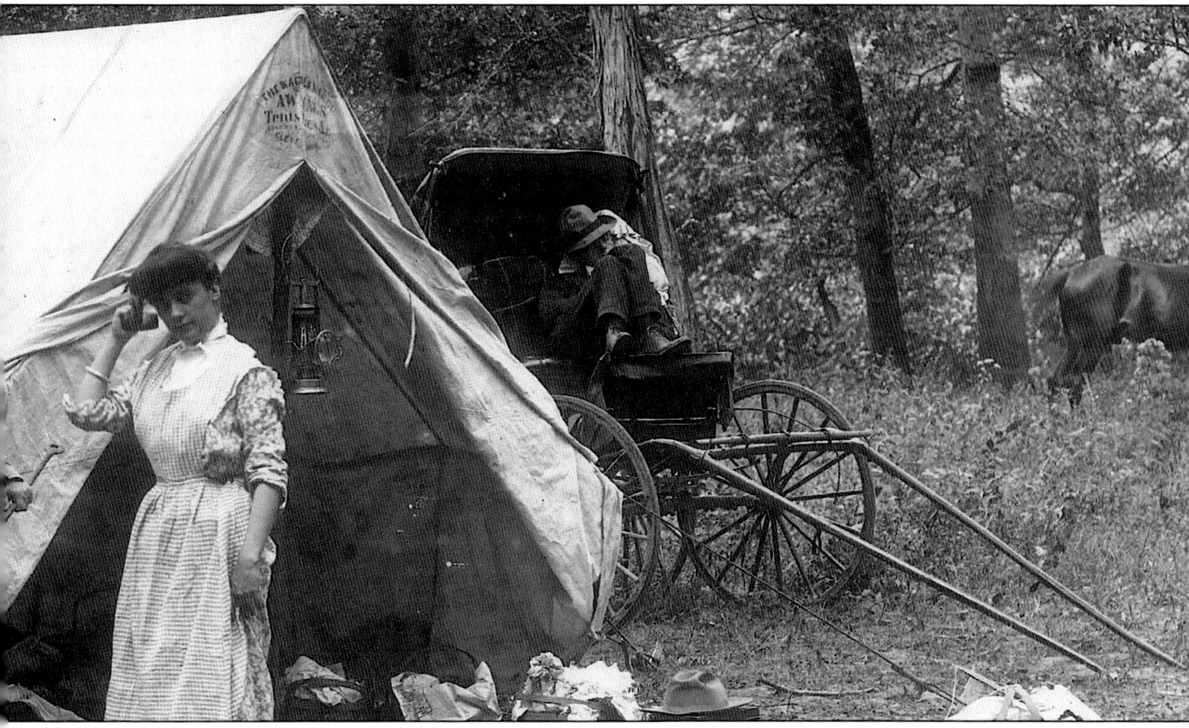

William Frederick Lichtenberger.)

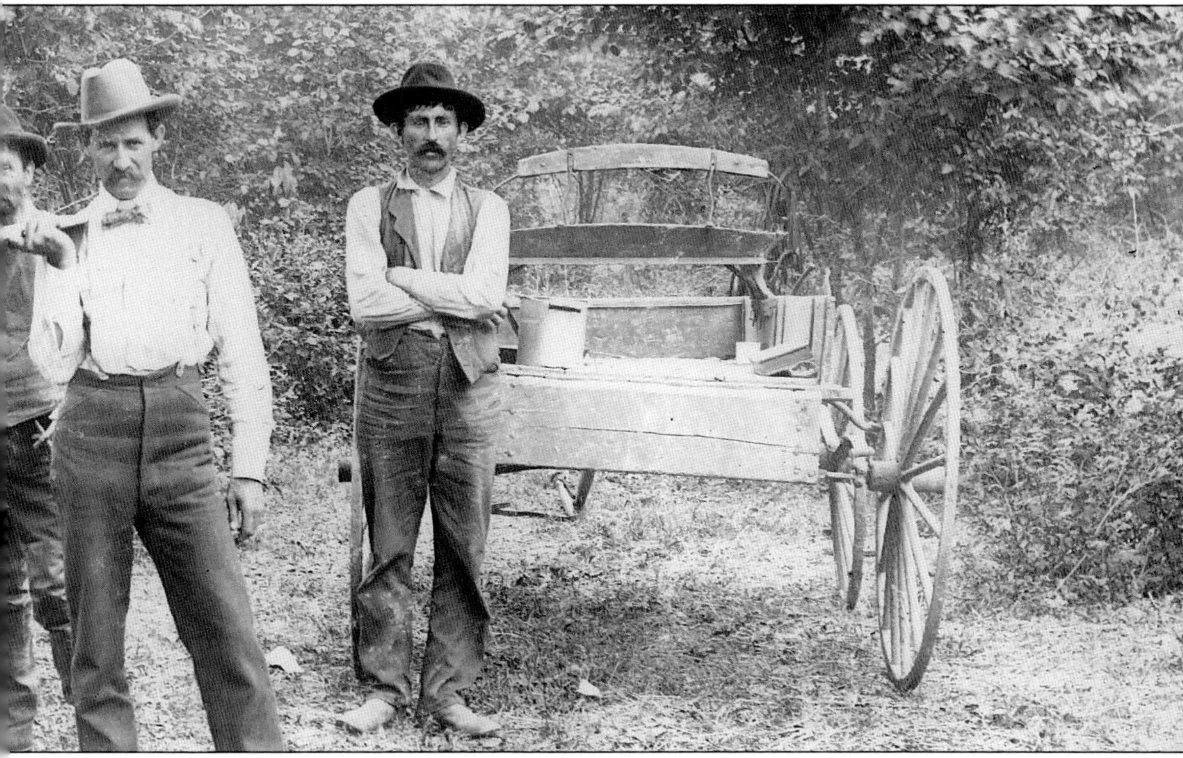

well as others. (Photographer: William Frederick Lichtenberger.)

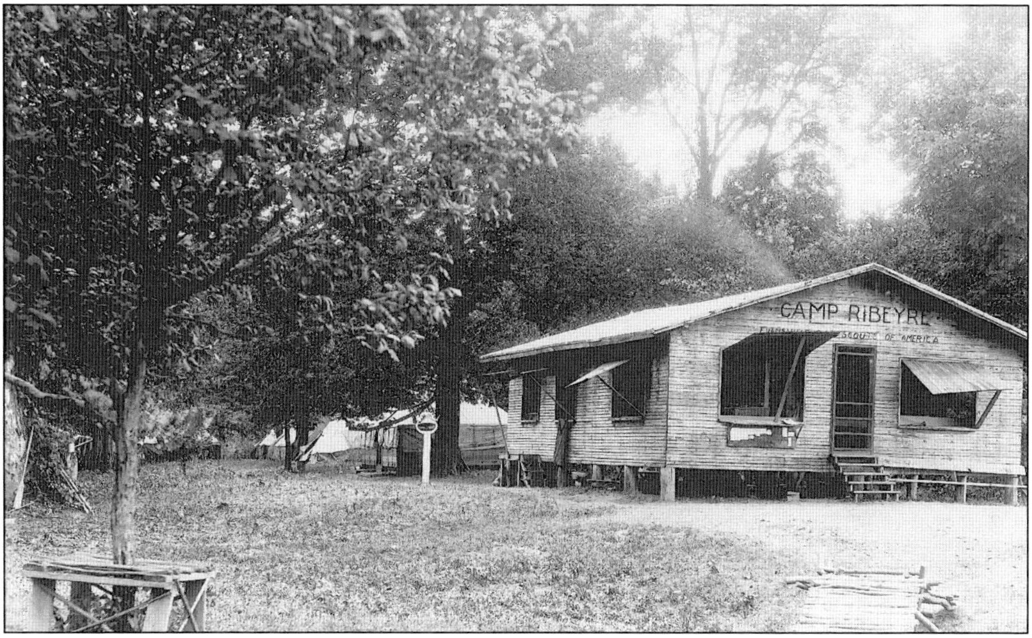

Pictured is Camp Ribeyre, home of the Evansville Boy Scouts of America. Note the tents pitched in the background of the photograph.

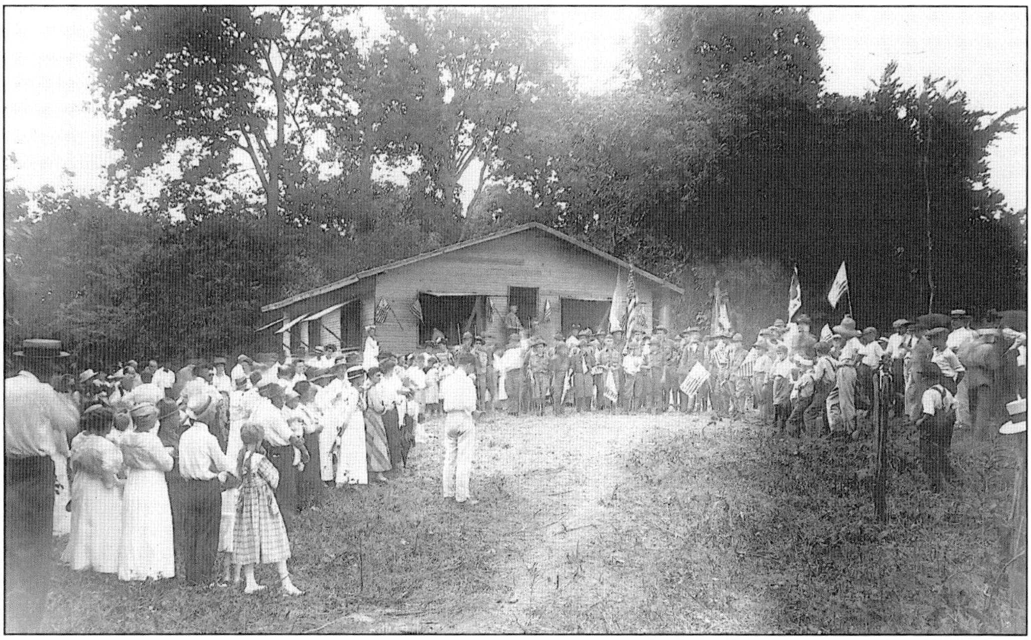

This crowd, some holding American flags, gathers at the Ribeyre Boy Scout camp. Note the Boy Scout troop assembled in the center of the photograph. (Photographer: William Frederick Lichtenberger.)

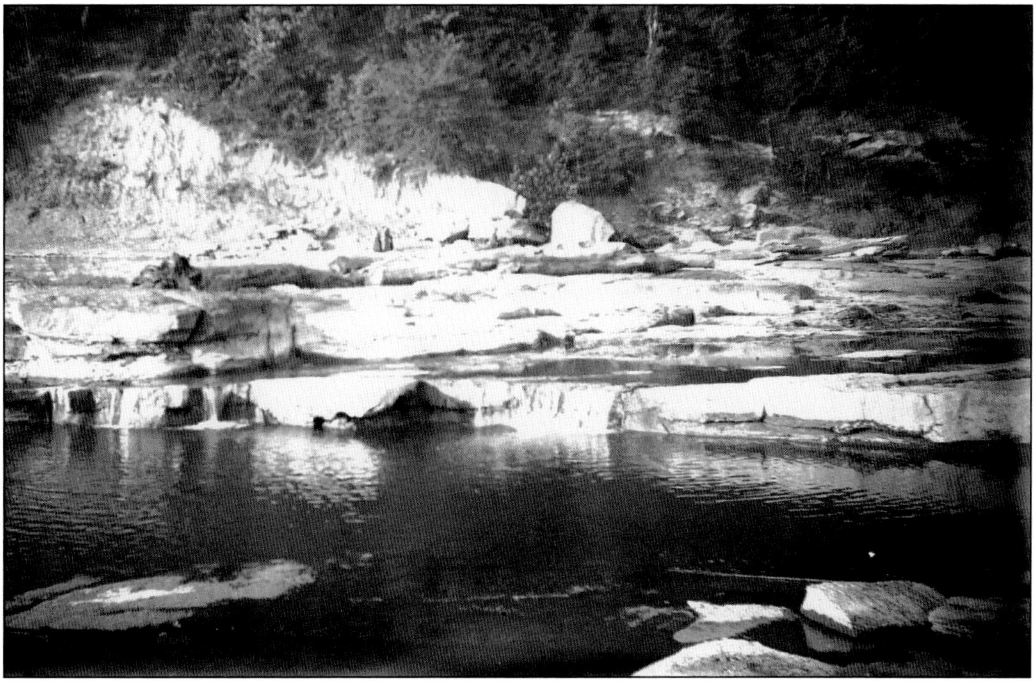

This October 16, 1901 photograph shows a view of the Old Dam of the Wabash River, south of New Harmony. Identified on the far bank are "Aunt Sue, Rachel Fauntleroy, and Homer Fauntleroy." (Photographer: Homer Fauntleroy.)

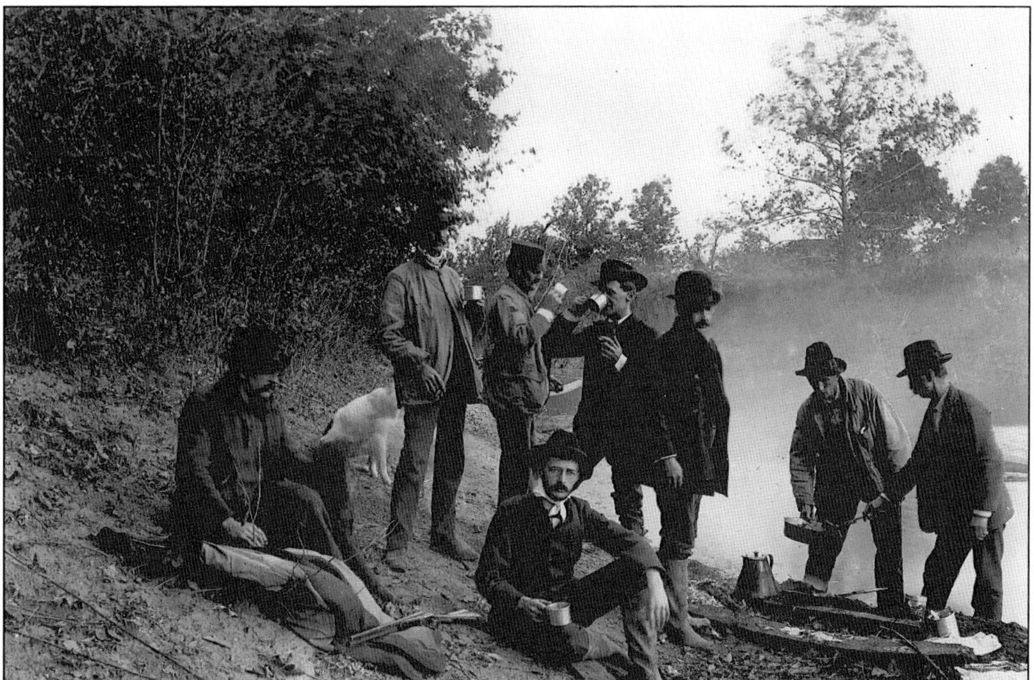

This camp photograph shows friends A.C. Thomas, Windy Dalzell, Watt Beau, Frank Miller, and others. (Photographer: William Frederick Lichtenberger.)

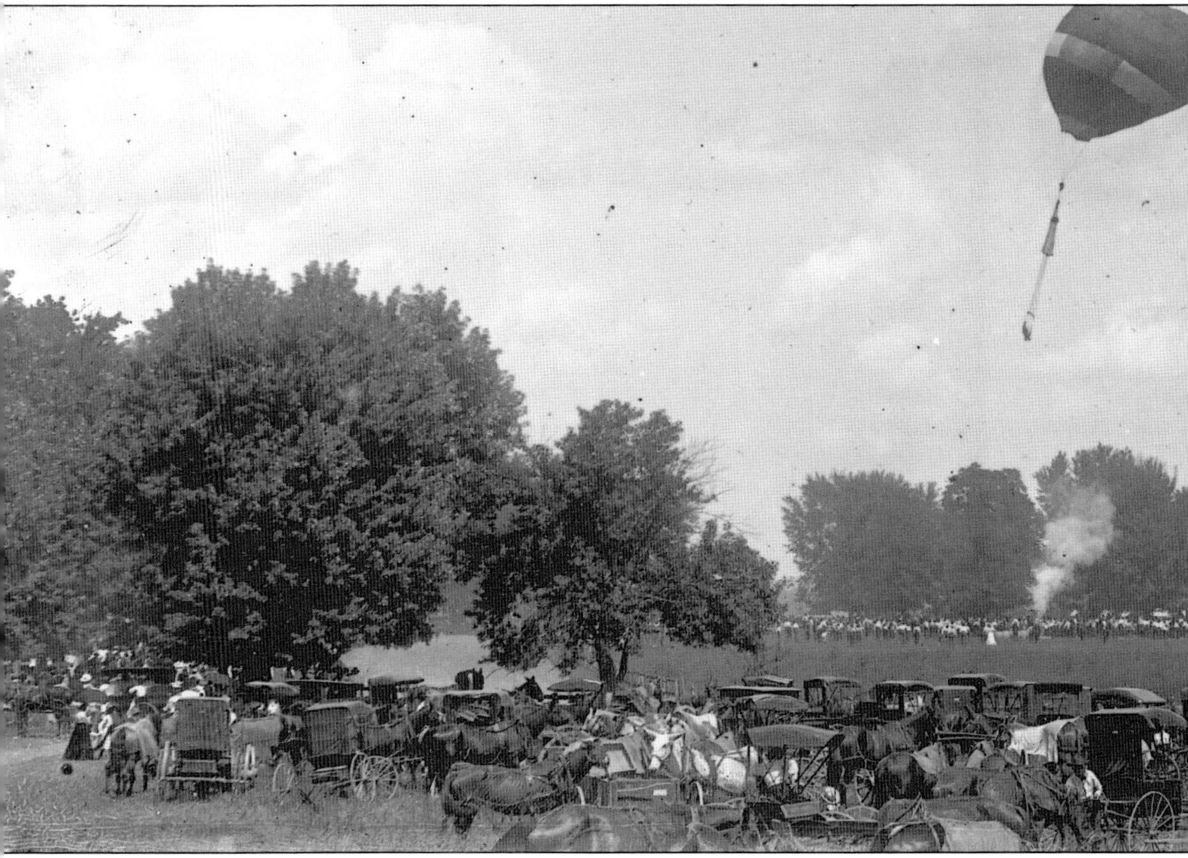

This balloon descent, photographed at the New Harmony Fairgrounds east of town, attracts a

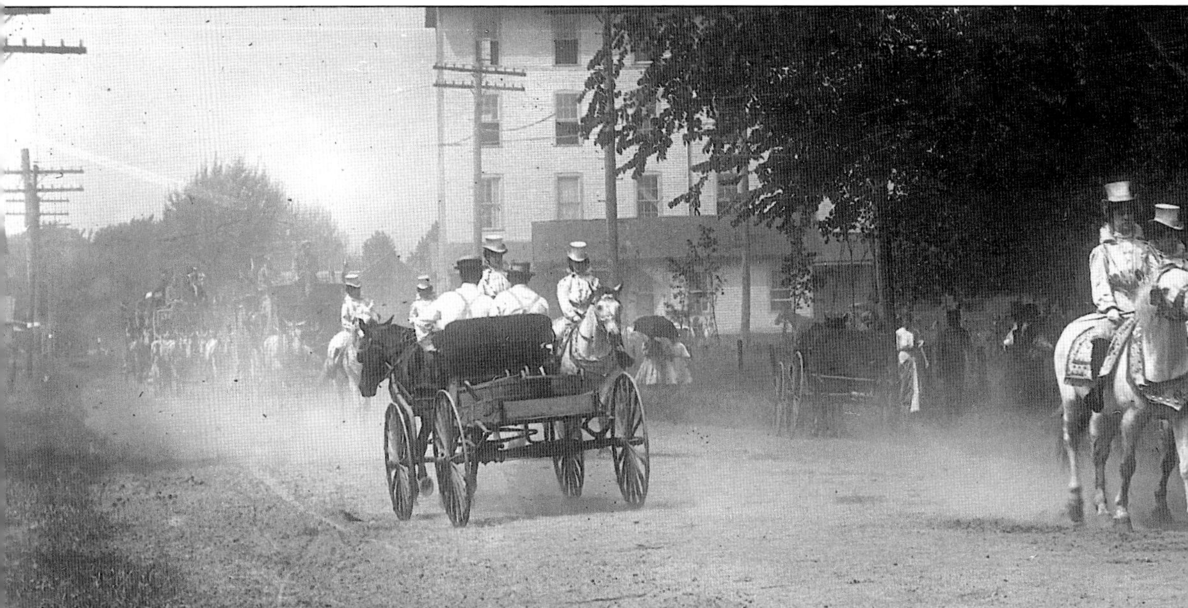

The Cole Brothers' Circus comes to New Harmony on August 29, 1907. (Photographer: William

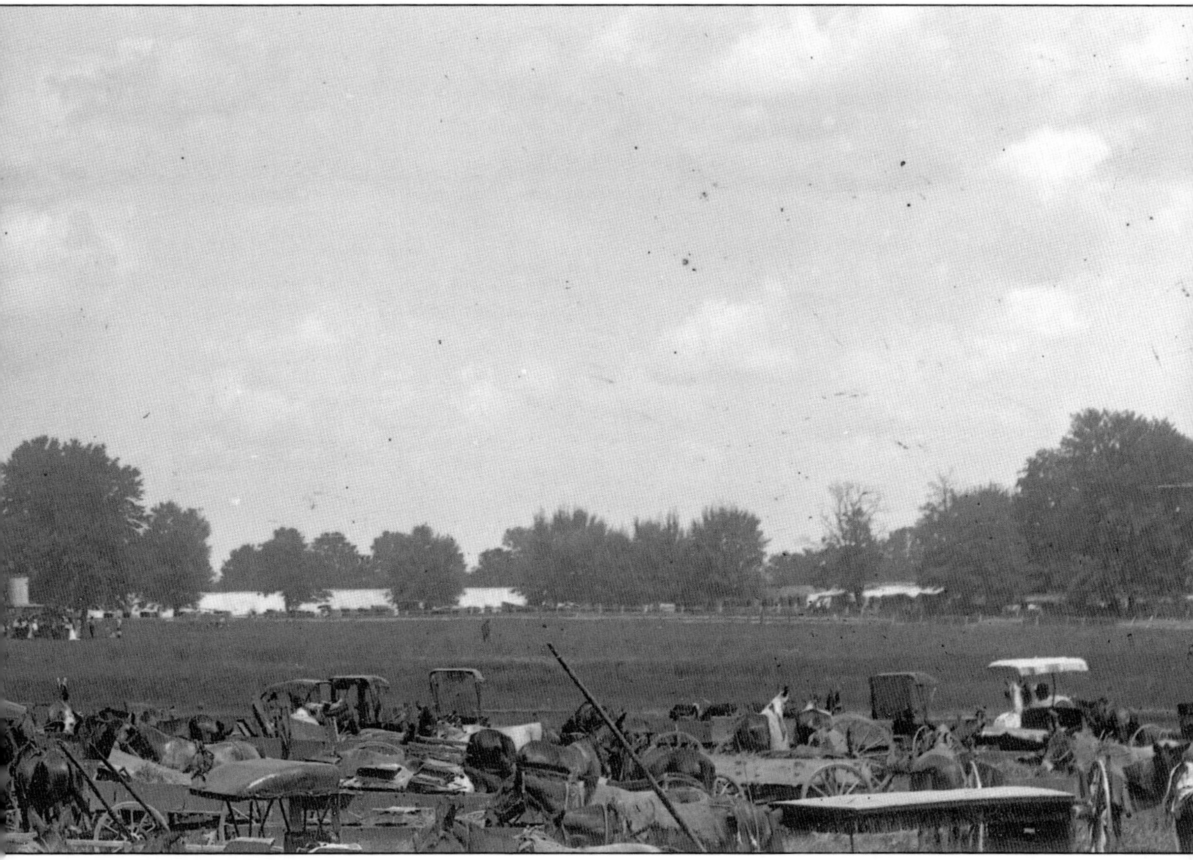

large crowd of onlookers.

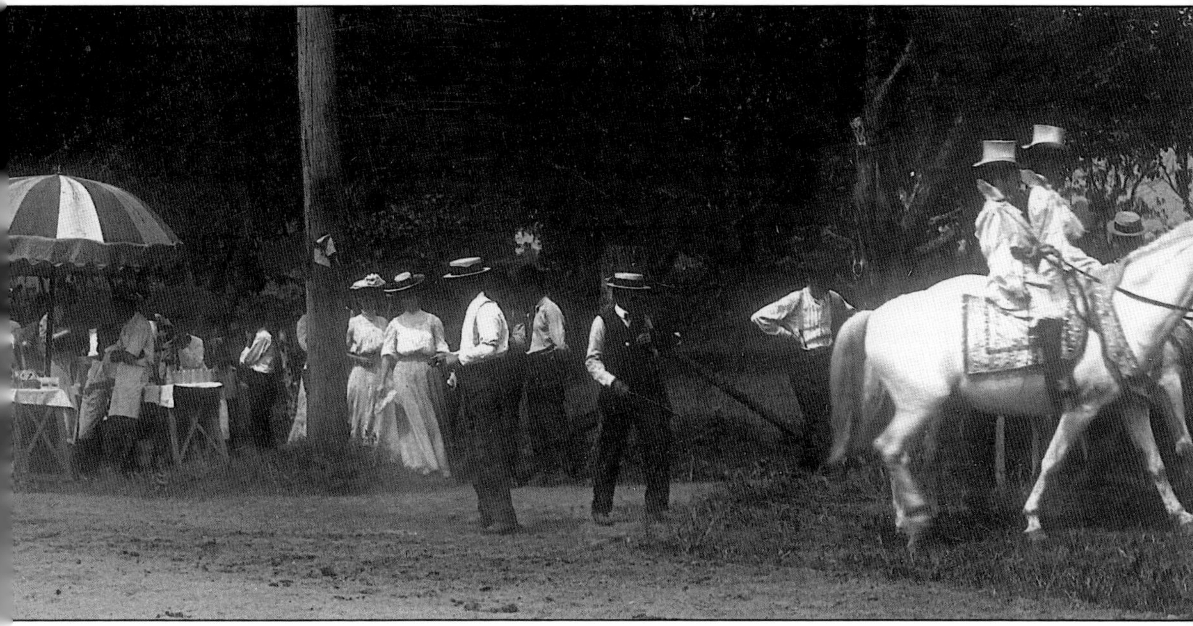

Frederick Lichtenberger.)

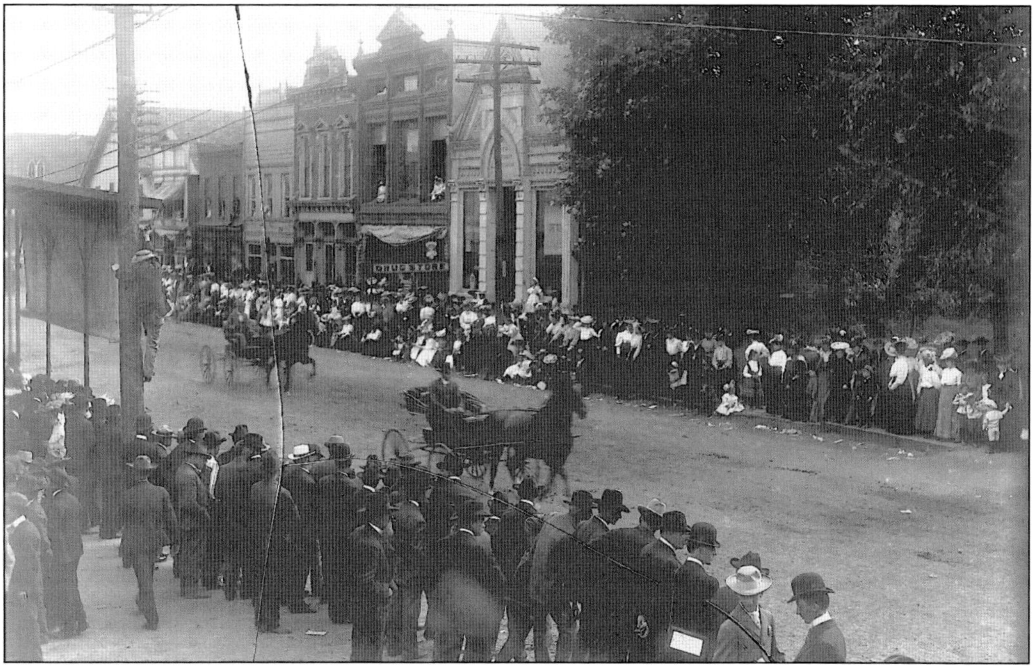

This 1906 photograph shows "Horse Show Day" on Main Street in New Harmony. Crowds line the sidewalks, and a young man has climbed a pole (on the left side of the image) to gain a better vantage point from which to view the events. (Photographer: William Frederick Lichtenberger.)

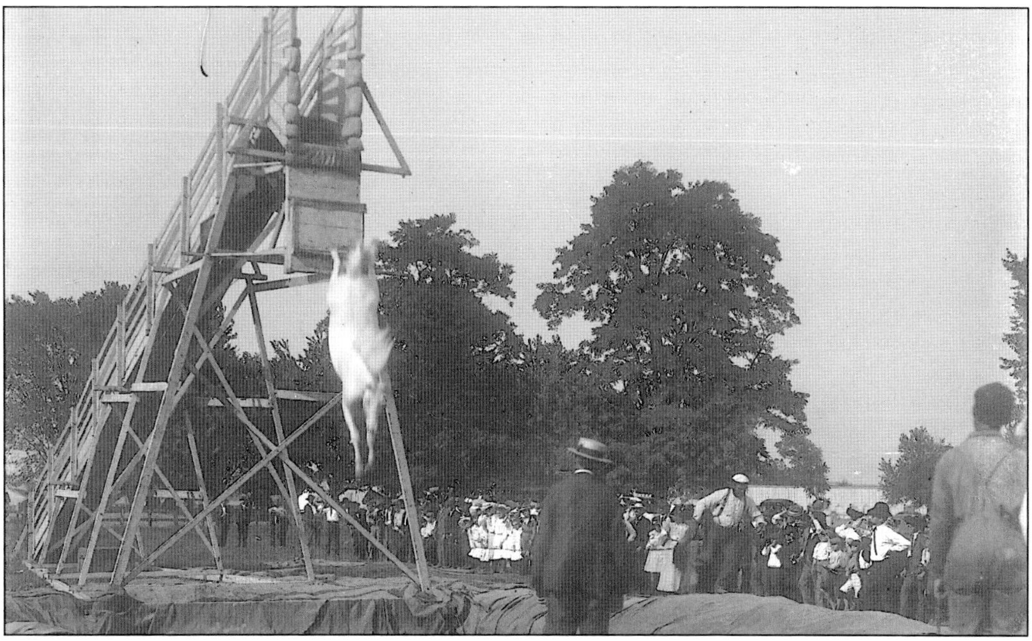

Among the historic forms of "animal entertainment" that fairs, circuses, and carnivals brought to towns were sights like this "diving" horse, photographed at the New Harmony Fairgrounds. Of course, today such events are prohibited, and animal protection laws regulate the treatment of animals by such enterprises.

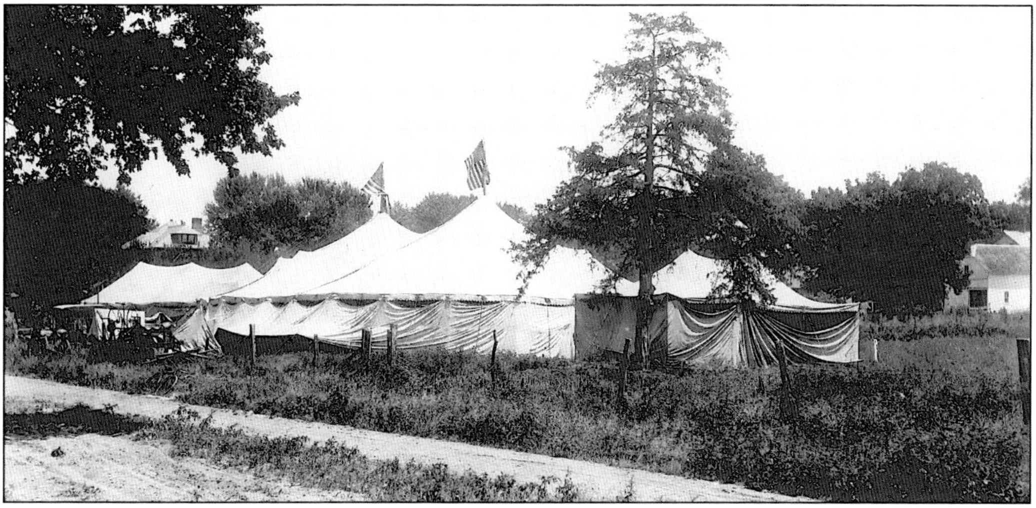

Shown in this view, circus tents are pitched on the edge of town. (Photographer: William Frederick Lichtenberger.)

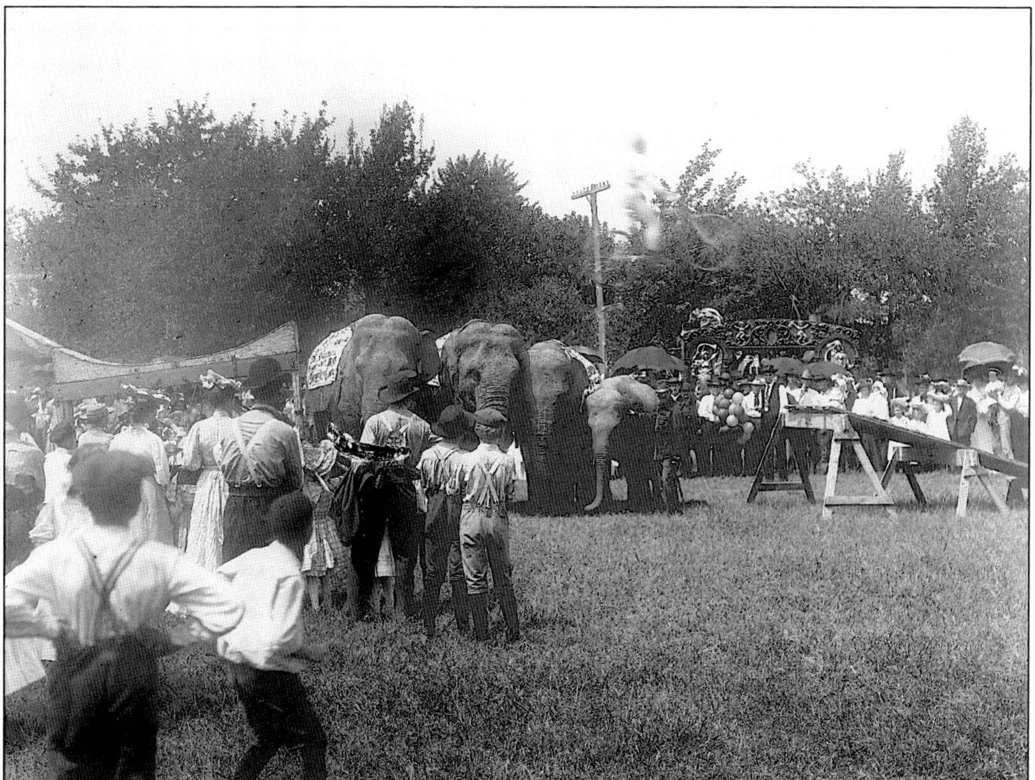

The elephants and entertainment acts of Cole's Circus gather in John Greve's field outside New Harmony. Note the cyclist in mid-air.

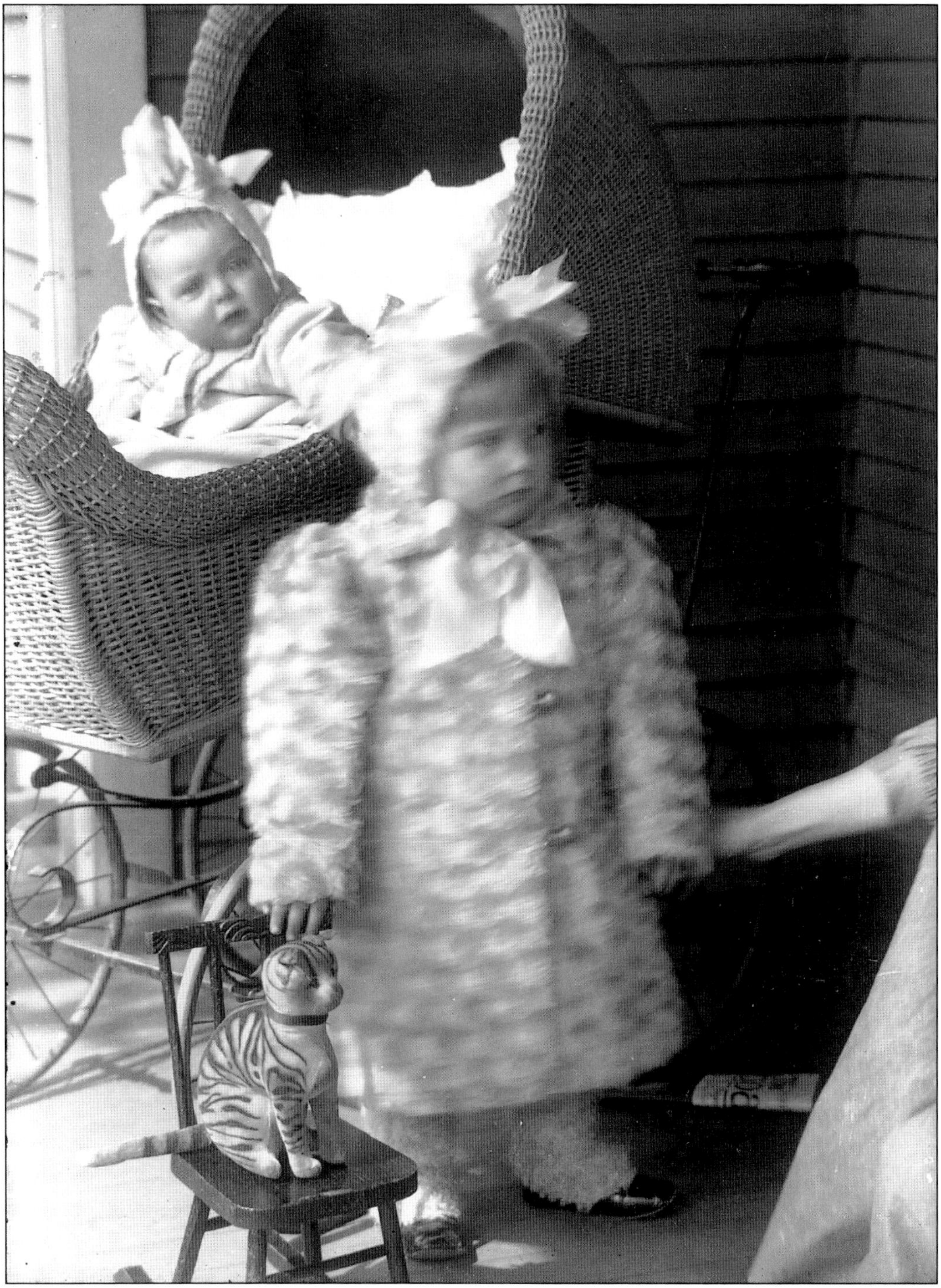

Young Mary Fretageot stands in her cloak and hood on March 25, 1908, near her younger sister, Cecilia, in the buggy. Their toy cat sits in its perfectly-sized chair. (Photographer: Homer Fauntleroy.)

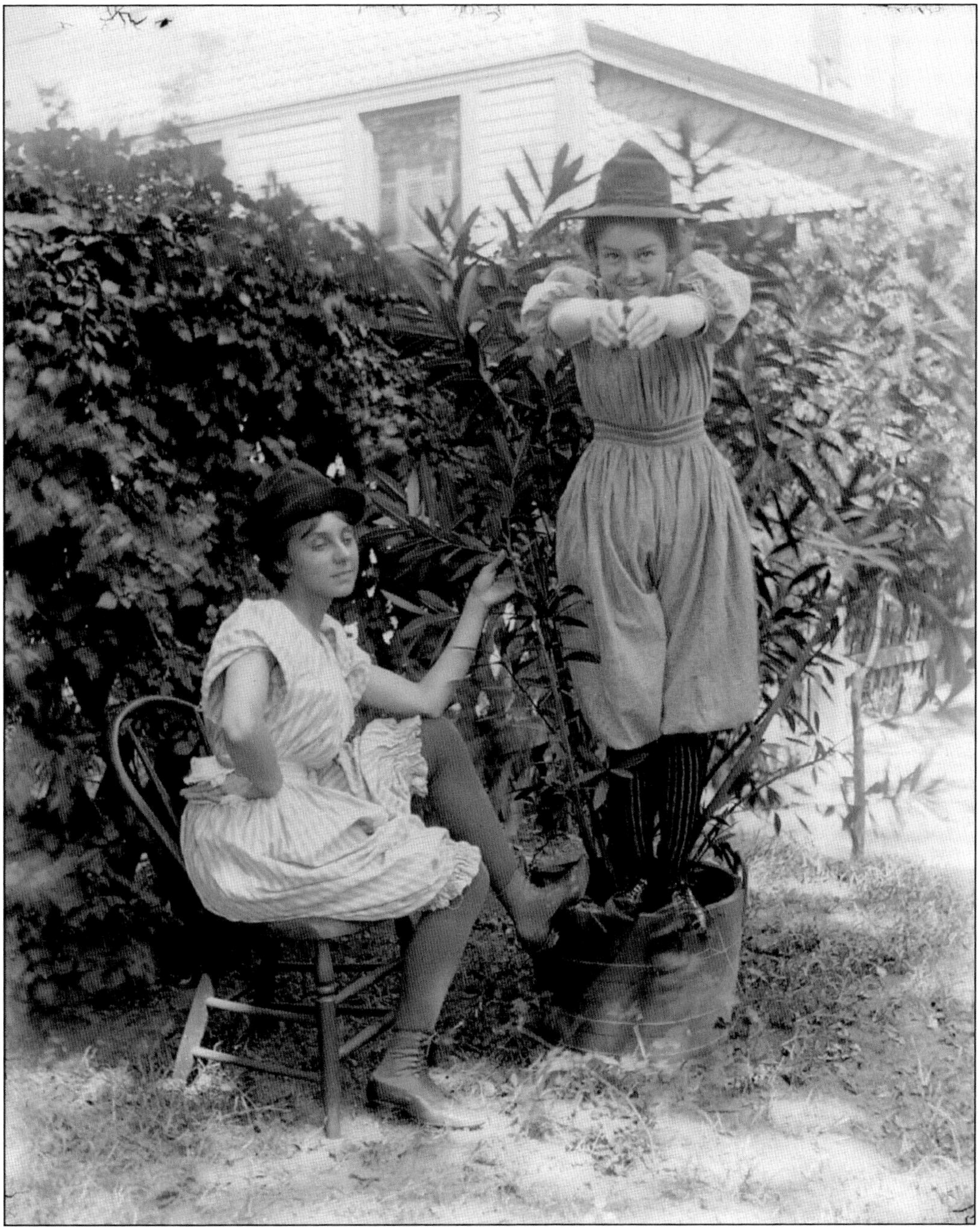

In this comical photograph, Eloise Mumford and Louise Hill, dressed in their bathing suits, practice diving for the camera.

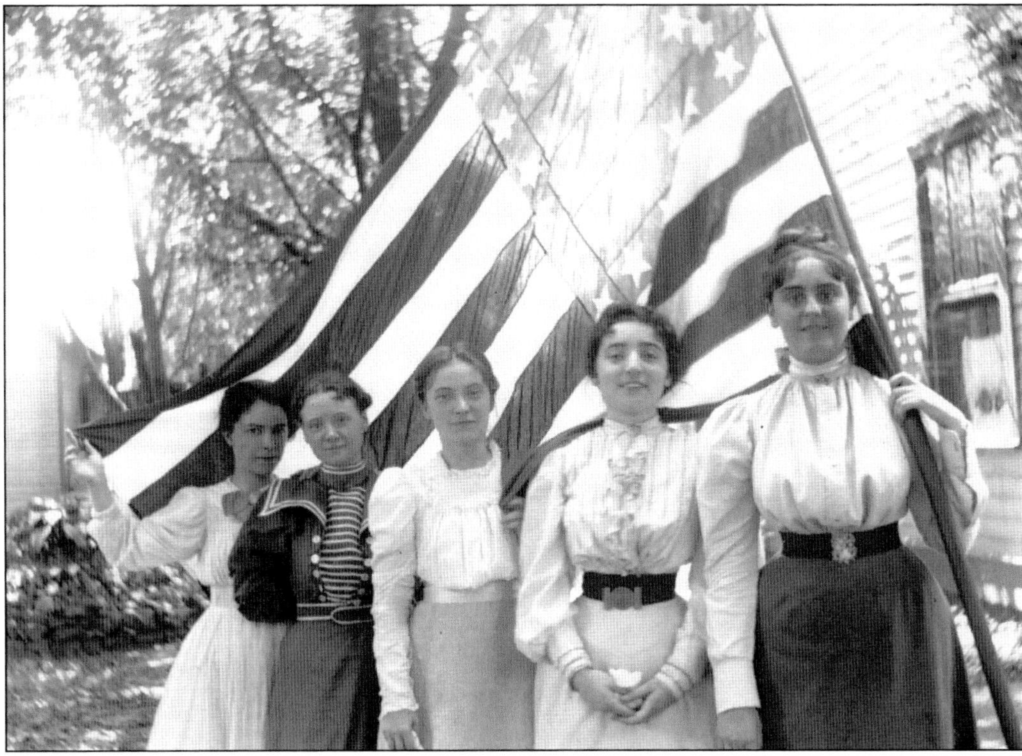

These friends gather at the Golden home in New Harmony. Pictured from front to back are: Marcia Corbin, Bessie Strauss, Carrie Parks, Connie Lynn, and Fannie Golden.

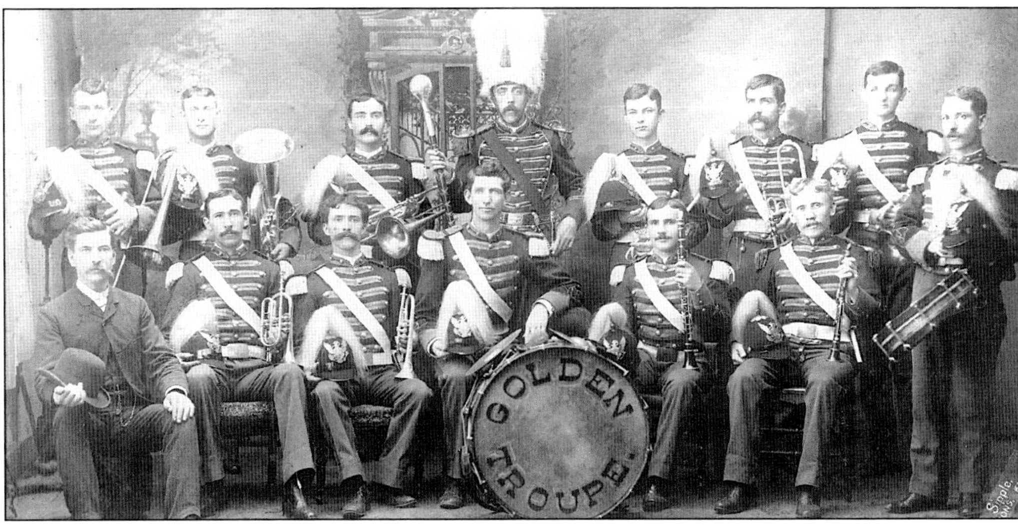

"The Golden Troupe Silver Band and Orchestra," sometimes known as the "Silver Cornet Band," accompanied the Golden Troupe on their theatrical tours. The orchestra would play an overture before the play, perform between acts, and parade through towns as a form of advertisement for the Troupe. Some of the musicians, such as Martin Golden Jr., pictured third from left in the front row, also performed as actors. Troupe manager Martin Golden Sr. sits on the left end of the front row. (Photo courtesy of the New Harmony State Historic Site Collection.)

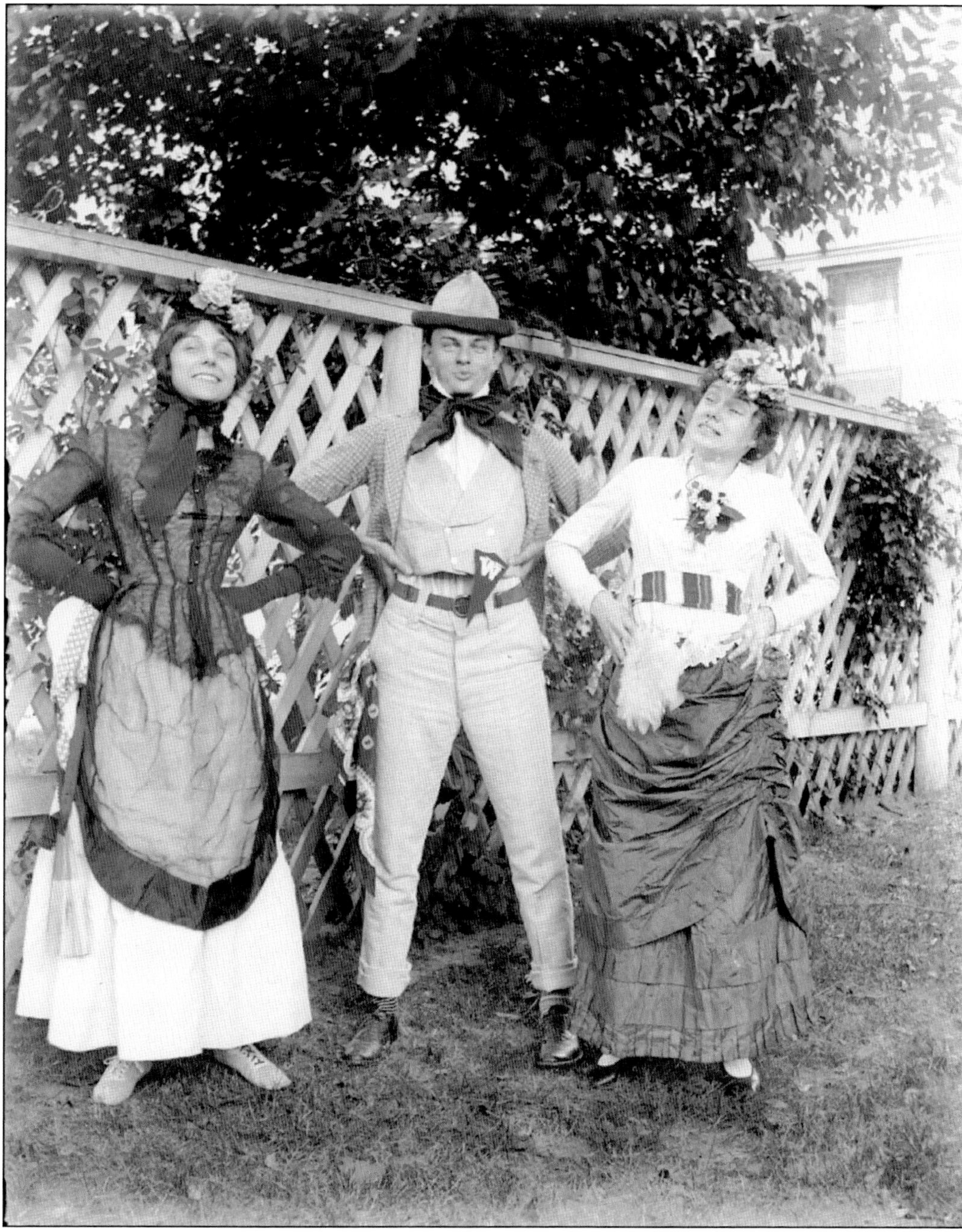

A group of young people, including Louise Hill and Eloise Mumford, dresses up in costume to attend a "Poverty Party" at the home of the Golden family in New Harmony. (Photographer: Homer Fauntleroy.)

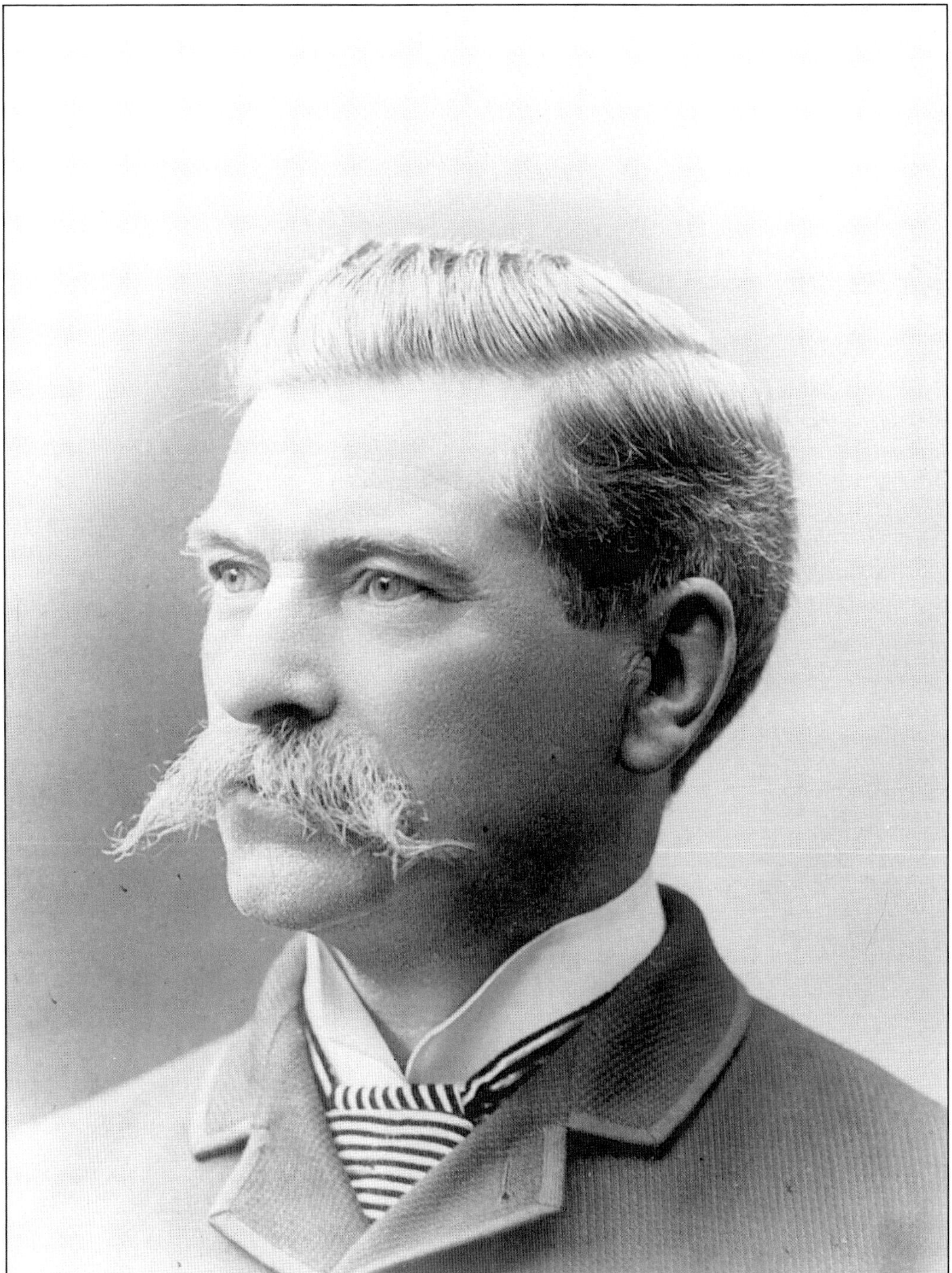

Martin Golden Sr., patriarch of the Golden family, was the son of Irish immigrants who died before establishing themselves in this country. He was raised by siblings in New York City and New Orleans, where he was exposed to the theater. He met his wife, also a young thespian, in St. Louis in 1855. They married in 1861, in St. Louis, and thus began their life together in the American theater. (Photo courtesy of the New Harmony State Historic Site Collection.)

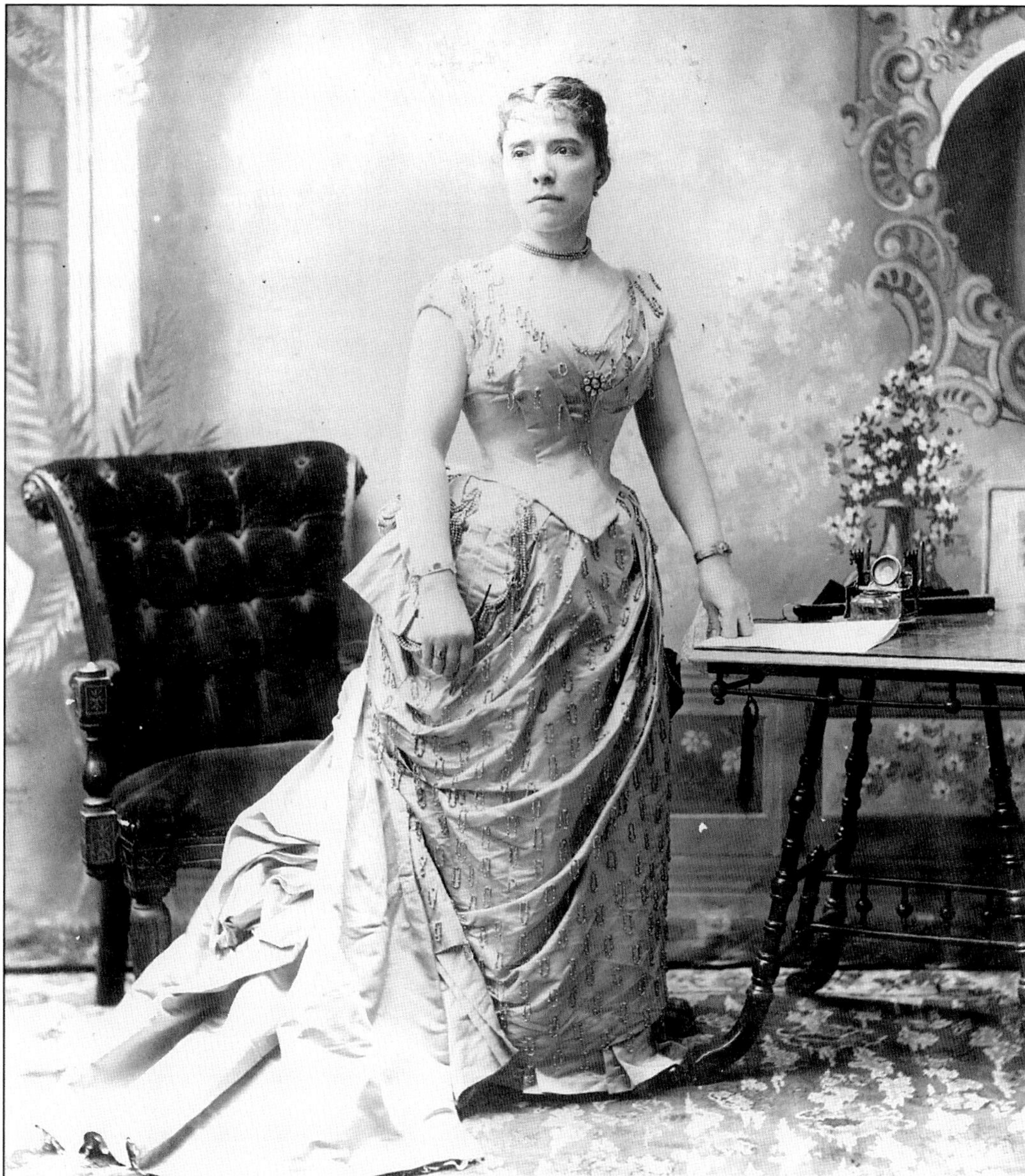

Emma Isabella Llewellyn Golden was the daughter of English immigrants, and was an orphan by the age of 17. She became involved in the theater when her father took a job as a doorman at a St. Louis establishment. Upon his death, the owners of the theater gave "Bella" a job as a performer, and her natural talents brought her acclaim. She went on to meet Martin Golden in 1855 and marry him in 1861. They had four talented children while she worked full-time as an actress on the early American stage. Their children were Martin Jr., actor and New Harmony businessman; William E., playwright and English professor at New York's Brooklyn Polytechnic Institute; Grace I., actress and opera singer; and Frances L., vaudevillian, music teacher, and one of the founders of Evansville's Civic Theater. (Photo courtesy of the New Harmony State Historic Site Collection.)

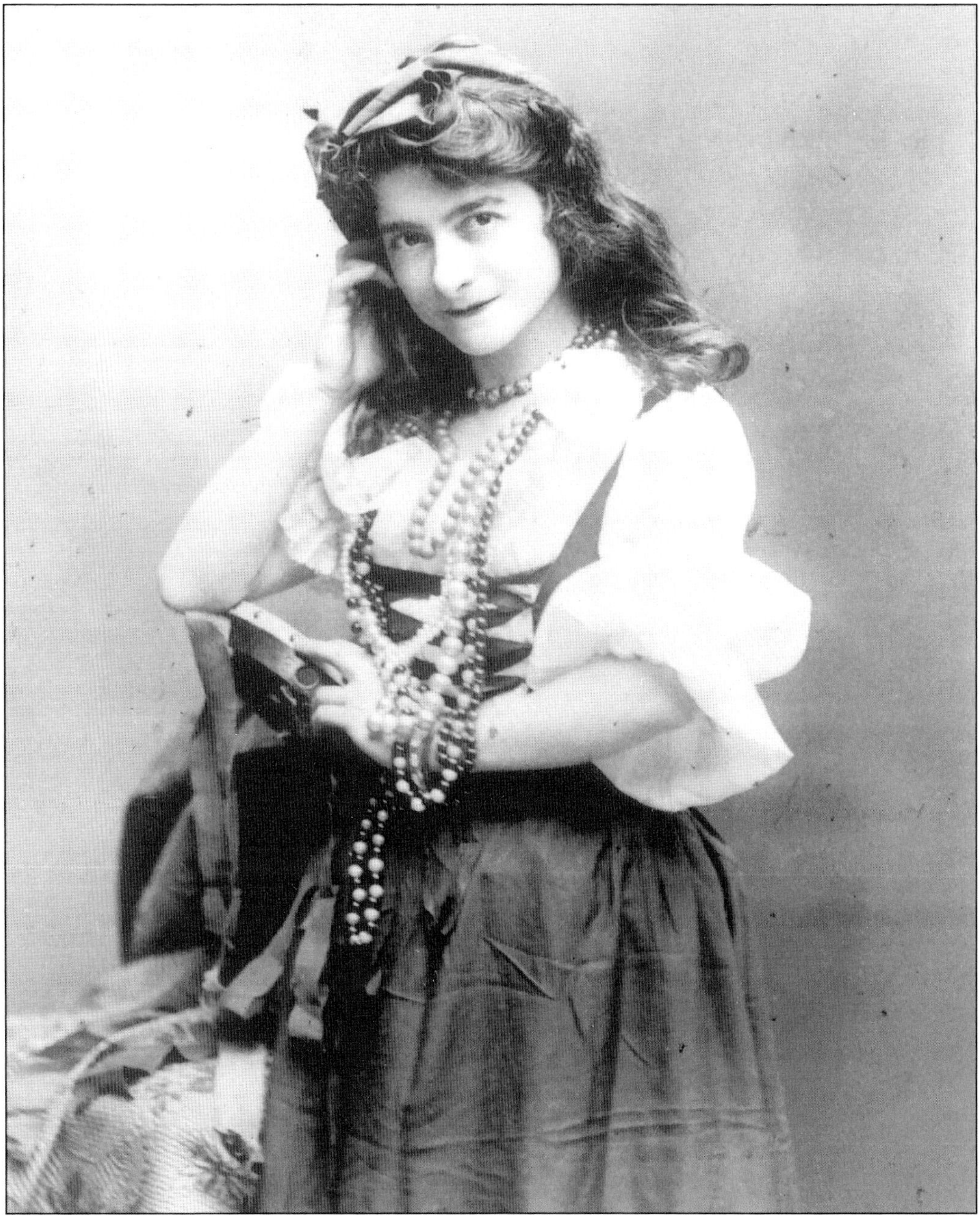

Grace Isabella Golden was born in New Harmony in 1867, and grew up on the stage, performing with her parents and older brothers, Martin Jr. and William; their younger sister, Frances, was not born until 1877. Grace's gift was for operatic singing, and she left New Harmony to seek her fortune, making her debut at the Metropolitan Opera Company in New York in 1883. This photograph shows Grace as "Santuzza," the lead soprano role in *Cavellaria Rusticana*, a role she assumed after serving as understudy to the prima donna soprano Lillian Russell. Tragically, Grace died of tuberculosis in 1903 at the age of 36. She is buried with her family at Maple Hill Cemetery in New Harmony. (Photo courtesy of the New Harmony State Historic Site Collection.)

Four

TOWN IN TRANSITION

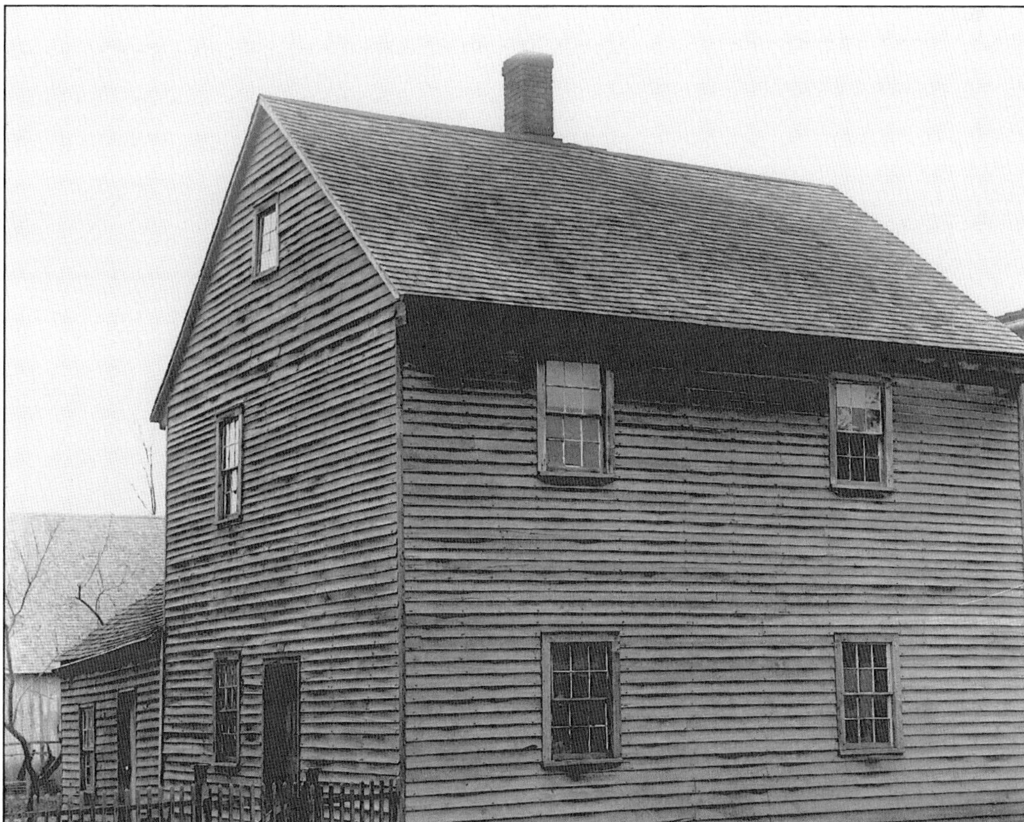

This March 9, 1906 photograph shows the Schuee (Schnee?) house, an original Harmonist dwelling. On the date of this photograph, it was still unaltered. (Photographer: Homer Fauntleroy.)

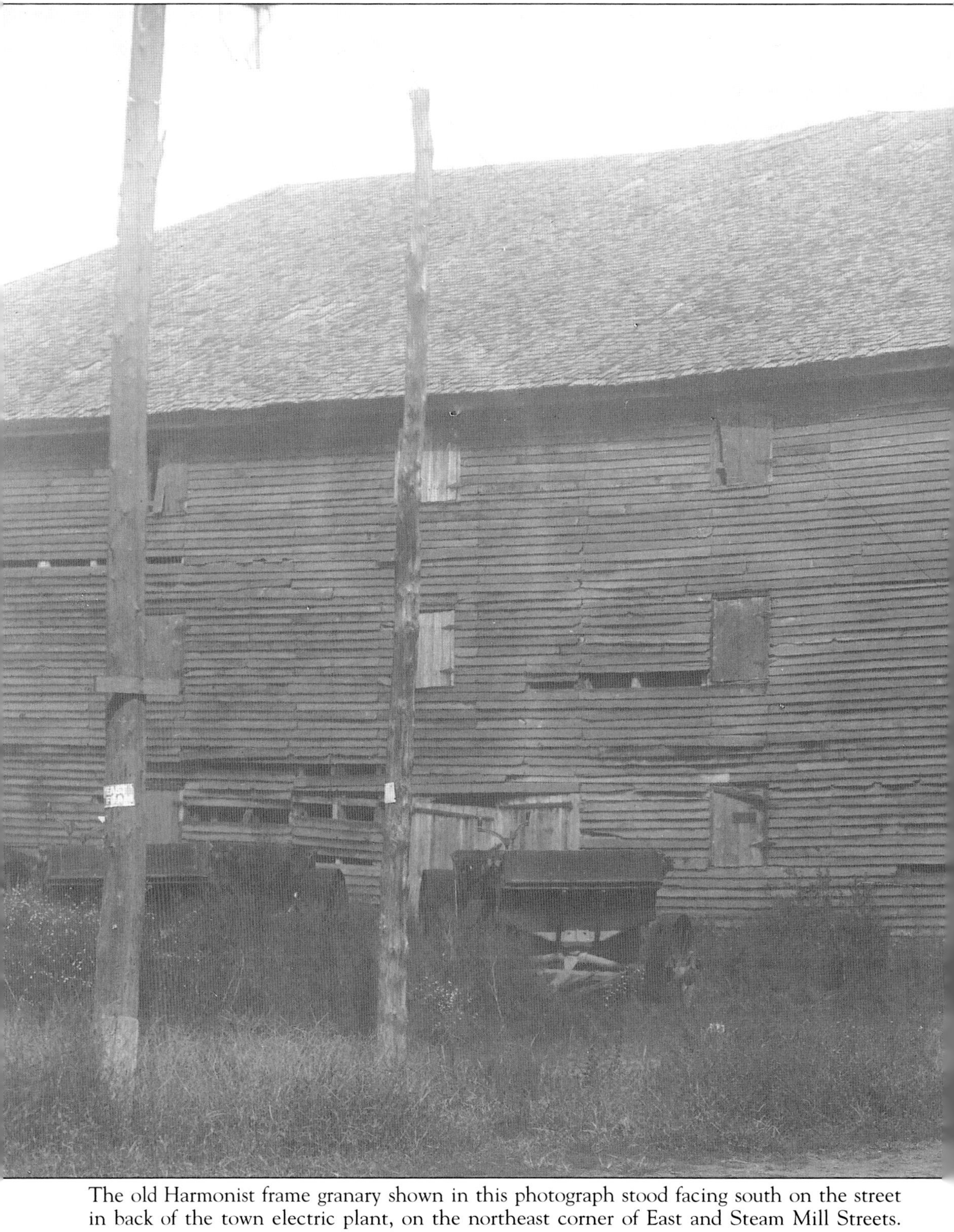

The old Harmonist frame granary shown in this photograph stood facing south on the street in back of the town electric plant, on the northeast corner of East and Steam Mill Streets.

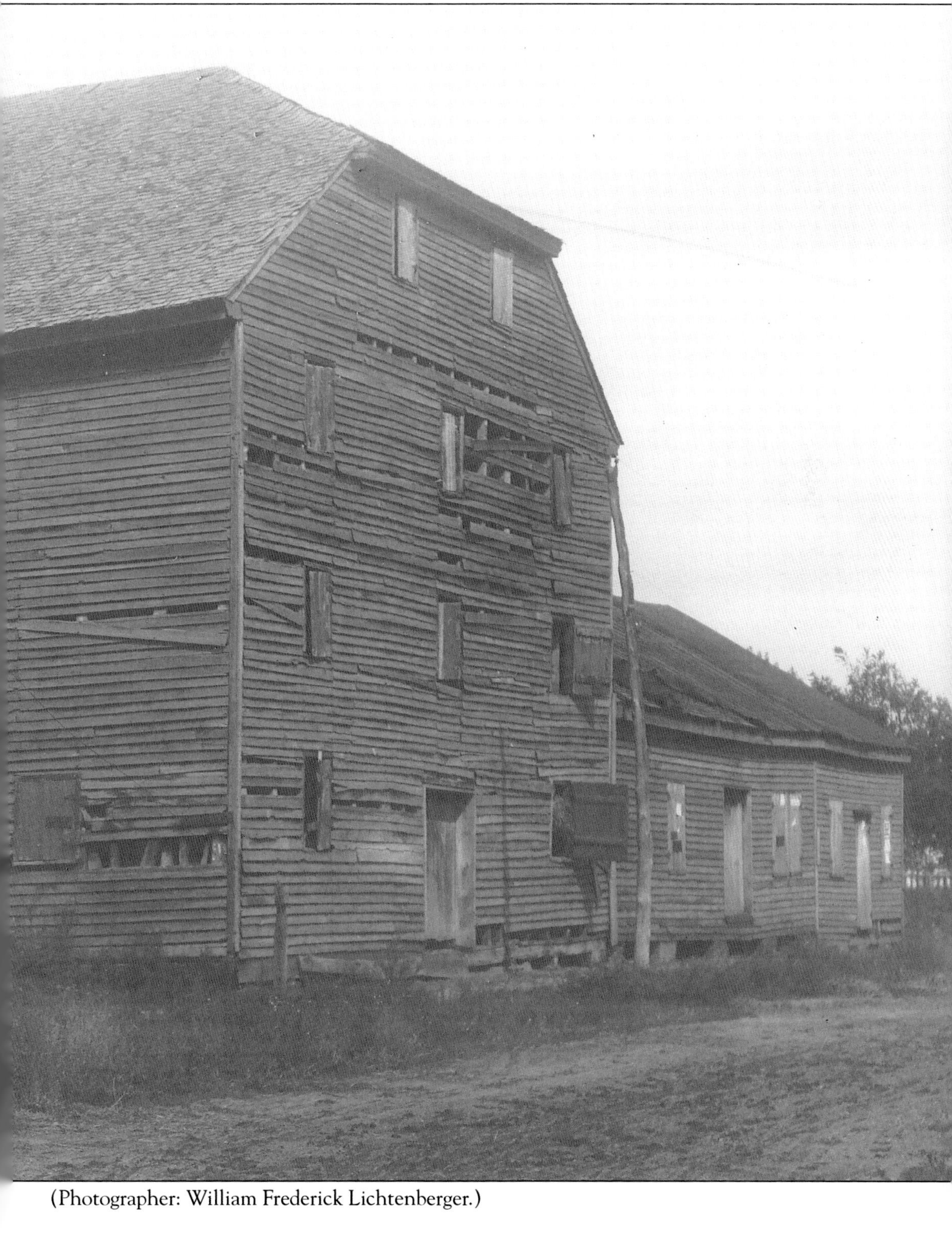

(Photographer: William Frederick Lichtenberger.)

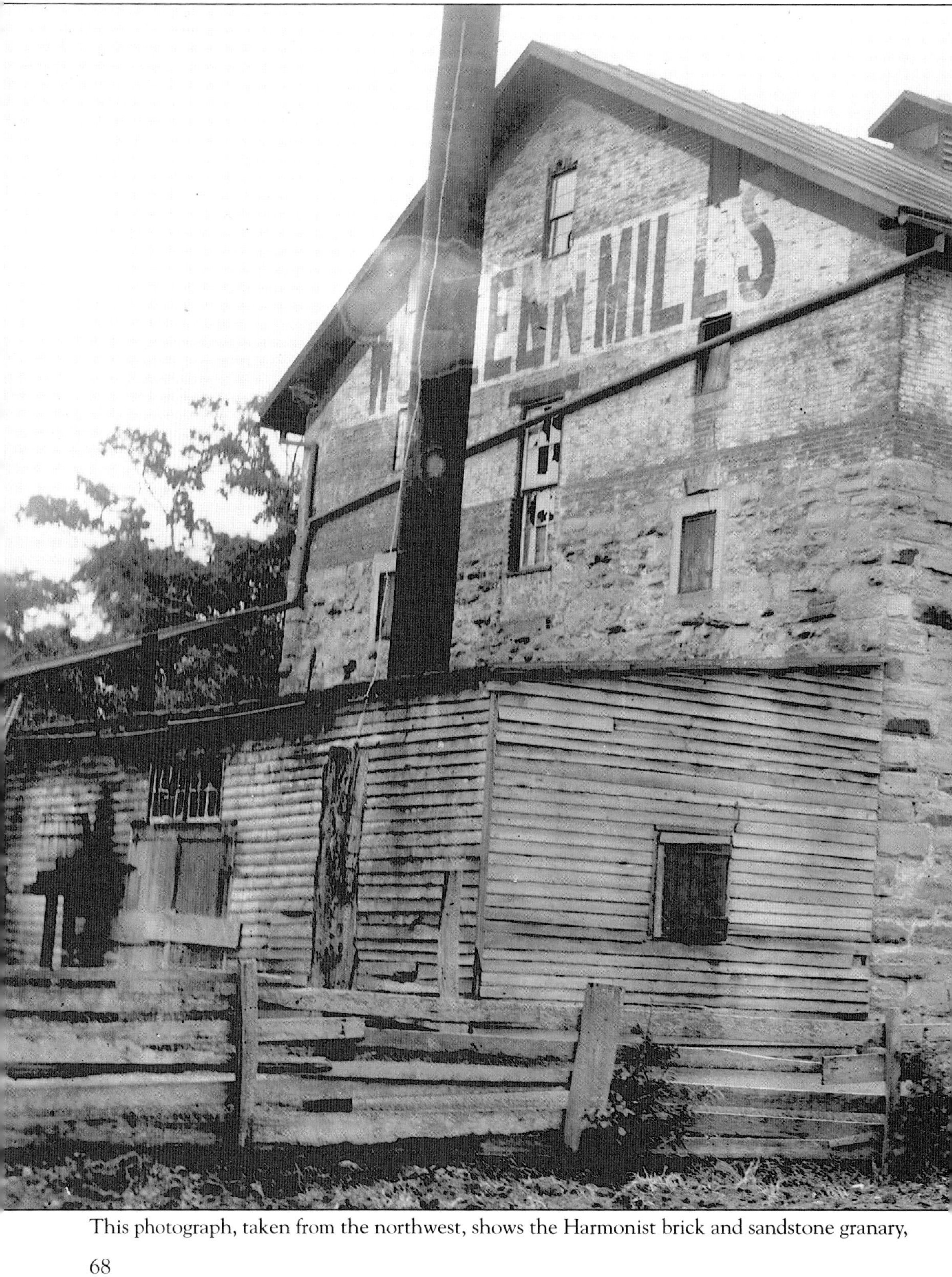

This photograph, taken from the northwest, shows the Harmonist brick and sandstone granary,

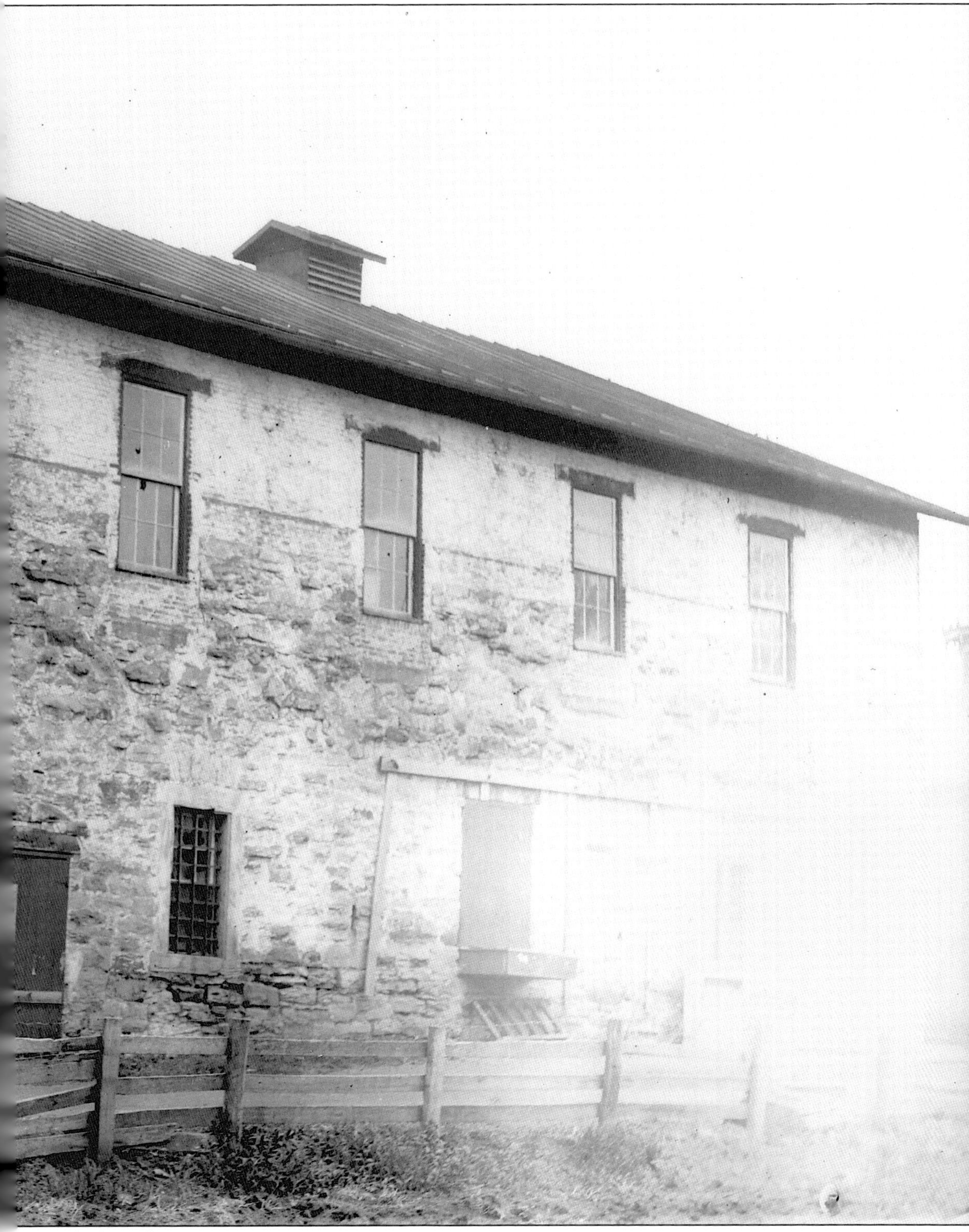

which underwent restoration in 1998-99.

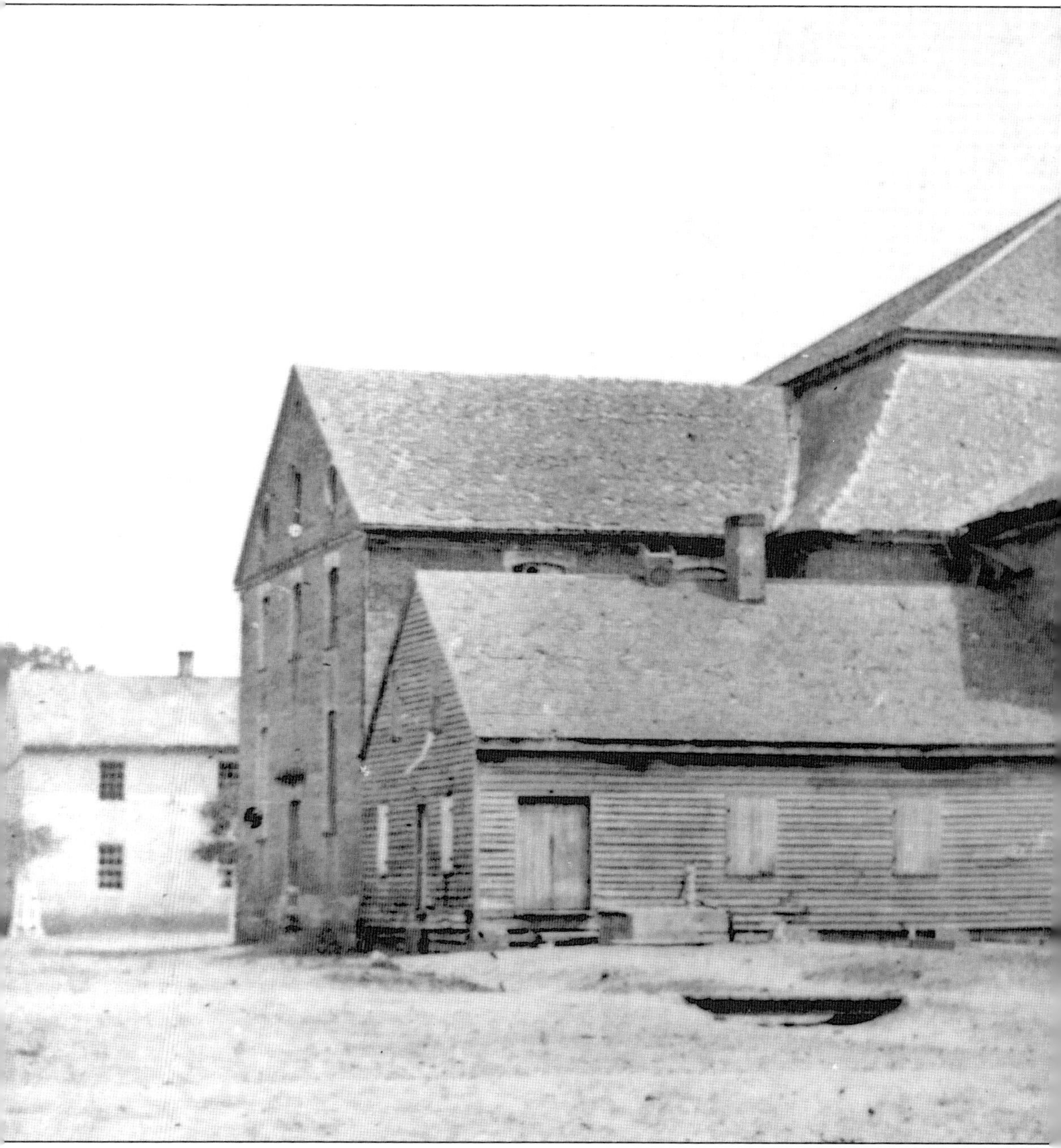

This photograph shows the Harmonist brick church before the demolition in 1874 of all but the building's east wing. The Harmonists purchased and then donated the lot and remaining wing to the town of New Harmony. They also gave $2000 towards the construction of the

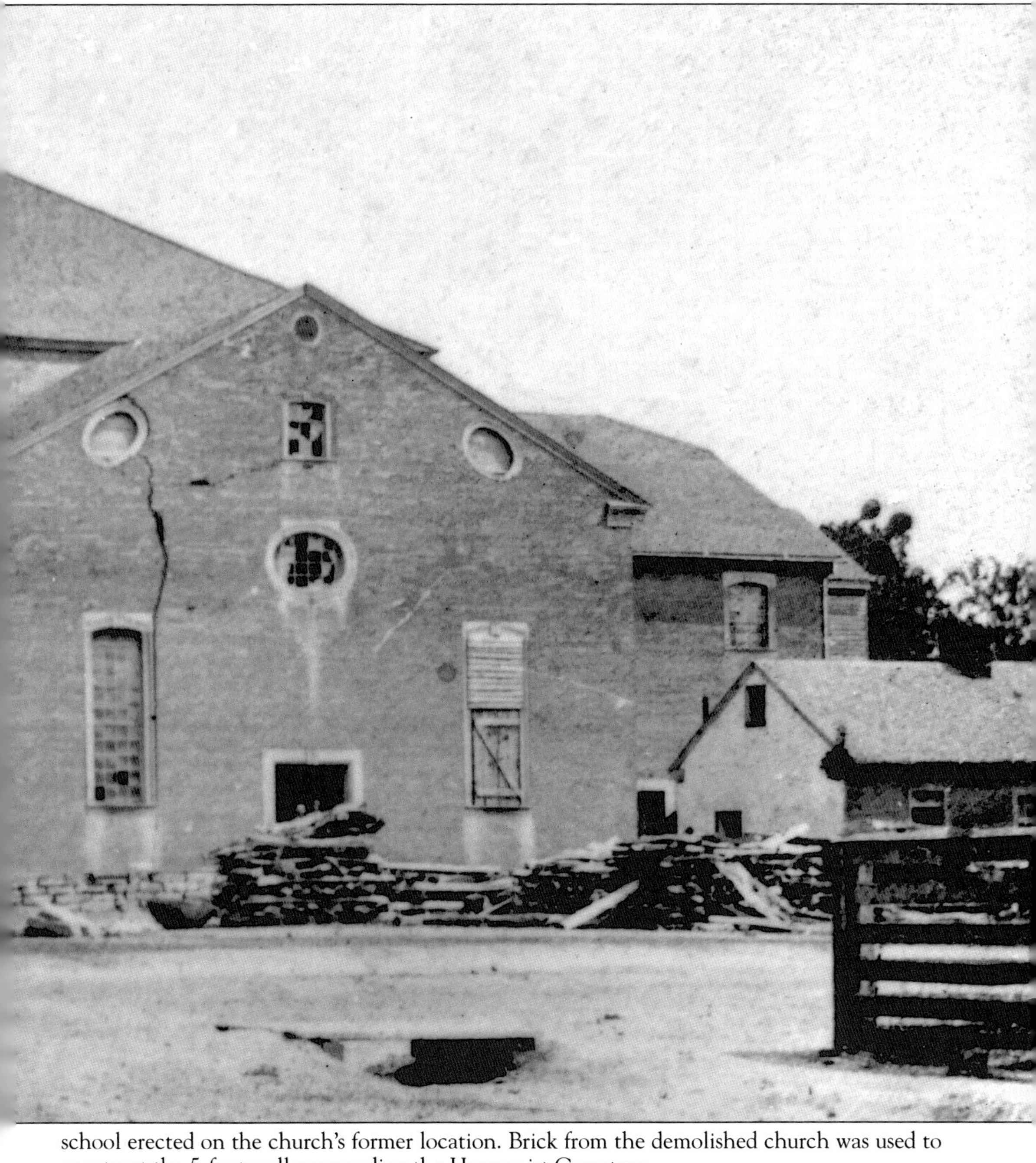

school erected on the church's former location. Brick from the demolished church was used to construct the 5-foot wall surrounding the Harmonist Cemetery.

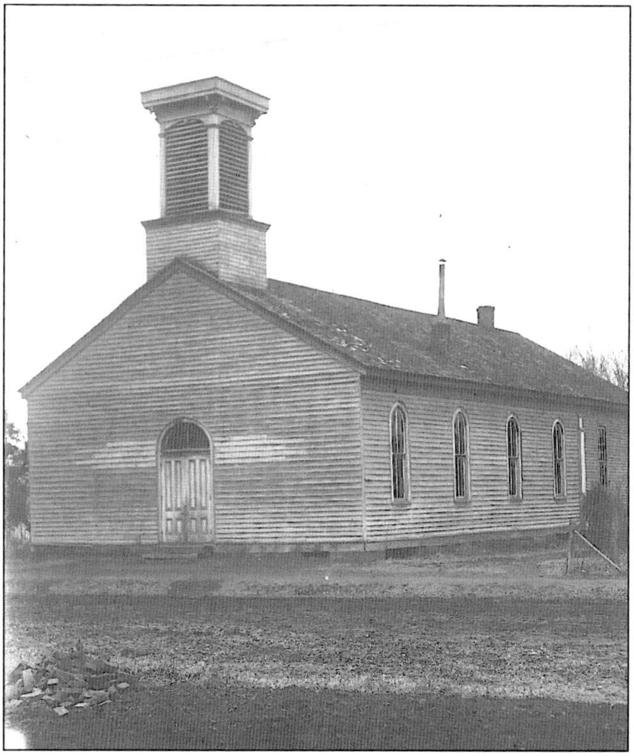

This is New Harmony's old Methodist church, photographed March 9, 1906. (Photographer: Homer Fauntleroy.)

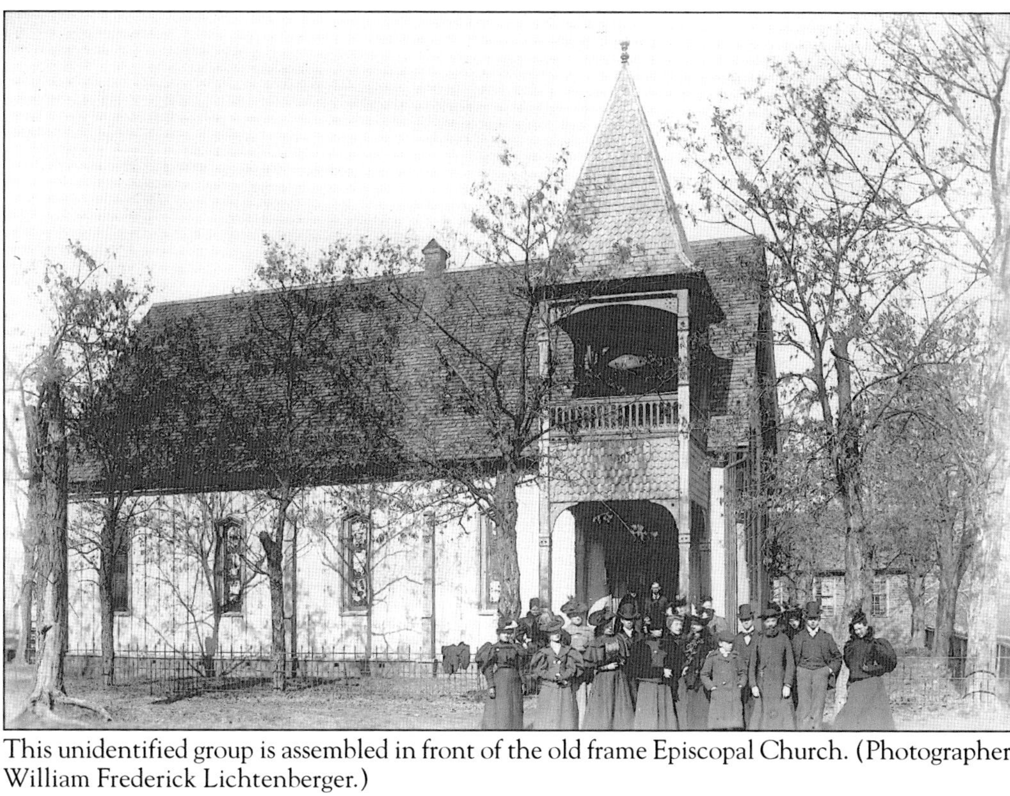

This unidentified group is assembled in front of the old frame Episcopal Church. (Photographer: William Frederick Lichtenberger.)

This is New Harmony's new Methodist church, photographed from the east on June 26, 1906. (Photographer: Homer Fauntleroy.)

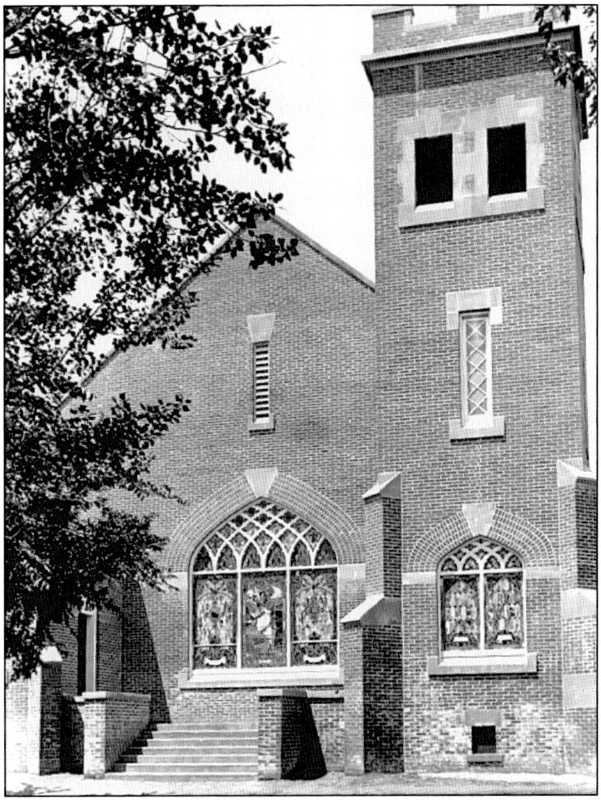

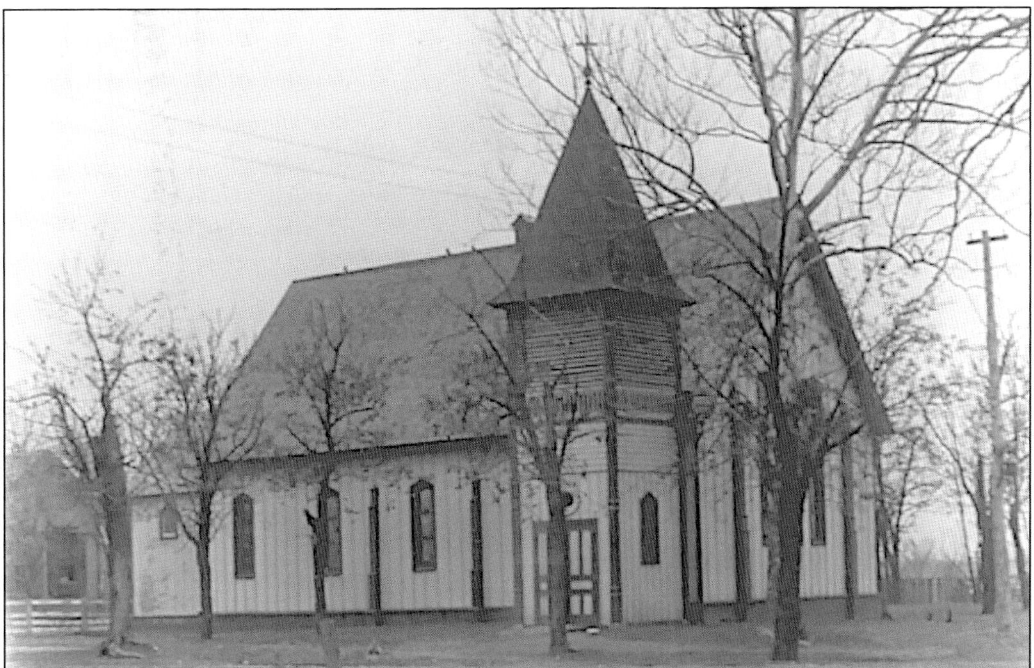

The "remodeled" Episcopal Church is shown here on March 11, 1906. (Photographer: Homer Fauntleroy.)

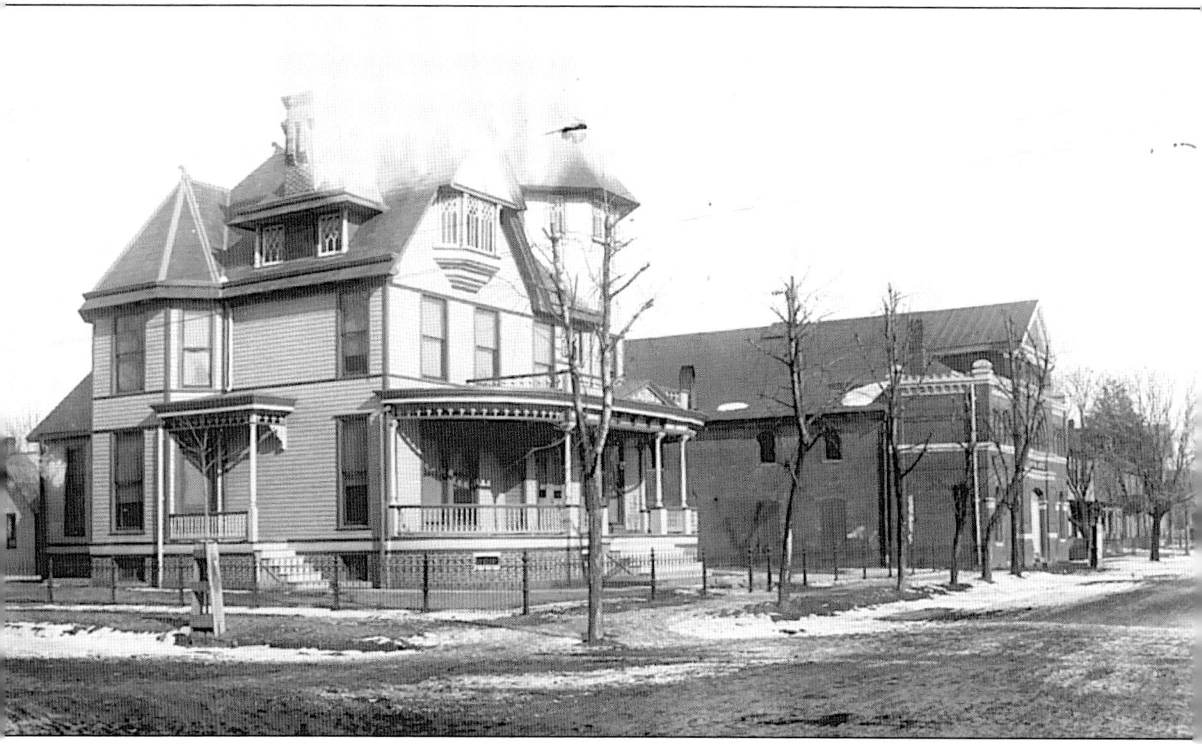

This photograph shows the Queen Anne-style Wilhelm House, which once stood on Church Street next to the Opera House. (Photographer: William Frederick Lichtenberger.)

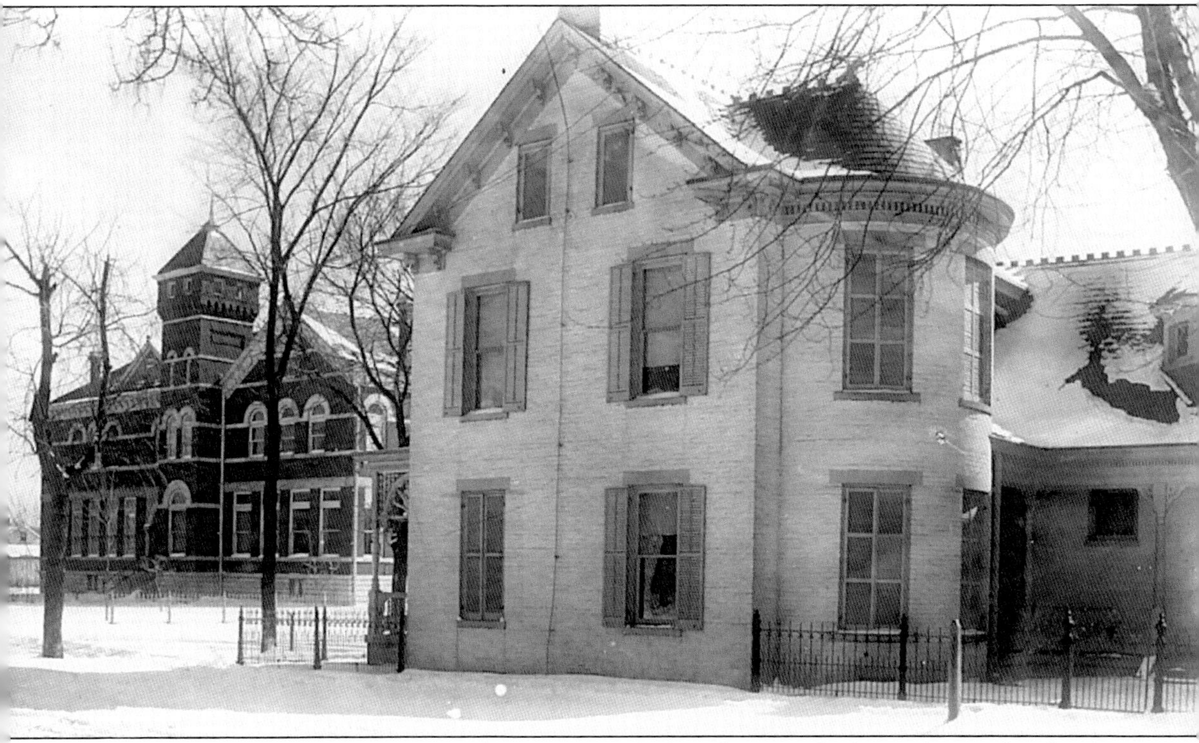

With the Workingmen's Institute in the background, this photograph shows the north side of the Schnee-Ribeyre-Elliott house. (Photographer: William Frederick Lichtenberger.)

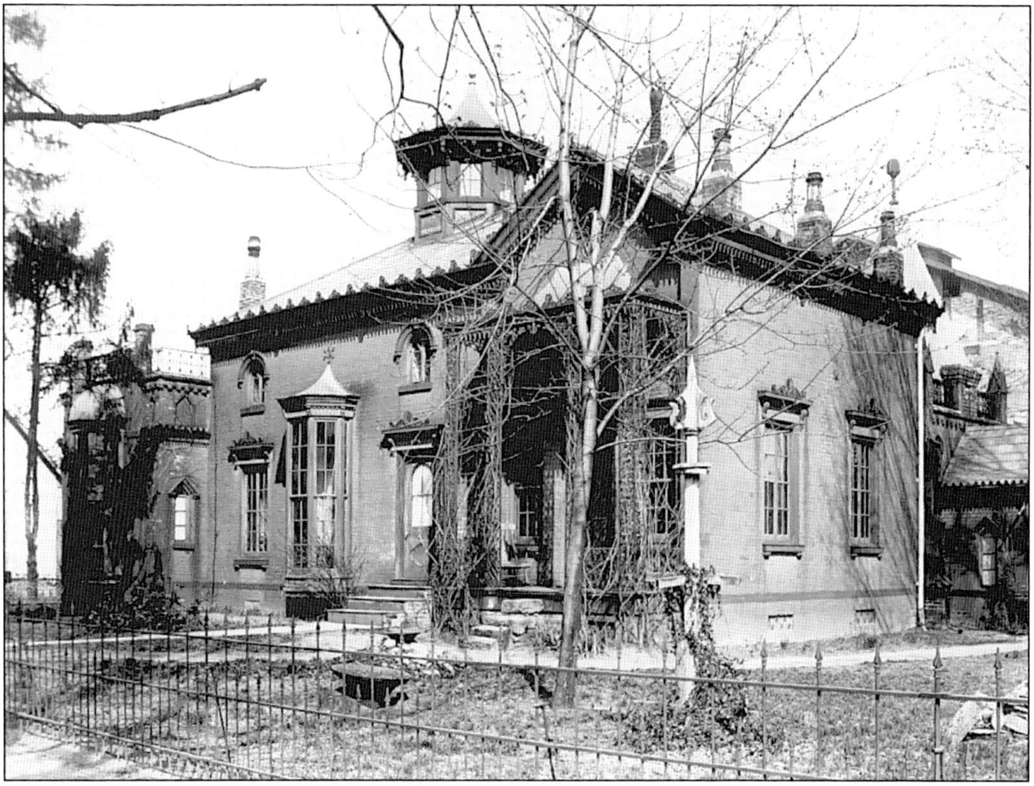

This photograph showcases David Dale Owen's Gothic Revival-style laboratory, which faces Church Street, and still stands south of the Harmonist Granary.

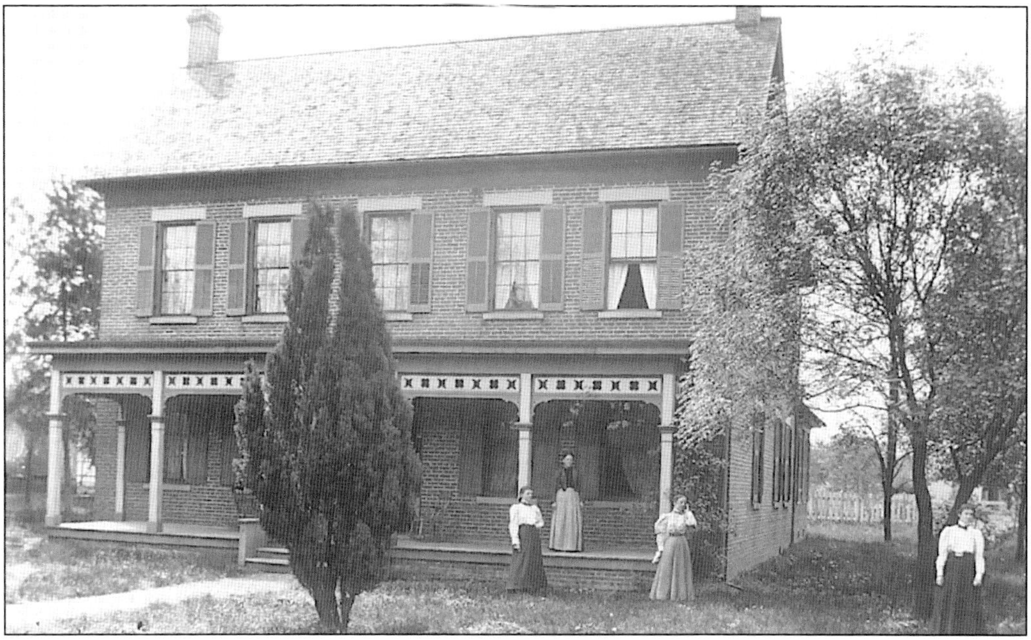

This is the New Harmony residence of T.J. Truscott. Pictured are Mary Truscott, Kate Mott, Margaret Stacer, and Lula Stacer.

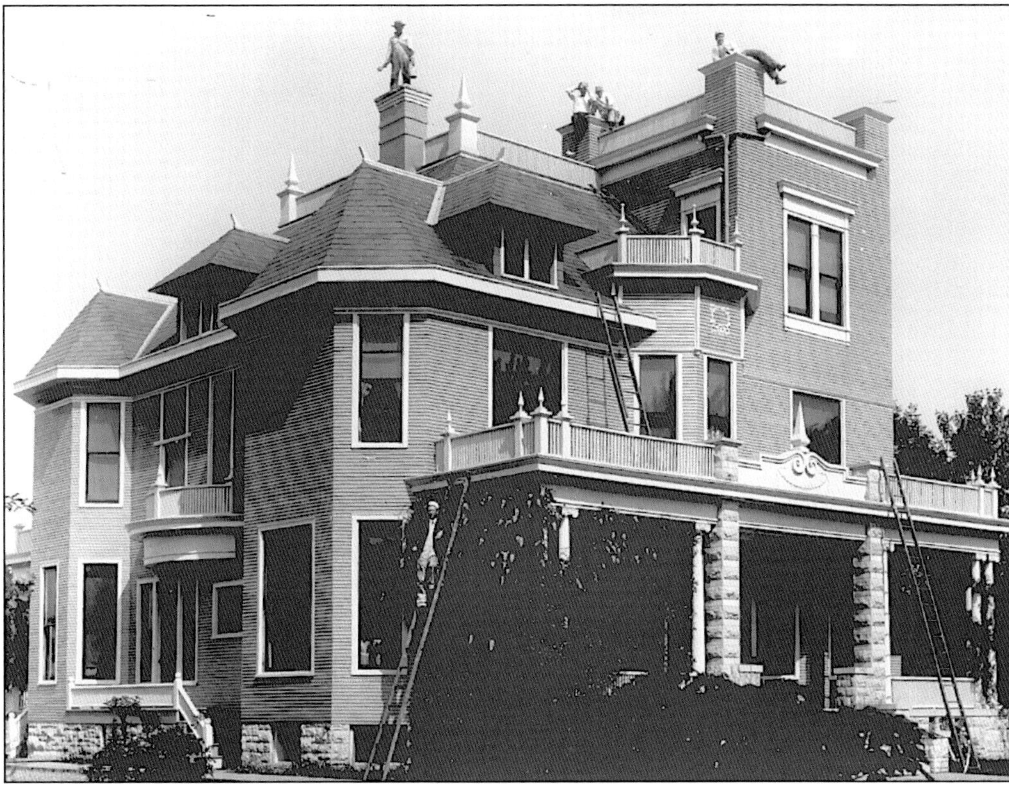

This 1906 photograph highlights the painting of Mrs. John Ribeyre's new home on Main Street. The painters take a break to pose for the camera. (Photographer: William Frederick Lichtenberger.)

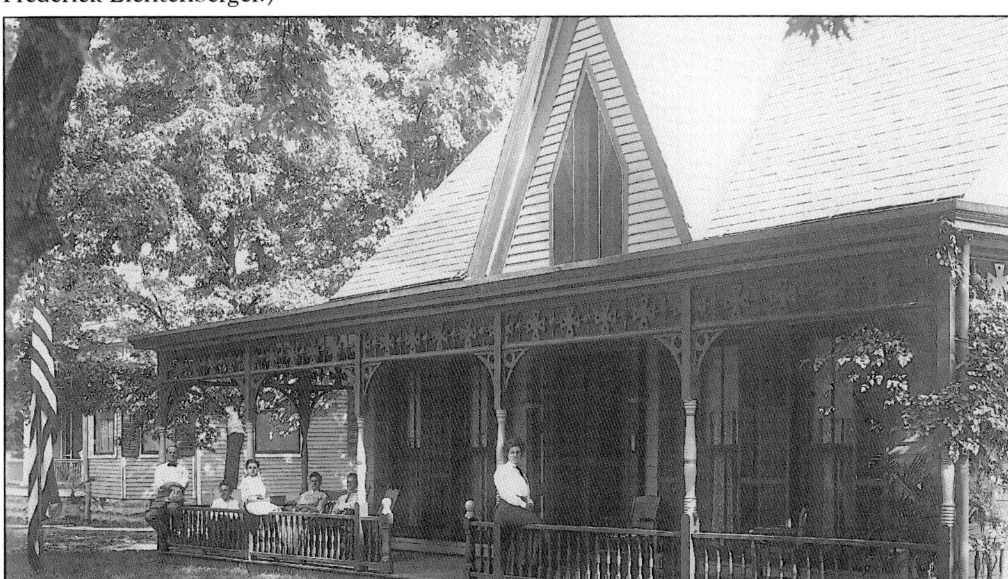

This is the New Harmony home of John Mott. (Photographer: William Frederick Lichtenberger.)

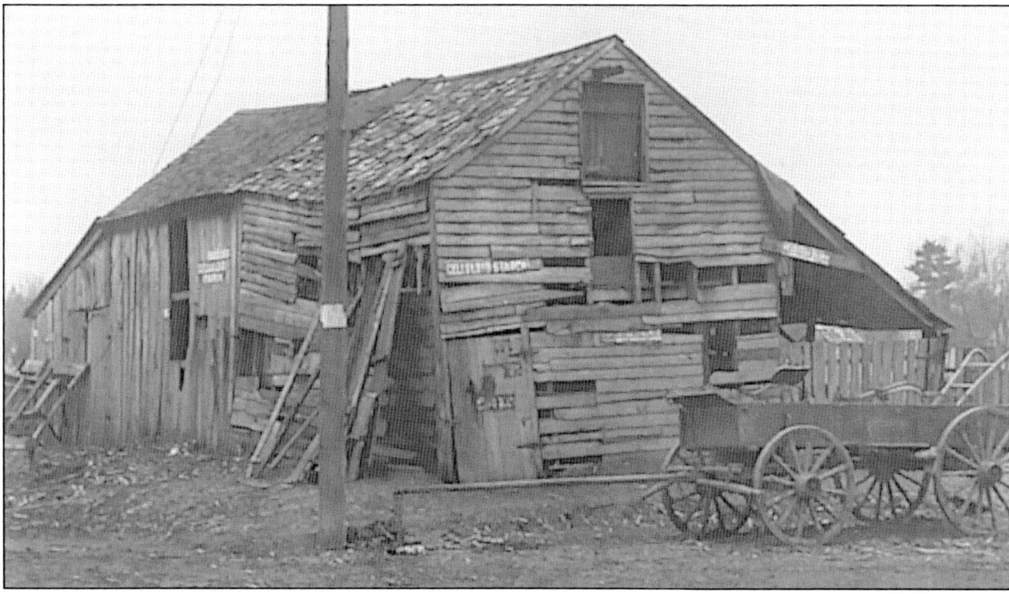

This old stable, located on the corner of Brewery and South Streets in New Harmony, was photographed March 11, 1906. (Photographer: Homer Fauntleroy.)

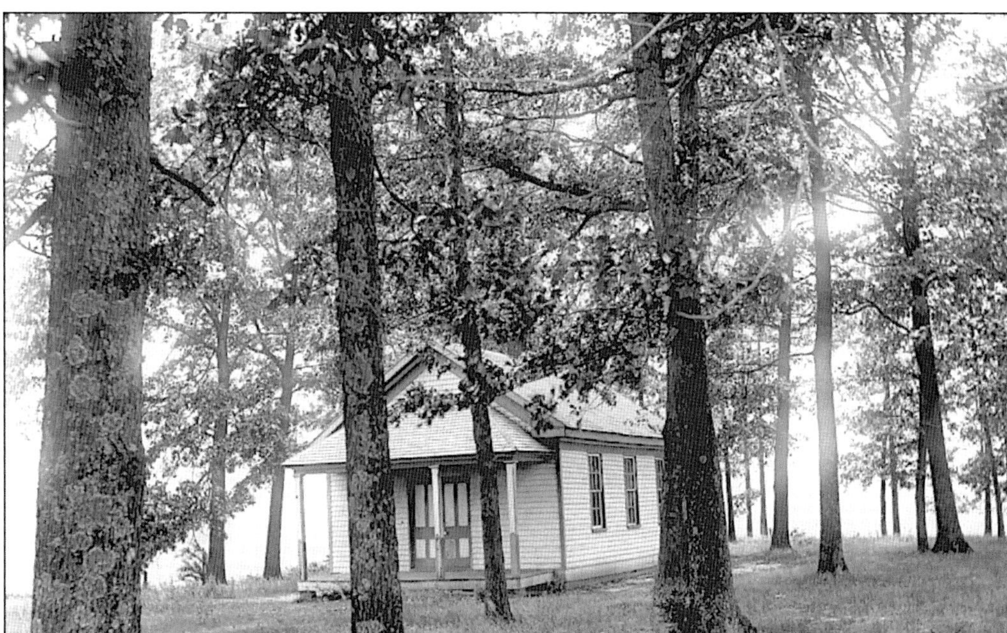

Shown here is the Wiley Schoolhouse, photographed June 17, 1906. (Photographer: Homer Fauntleroy.)

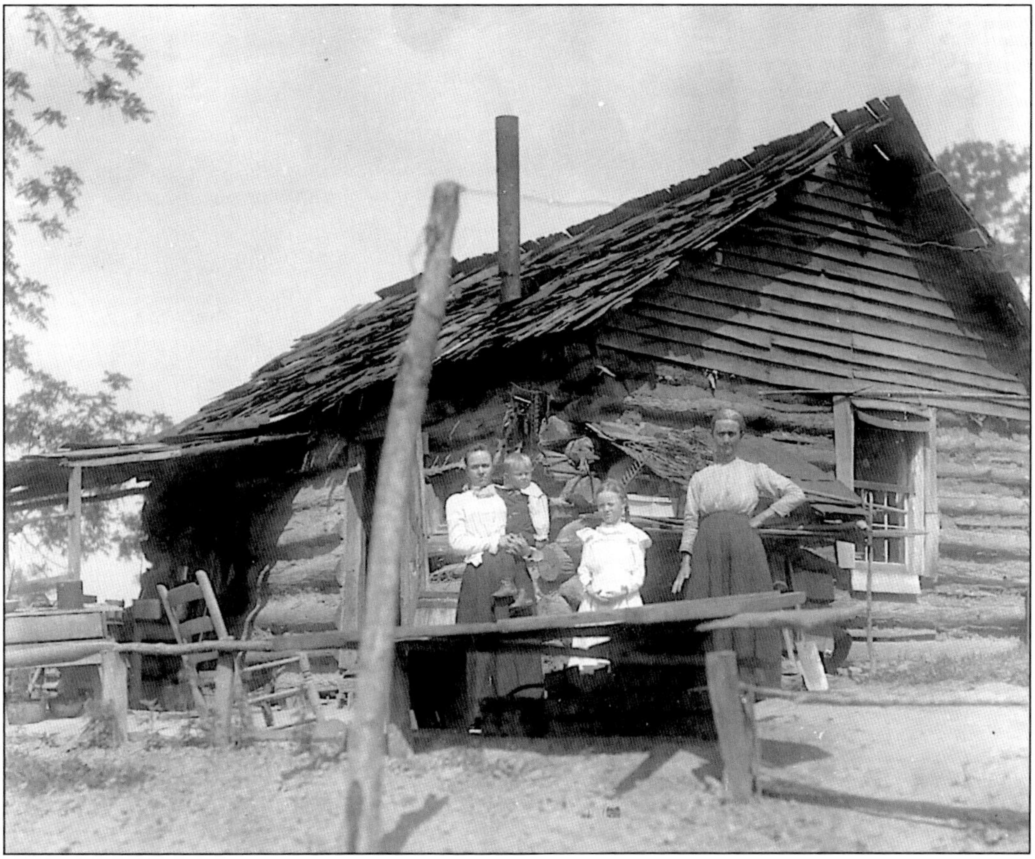

This photograph of rural life in Posey County—identified in the archive as the Hardy cabin—shows two unidentified women with two young children. (Photographer: William Frederick Lichtenberger.)

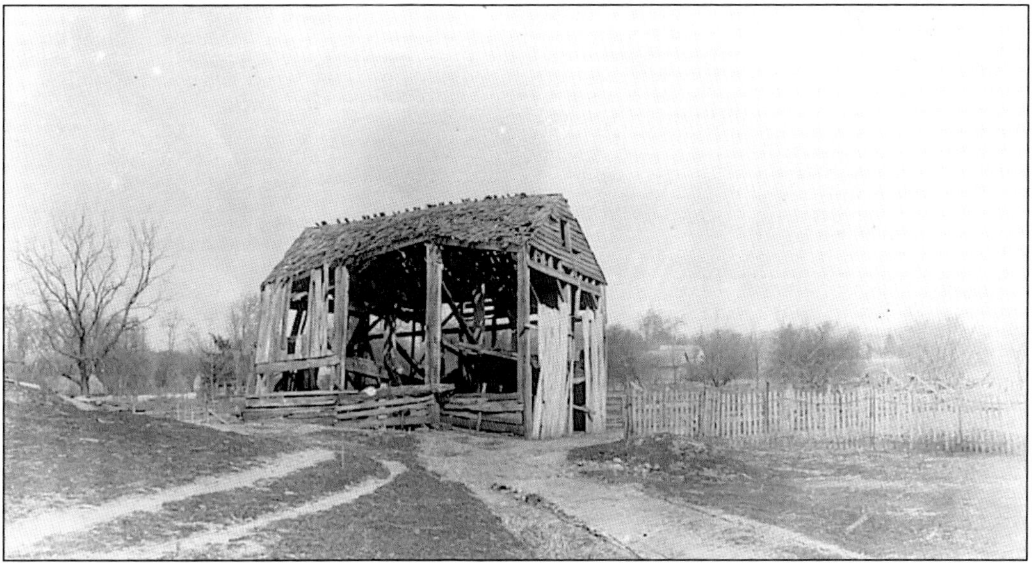

This crumbling frame building is identified as the old Lichtenberger mill.

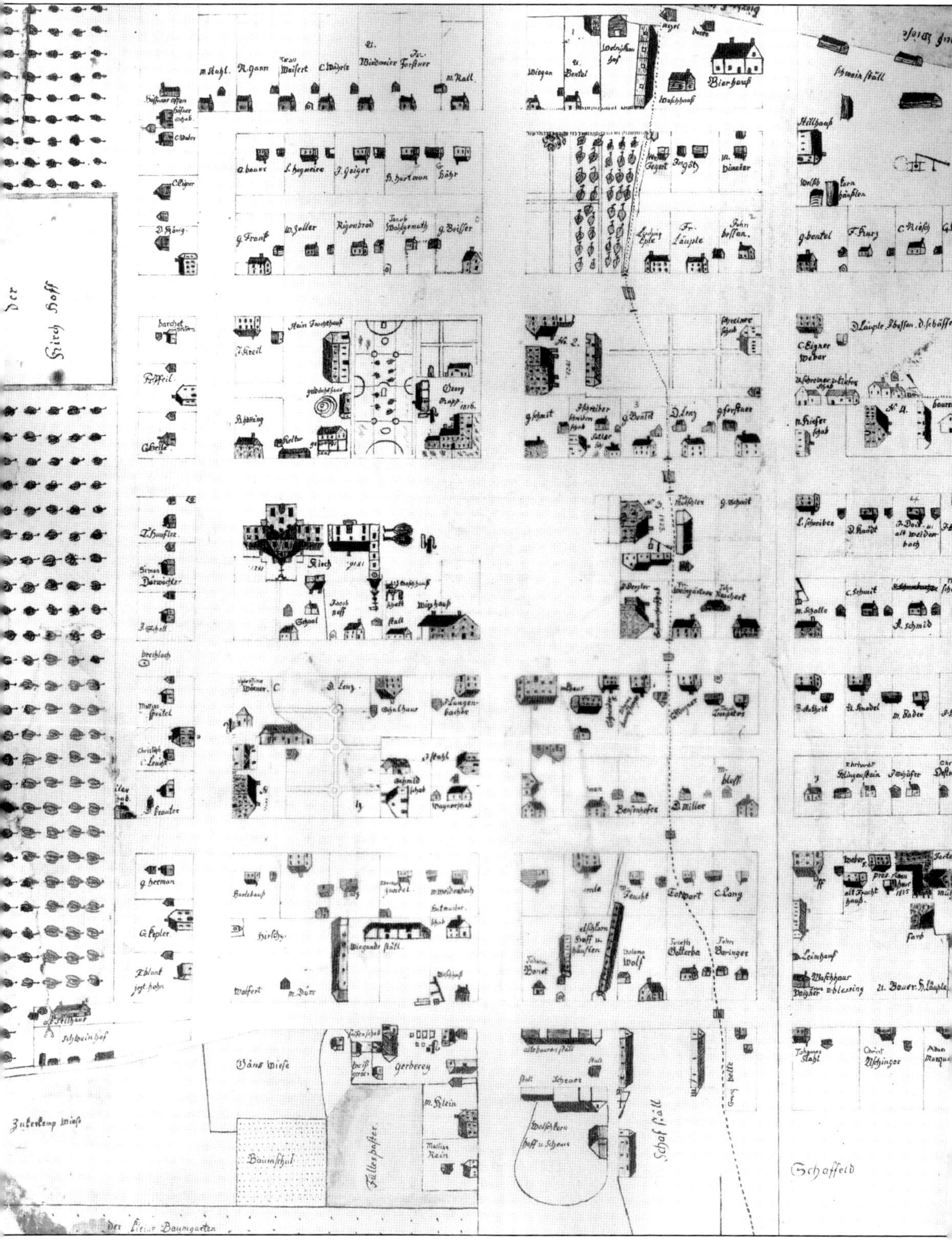

Der Hirsch Hoff
Bierhauß
Kirch
Gerberey
Gäns Wiese
Baumschul
Schaffeld
der kleine Baumgarten

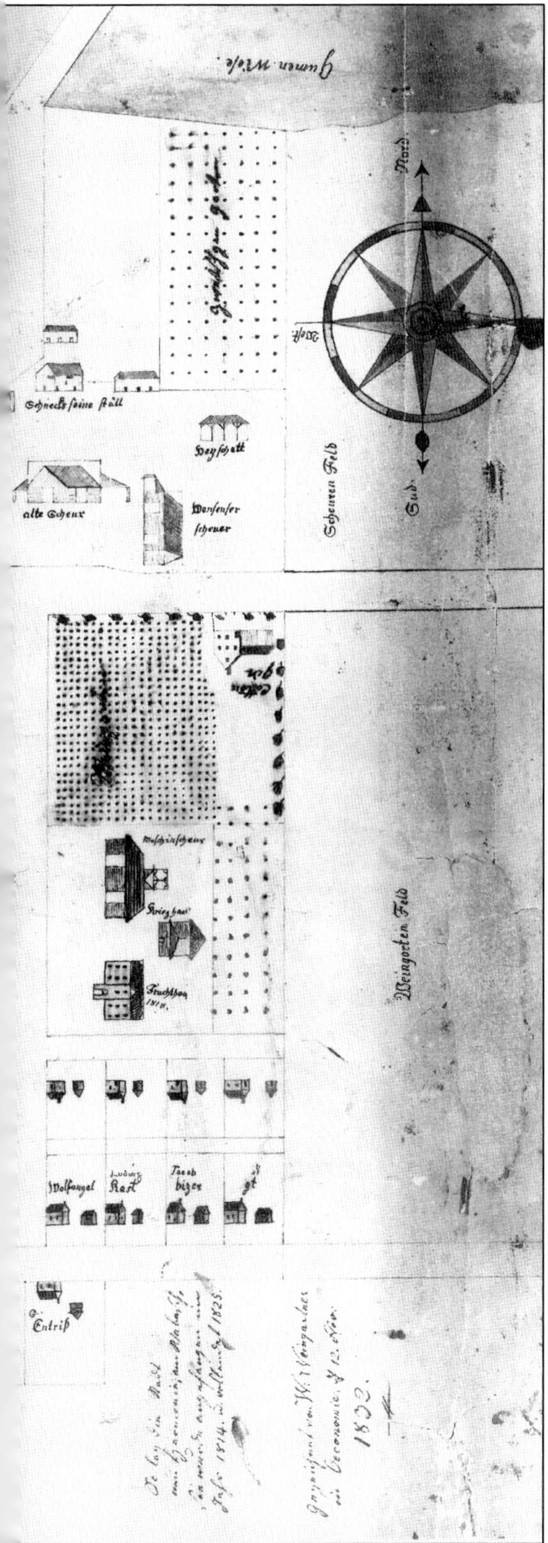

A pictorial map of New Harmony drawn by W. Weingartner in 1832, Economie, PA, shows specific buildings and manufactories at the time of the 1825 sale of the town from George Rapp and the Harmonists to Robert Owen of New Lanark, Scotland. (Photograph from the collection of Historic New Harmony.)

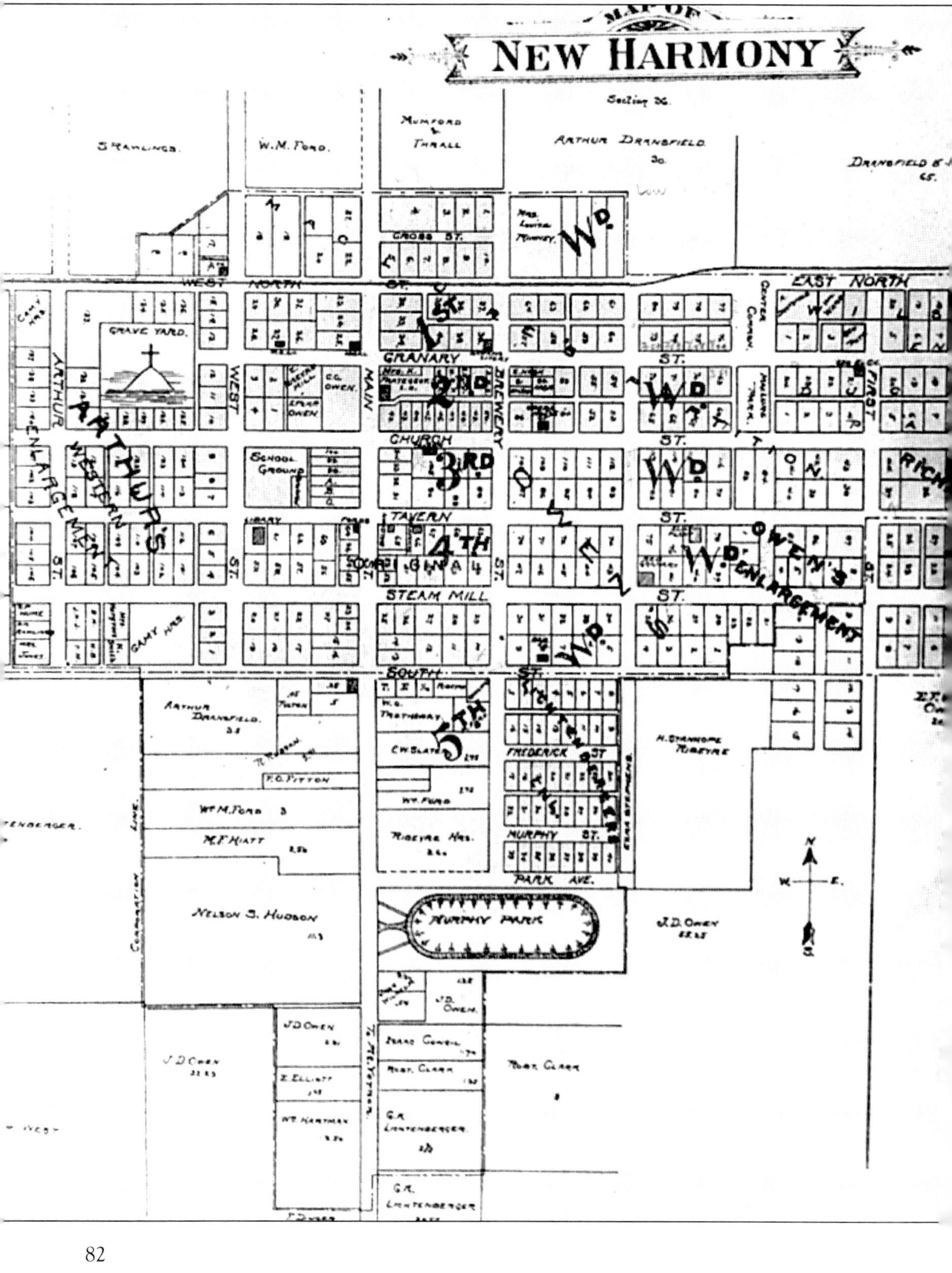
MAP OF
NEW HARMONY
Section 26.
S. Rawlings.
W. M. Ford.
Mumford & Thrall
Arthur Dransfield.
Cross St.
West North St.
East North
Grave Yard.
Granary
Main
Brewery
Church
Tavern
Steam Mill
South St.
School Ground
Library
West
Arthur
Arthur's Western Enlargement
Owen's Enlargement
1st Wd.
2nd Wd.
3rd Wd.
4th Wd.
5th Wd.
Center Common
Frederick St.
Murphy St.
Park Ave.
Murphy Park
Nelson S. Hudson
J. D. Owen
Rob't. Clark
G. R. Lichtenberger
H. Stanhope Ribeyre
Ribeyre Hrs.
C. W. Slater
W. M. Ford
M. F. Hiatt
F. C. Pitton
Arthur Dransfield.
E. Elliott
Wm. Hartman
To Mt. Vernon
Corporation Line.
N
W
E
S

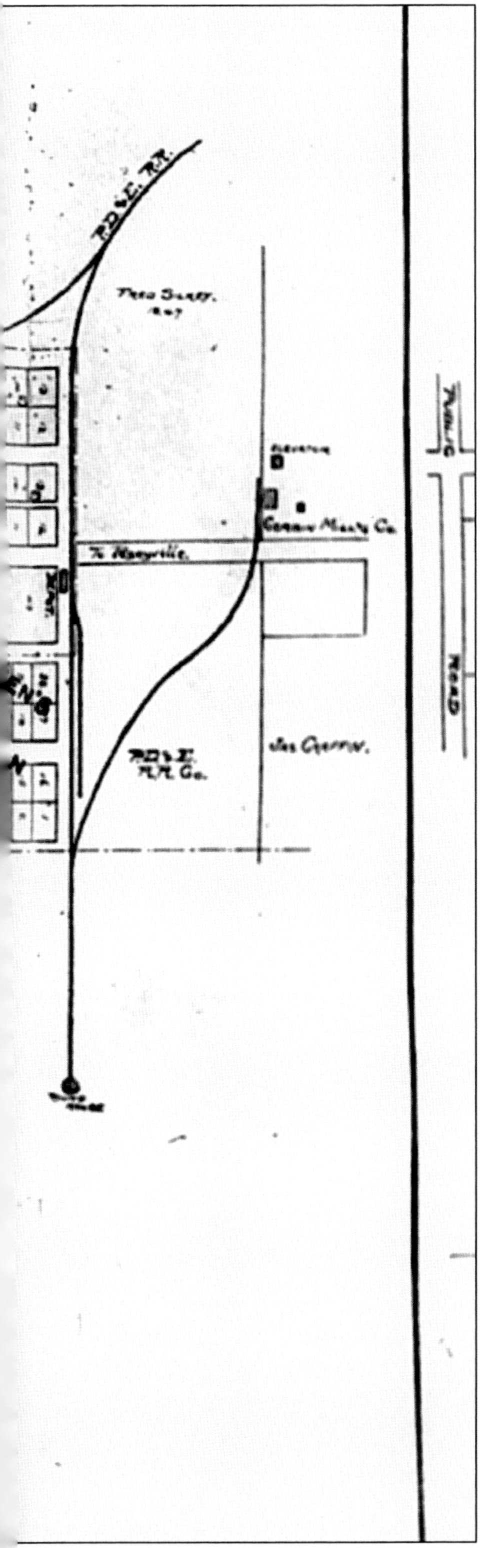

This 1900 map of New Harmony is included in the *Illustrated Atlas of Posey County, Indiana*, published by Keller & Fuller of Evansville, Indiana.

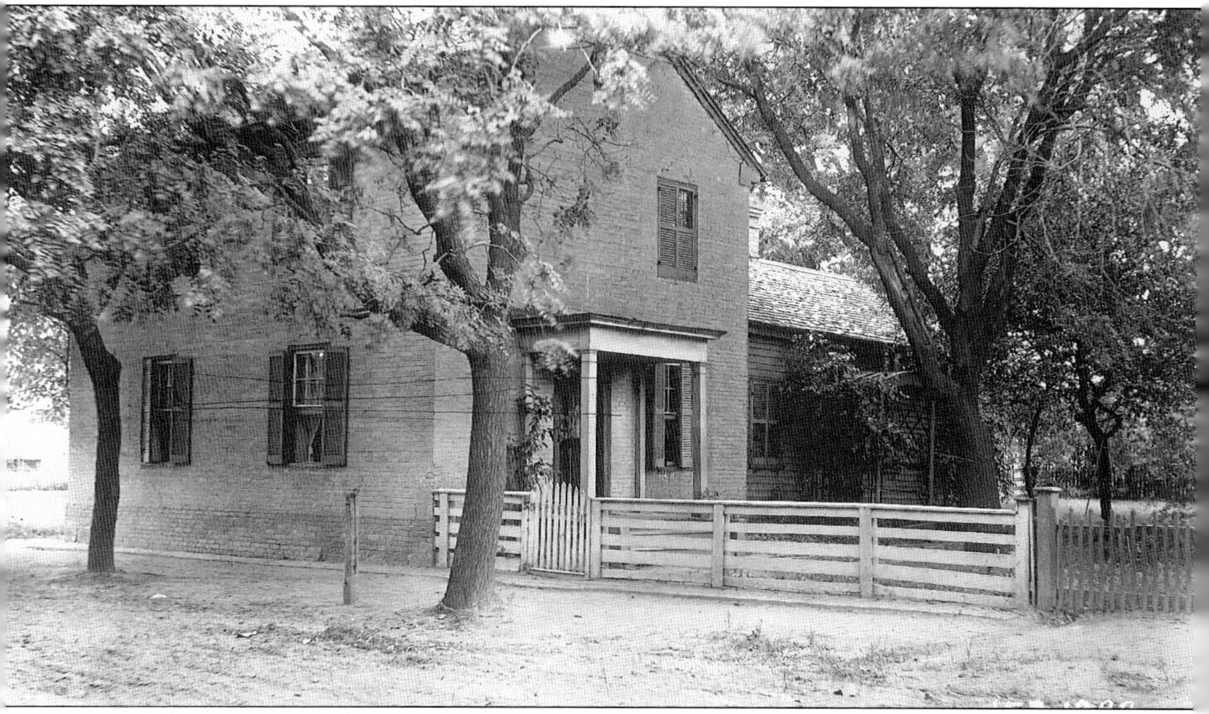

A July 12, 1898 photograph shows the former Joseph Neef house, located at the northeast corner of Church and West Streets. This Harmonist structure today houses the offices of University of Southern Indiana President Emeritus David L. Rice. (Photographer: Homer Fauntleroy.)

Five

Fire and Flood

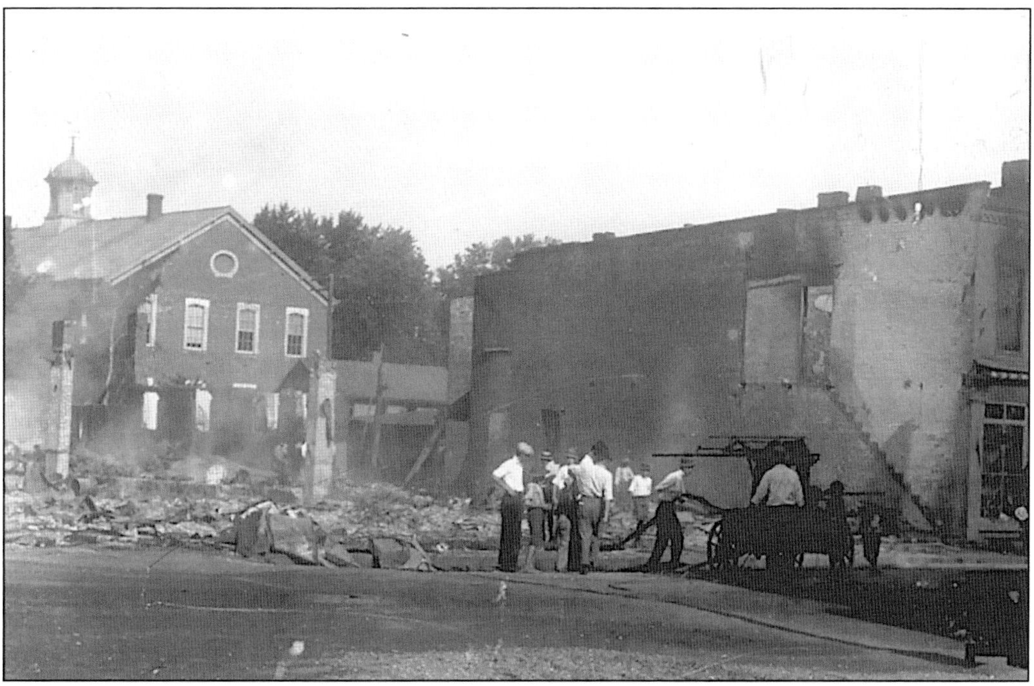

The Harmonist fire wagon, known as "Pat Lyon" (nicknamed for its manufacturer), stands near the ruins of Monitor Corner on August 17, 1908. Incredibly, this same group of Main Street buildings burned to the ground May 11, 1998.

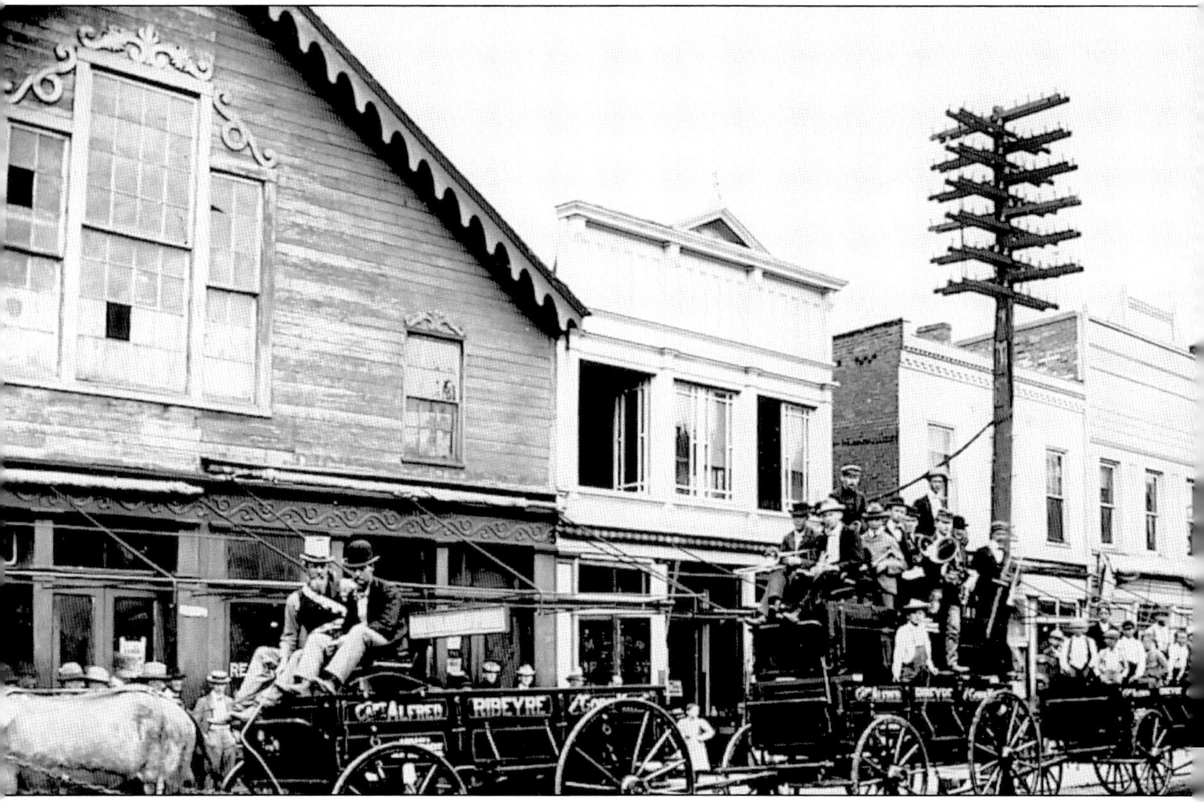

New Harmony "Corn King" Alfred Ribeyre sponsored this wagon parade, photographed proceeding south on Main Street past Monitor Corner, site of the August 17, 1908 fire. Notice the appearance of this building and its subsequent alterations in the next photograph. (Photographer: William Frederick Lichtenberger.)

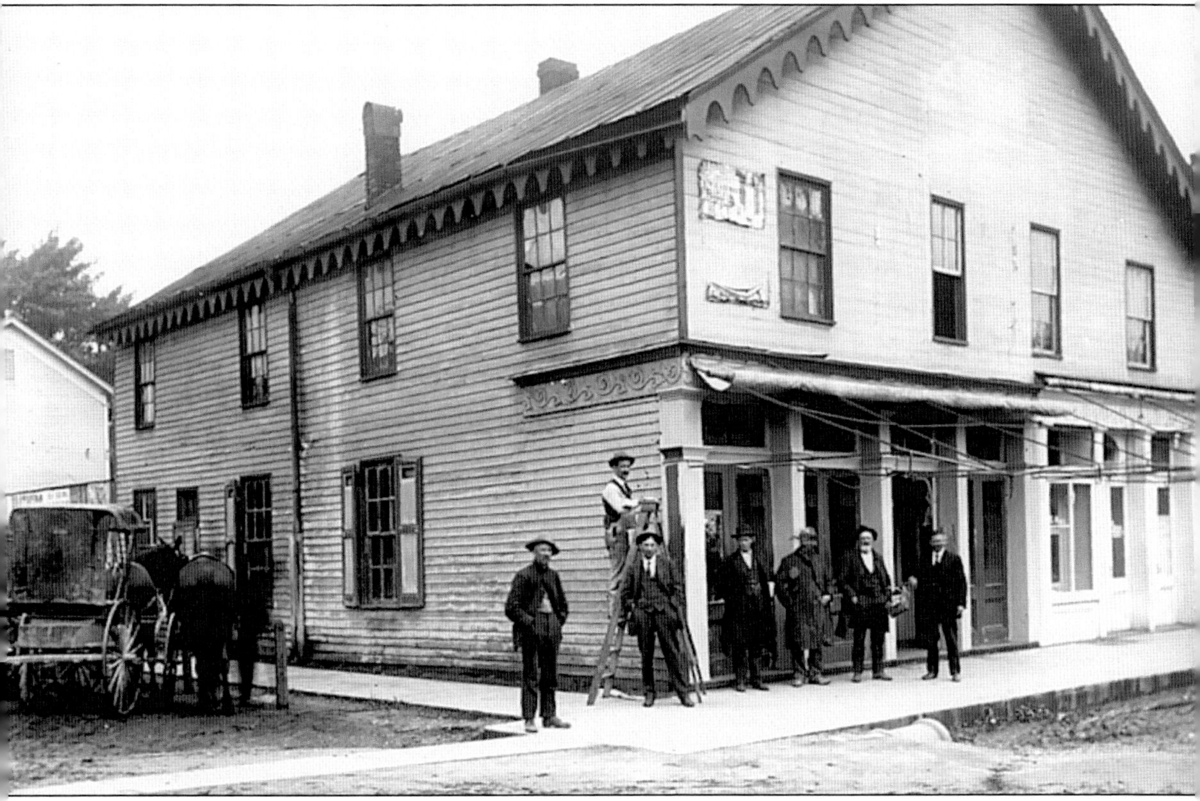

Pictured here is Monitor Corner in 1903. (Photographer: William Frederick Lichtenberger.)

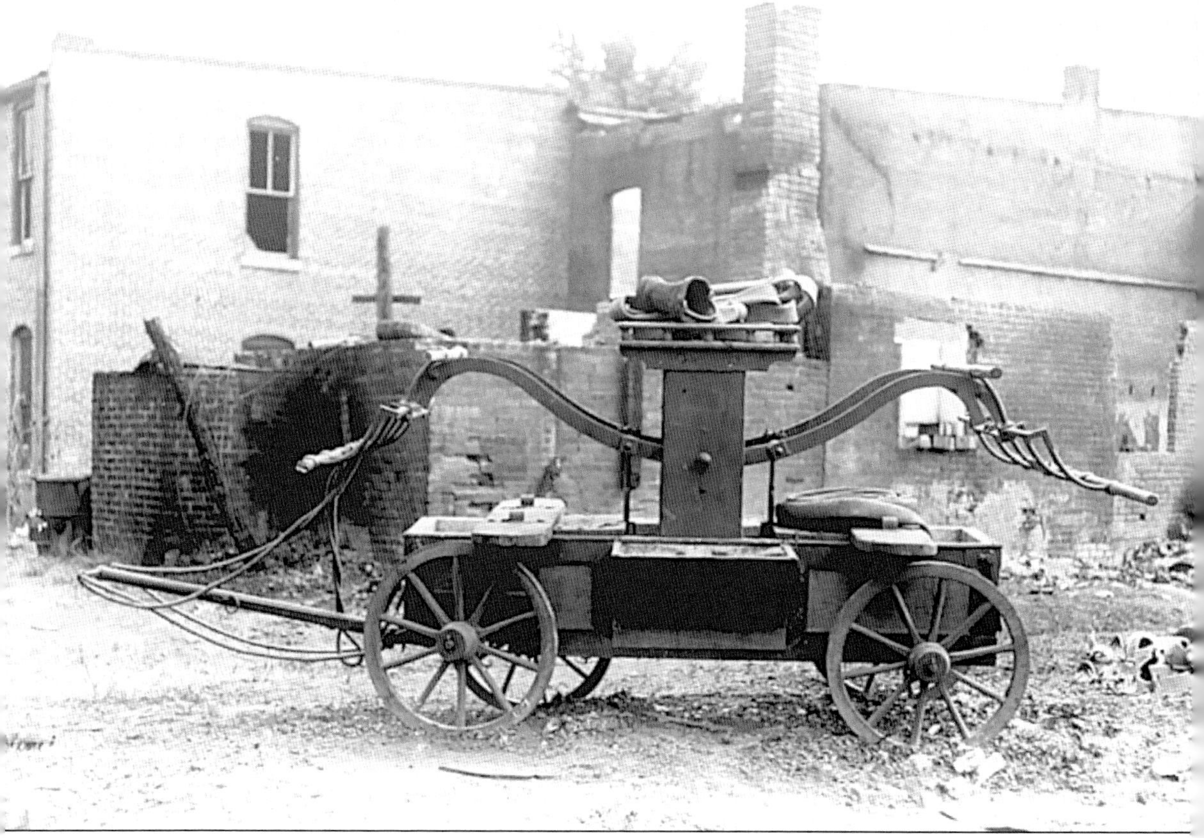

"Pat Lyon," the Harmonist fire wagon, is shown at the scene of the Monitor Corner fire on August 17, 1908. (Photographer: Homer Fauntleroy.)

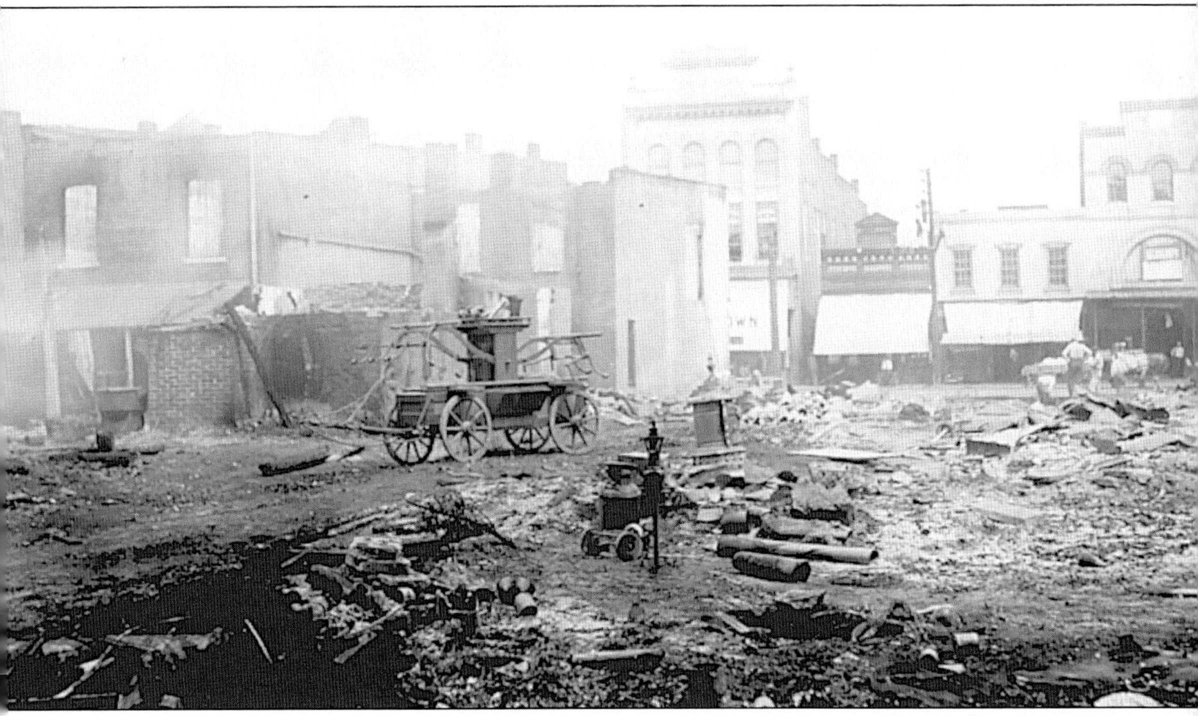

This August 17, 1908 photograph, looking east across Main Street, shows the damage left behind by the Monitor Corner fire. "Pat Lyon" stands sentinel. (Photographer: Homer Fauntleroy.)

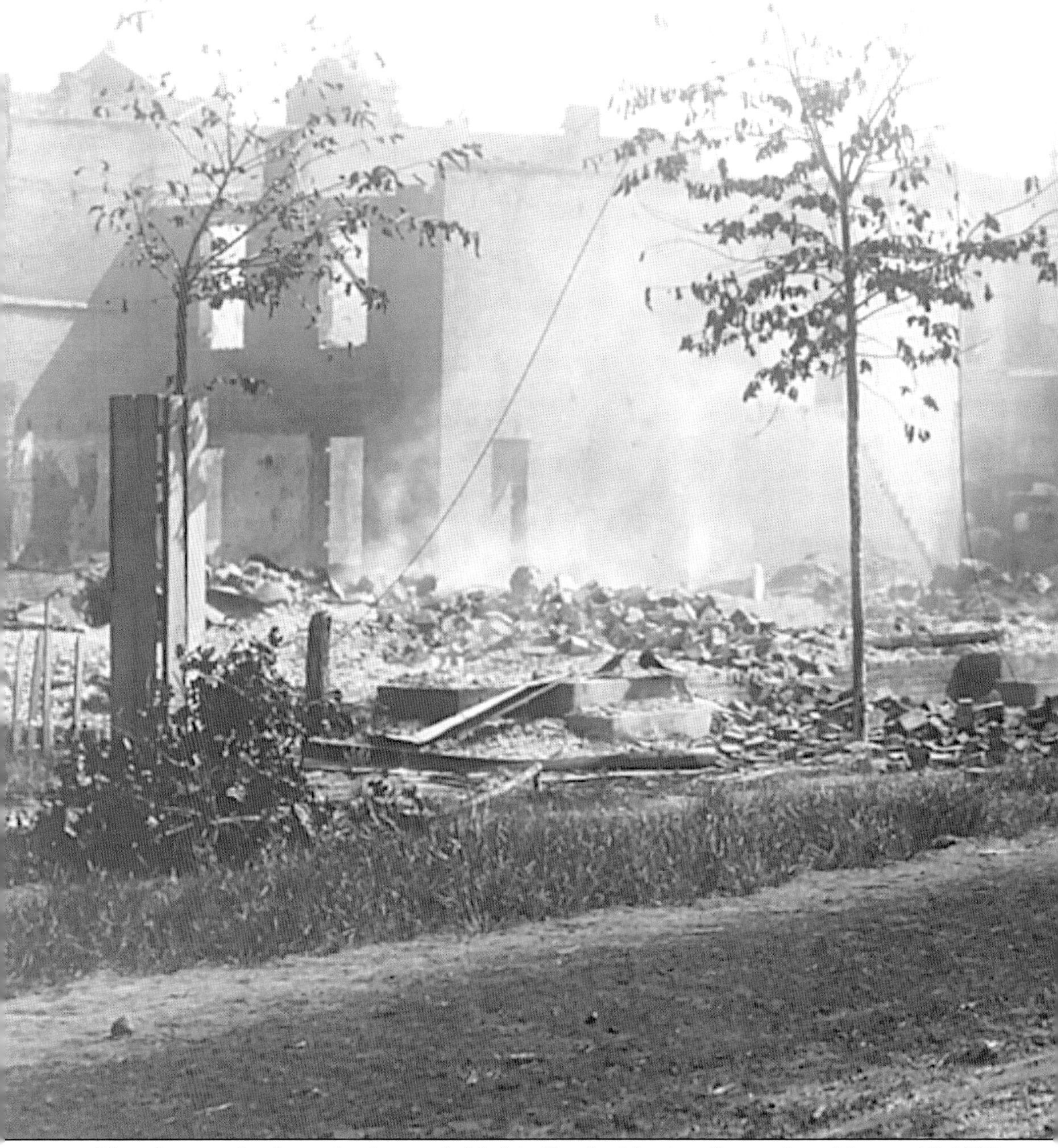

This photographs shows the damage left behind by the Monitor Corner fire of August 17, 1908. According to the inscription on the photograph: "Destroyed were: residence occupied by Mrs. Bump; Monitor Saloon; Loren Davis Ice Cream parlor; F.J. Miller & Company Drug Store (with Posey County Telephone exchange upstairs); H.D. Long Butcher shop (building included

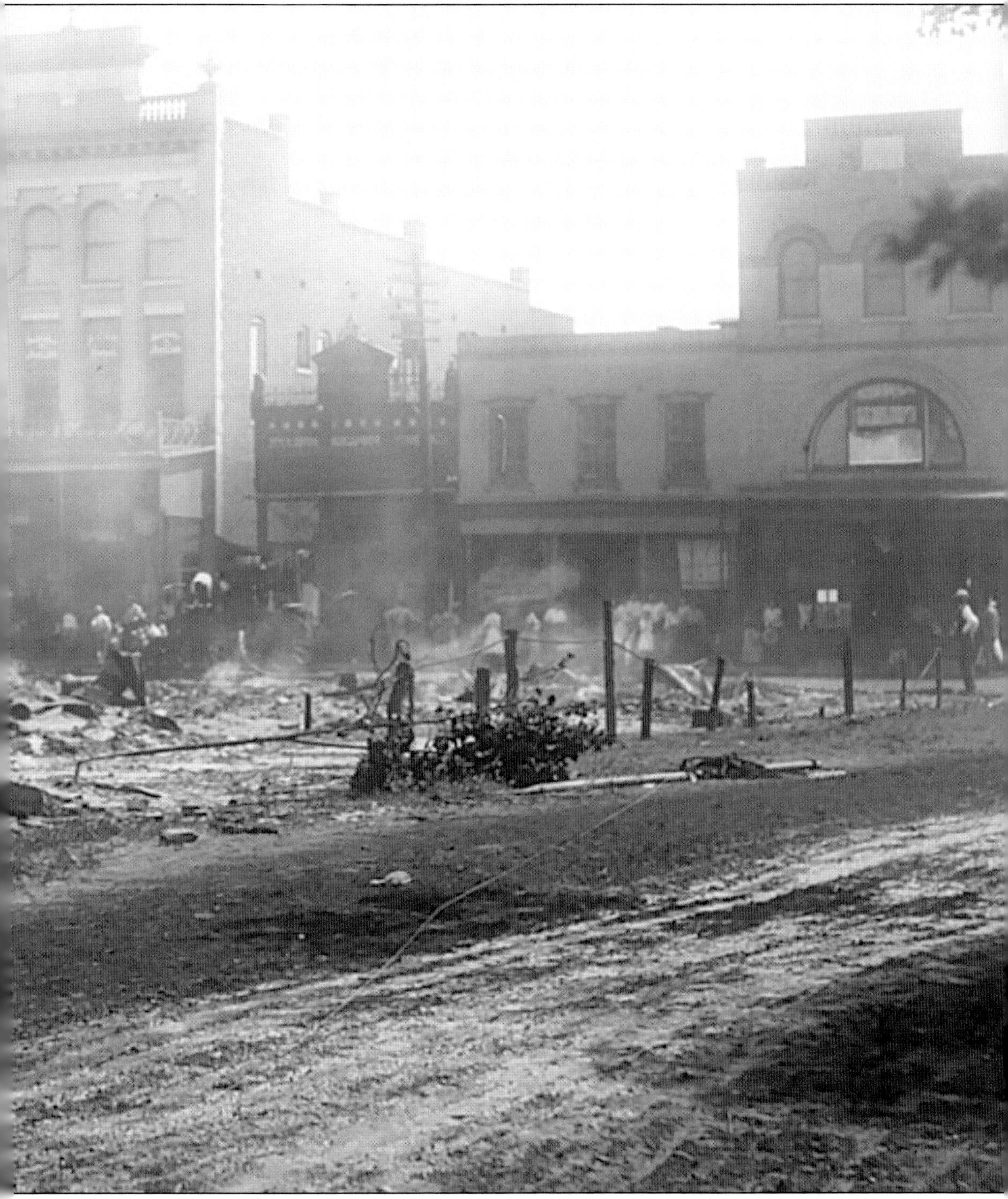

a residence and a millinery shop); and Lyric Theatorium run by E. A. Wilson. Left standing were the walls of H.D. Long's shop; the Lyric Theatorium owned by Charles Pretzsch (drug store not burned); Charles Pretzsch Hardware; Wilnoth and Wheatcroft; New Harmony Banking Co."

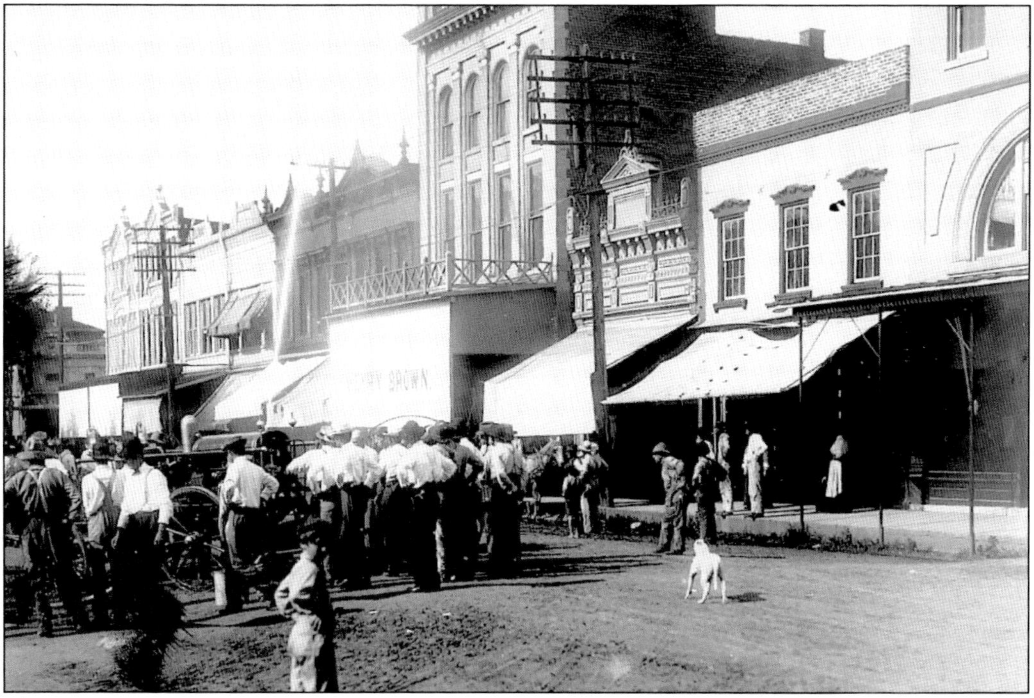

This crowd is assembled on Main Street on August 17, 1908, spraying down buildings located on the east side of the street, to prevent them from catching fire during the devastating Monitor Corner Fire.

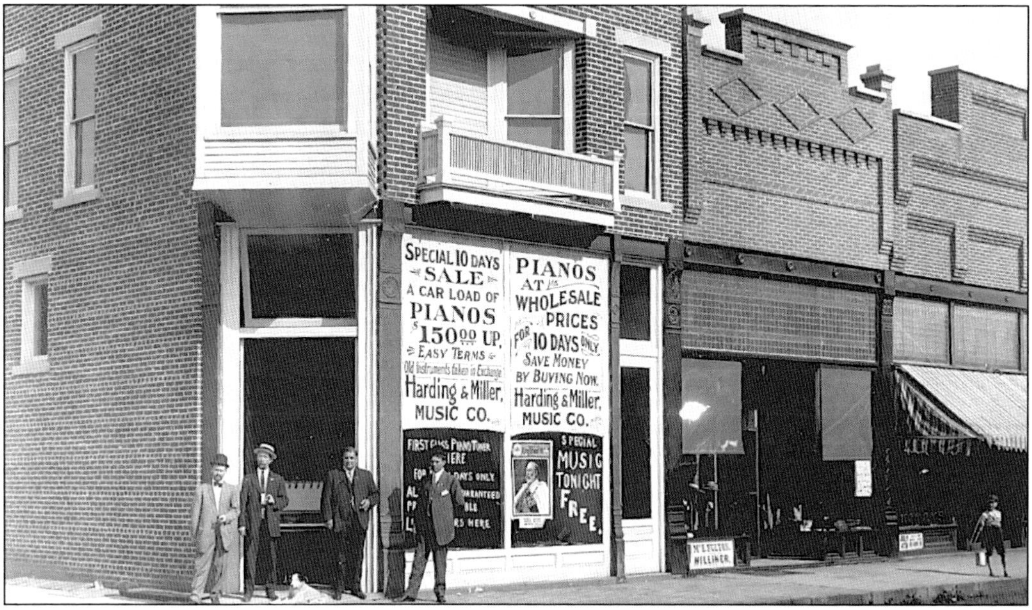

This photograph shows the new construction placed at the location of the 1908 Monitor Corner fire. Shown are the Eagle Building and adjacent structures, which housed the following businesses: Harding and Miller Music Company; Mrs. E. Fulton, milliner; and another store—possibly a camera/photography shop—which features a painted sign reading "Kodaks" on its front window. (Photographer: William Frederick Lichtenberger.)

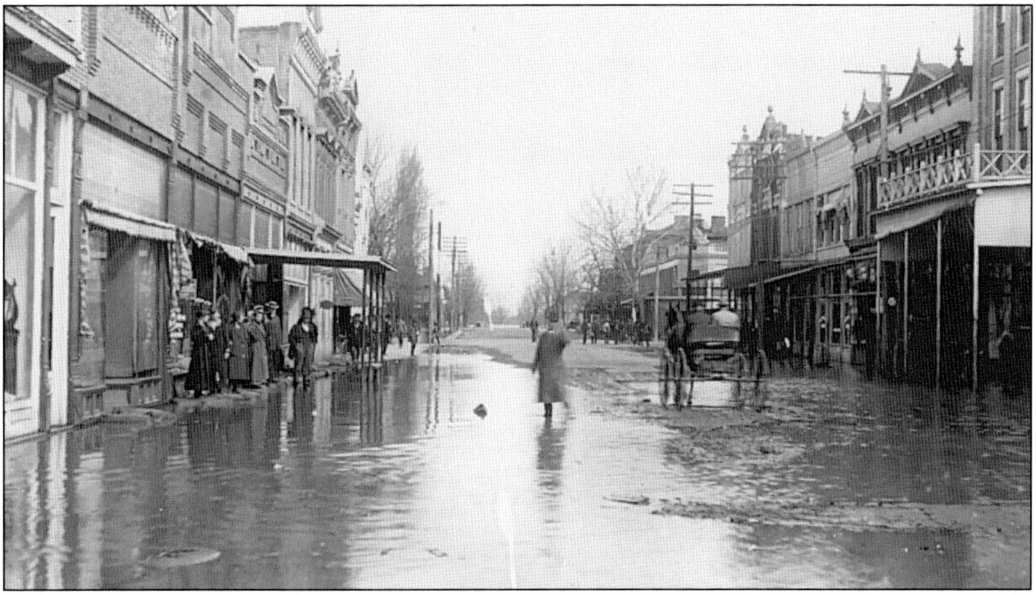

Unidentified individuals stand in Main Street during the flood of 1913.

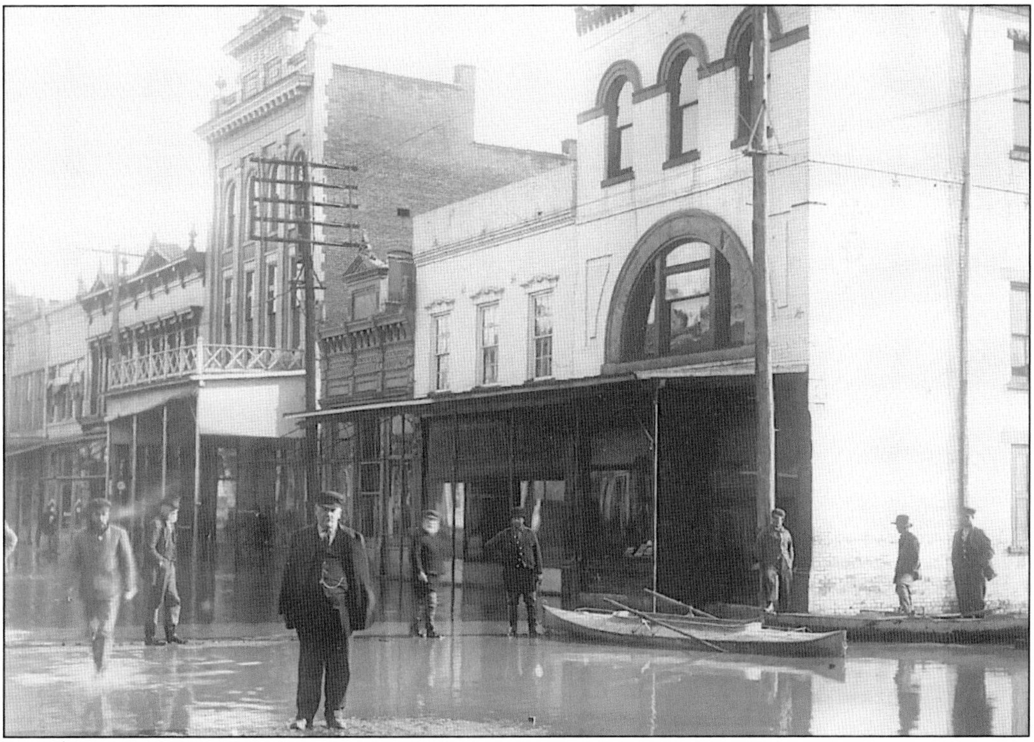

An unidentified man faces the camera in the middle of the flooded street while his fellow townsfolk emerge from the boats they have used as modes of transportation during the flood of 1913. (Photographer: William Frederick Lichtenberger.)

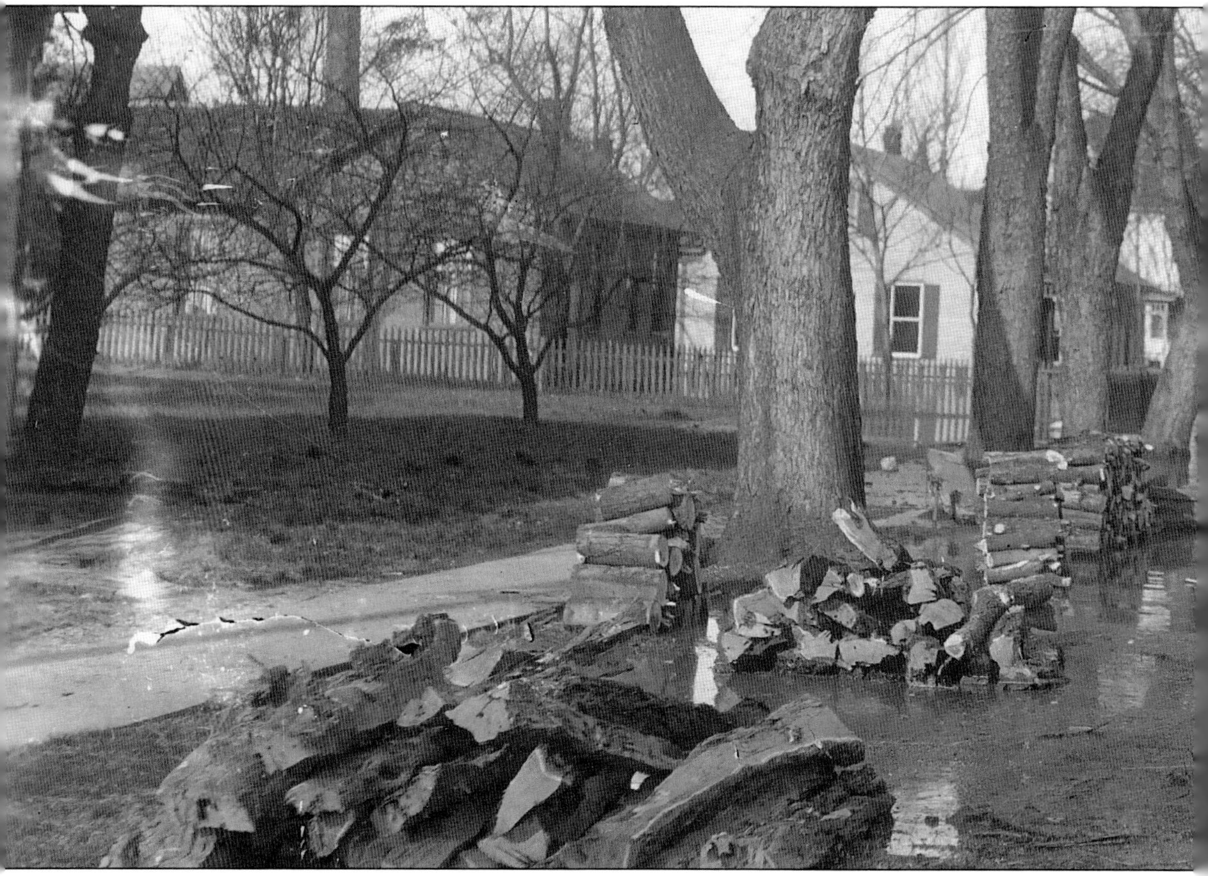

An unidentified woman seems to gaze forlornly at the flooded streets of New Harmony during the flood of 1913. Note the boat that she may have used to travel those streets at left,

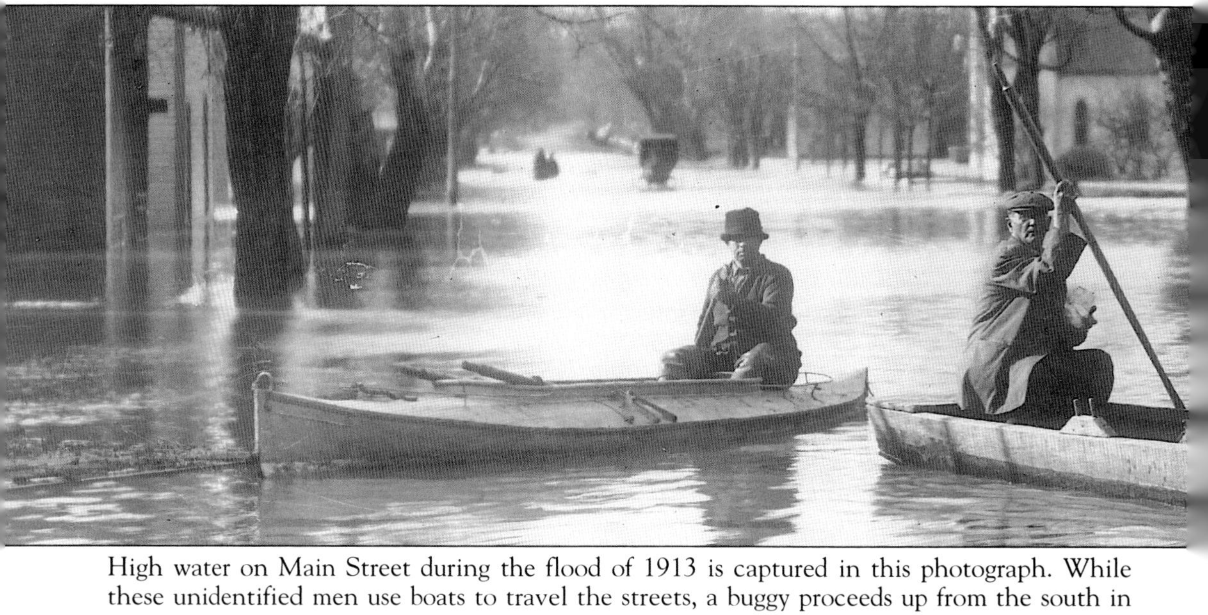

High water on Main Street during the flood of 1913 is captured in this photograph. While these unidentified men use boats to travel the streets, a buggy proceeds up from the south in

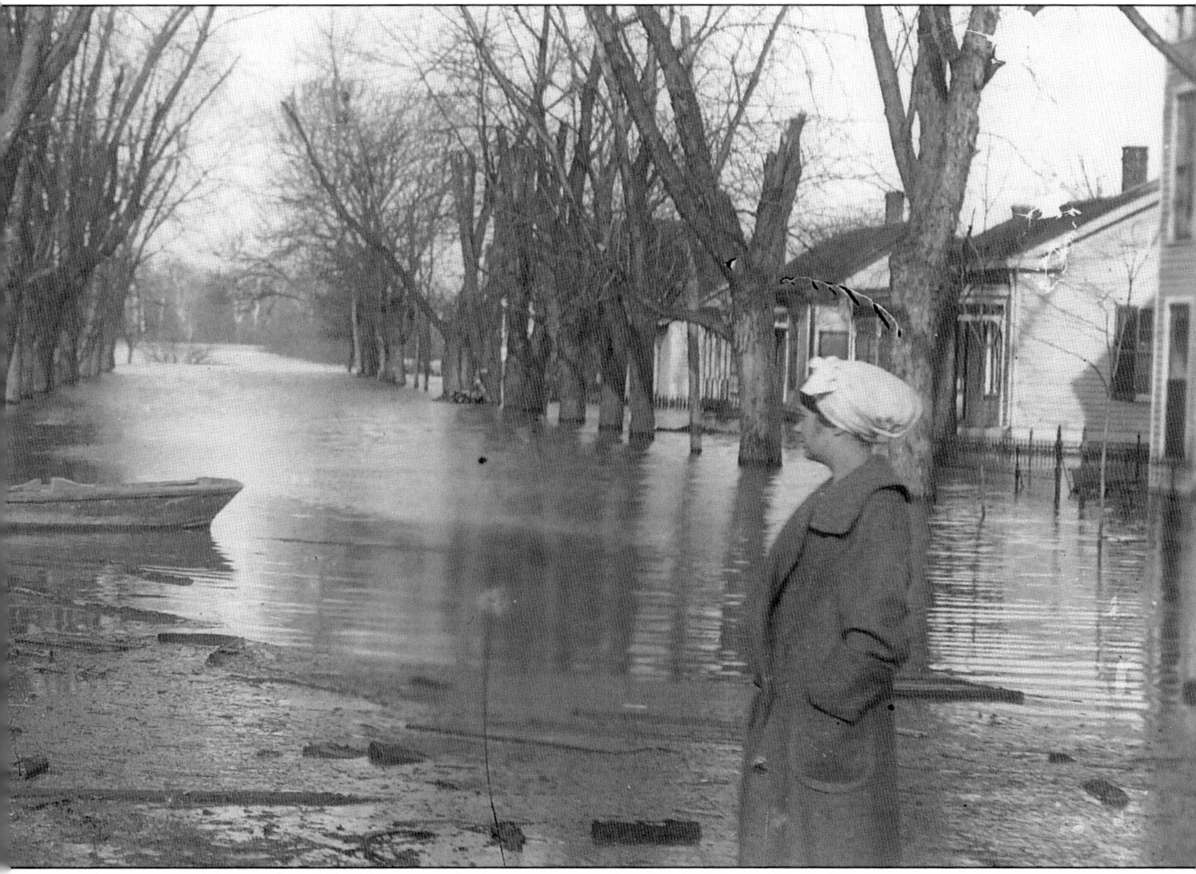

behind the piles of logs. (Photographer: Homer Fauntleroy.)

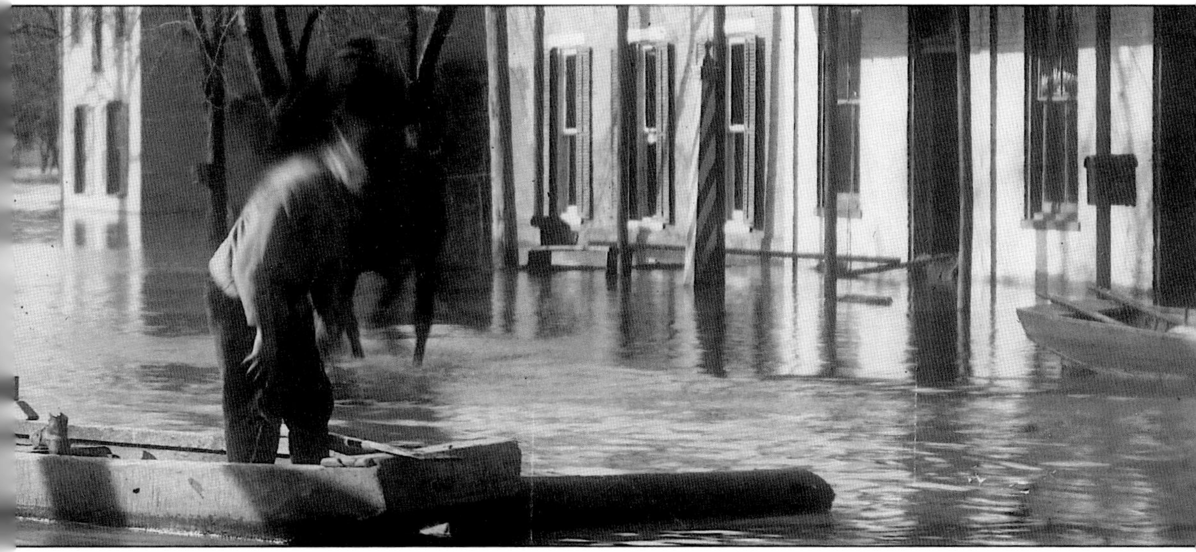

the center of the road. Holy Angels Catholic Church is visible in the distance on the right. (Photographer: William Frederick Lichtenberger.)

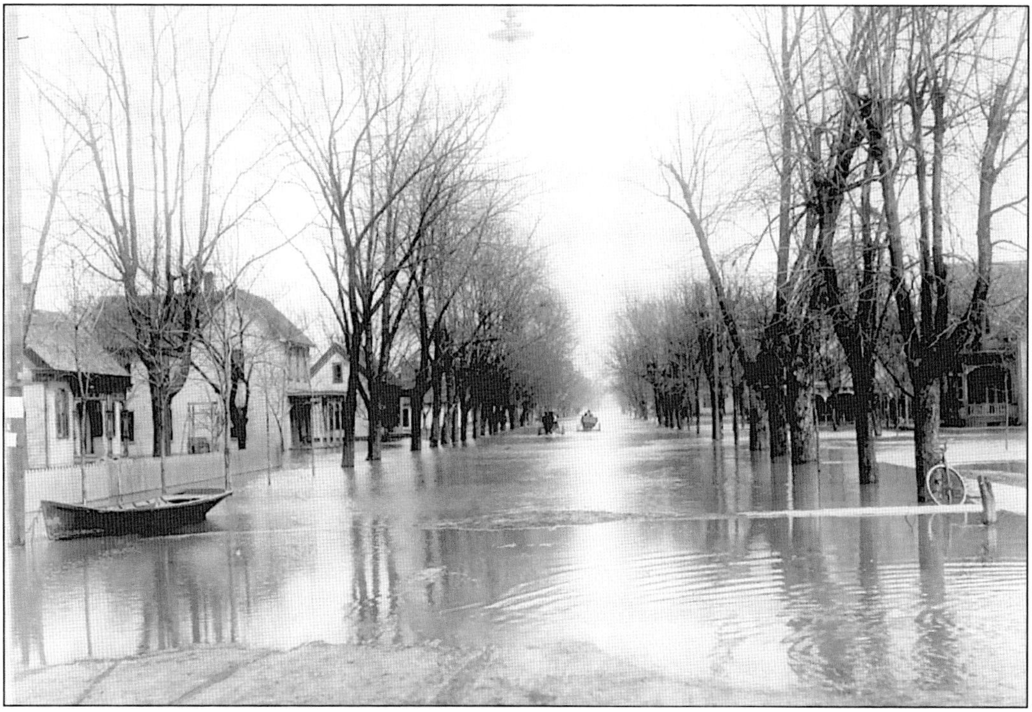

This 1913 photograph shows buggies in front of the L. Wade Wilson residence. (Photographer: William Frederick Lichtenberger.)

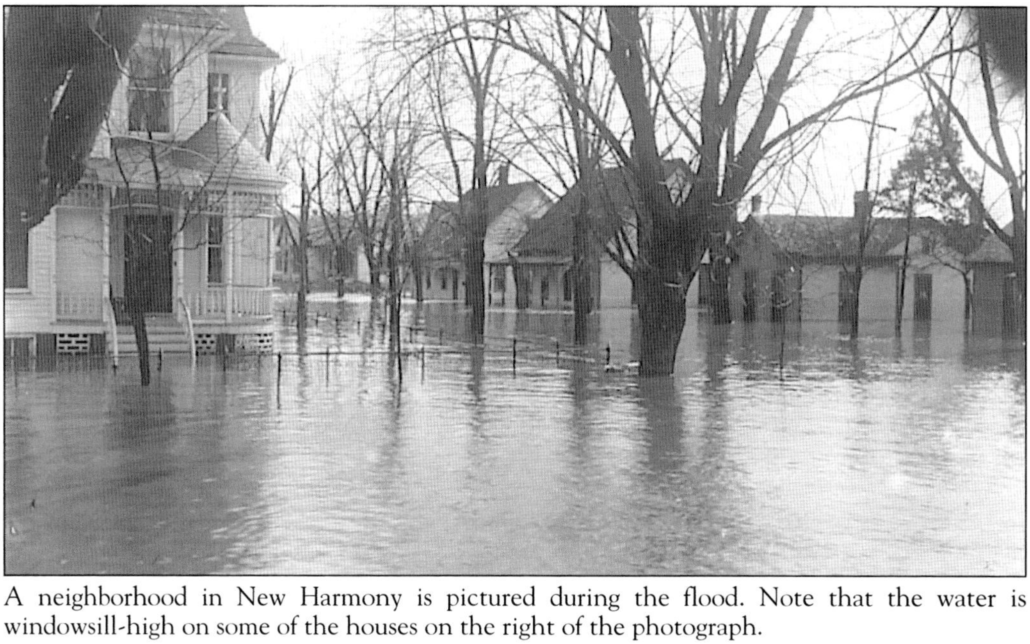

A neighborhood in New Harmony is pictured during the flood. Note that the water is windowsill-high on some of the houses on the right of the photograph.

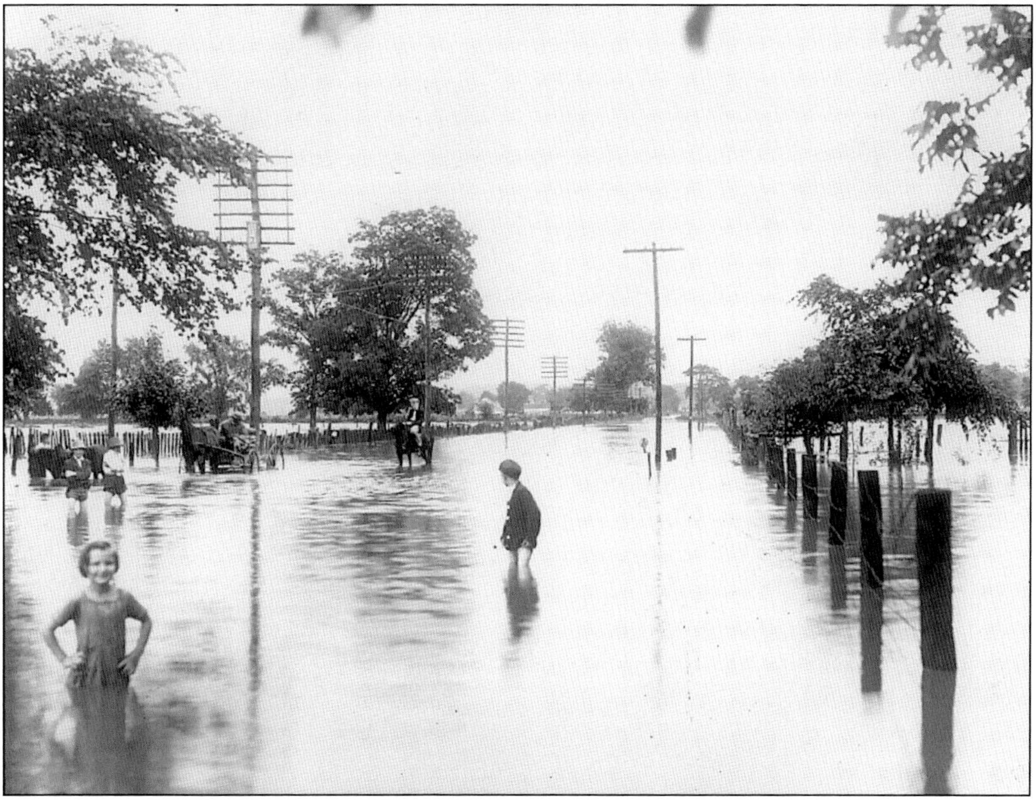

Unidentified residents walk, ride horses, and travel in buggies after a big rain on July 4, 1912. The little girl in the foreground of the photograph seems to be particularly enjoying the soggy circumstances. (Photographer: William Frederick Lichtenberger.)

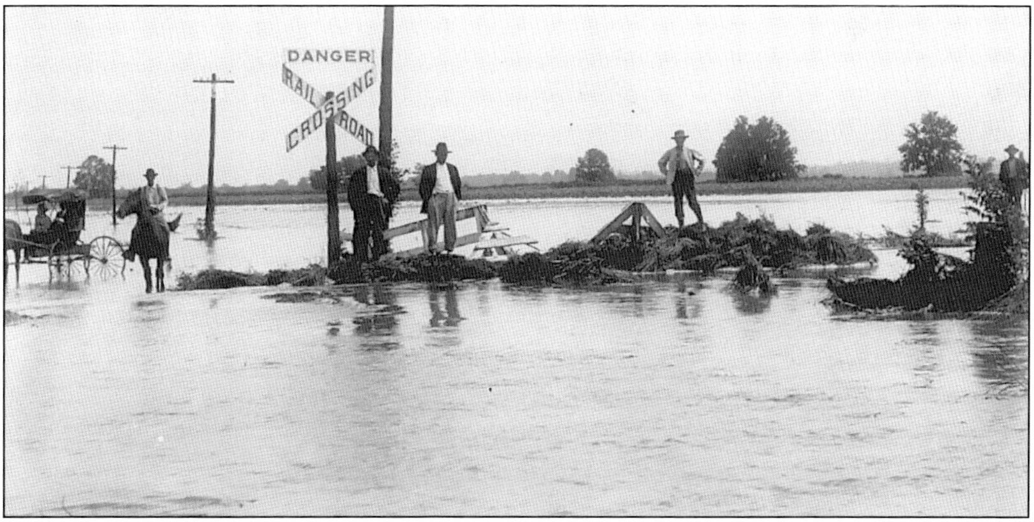

This 1913 photograph shows the flood waters at the intersection of Old Griffin Road and the railroad tracks on the east side of New Harmony. Unidentified men stand atop debris piles. (Photographer: William Frederick Lichtenberger.)

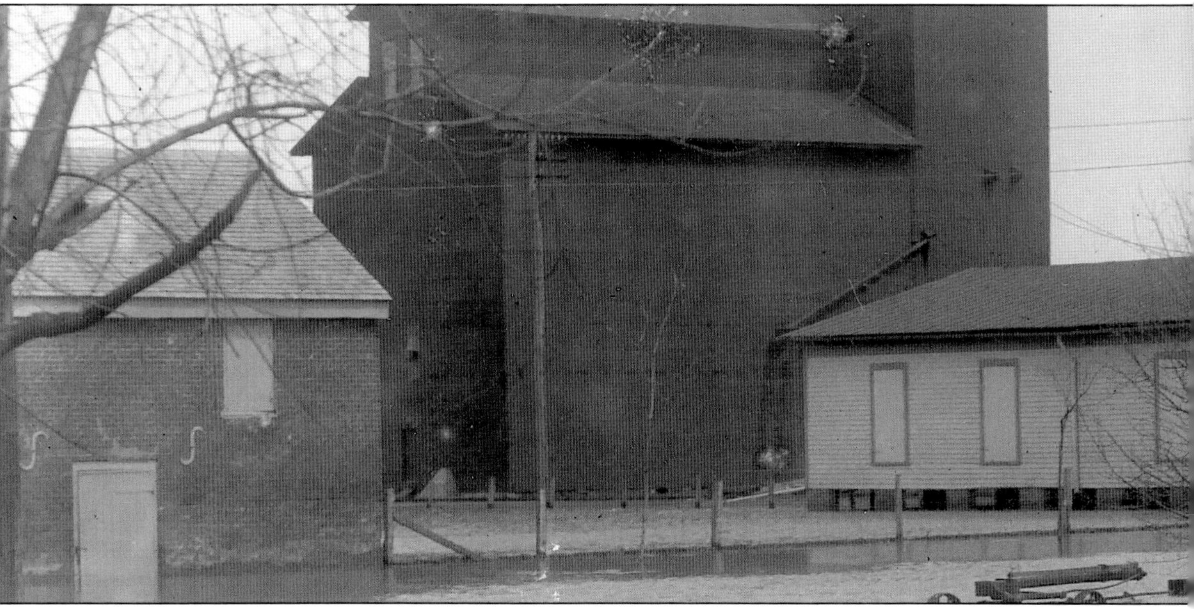

This photograph, taken in 1913, shows the flood waters surrounding the Corbin Milling Company on New Harmony's east side. Note the unidentified man, his arms crossed, standing

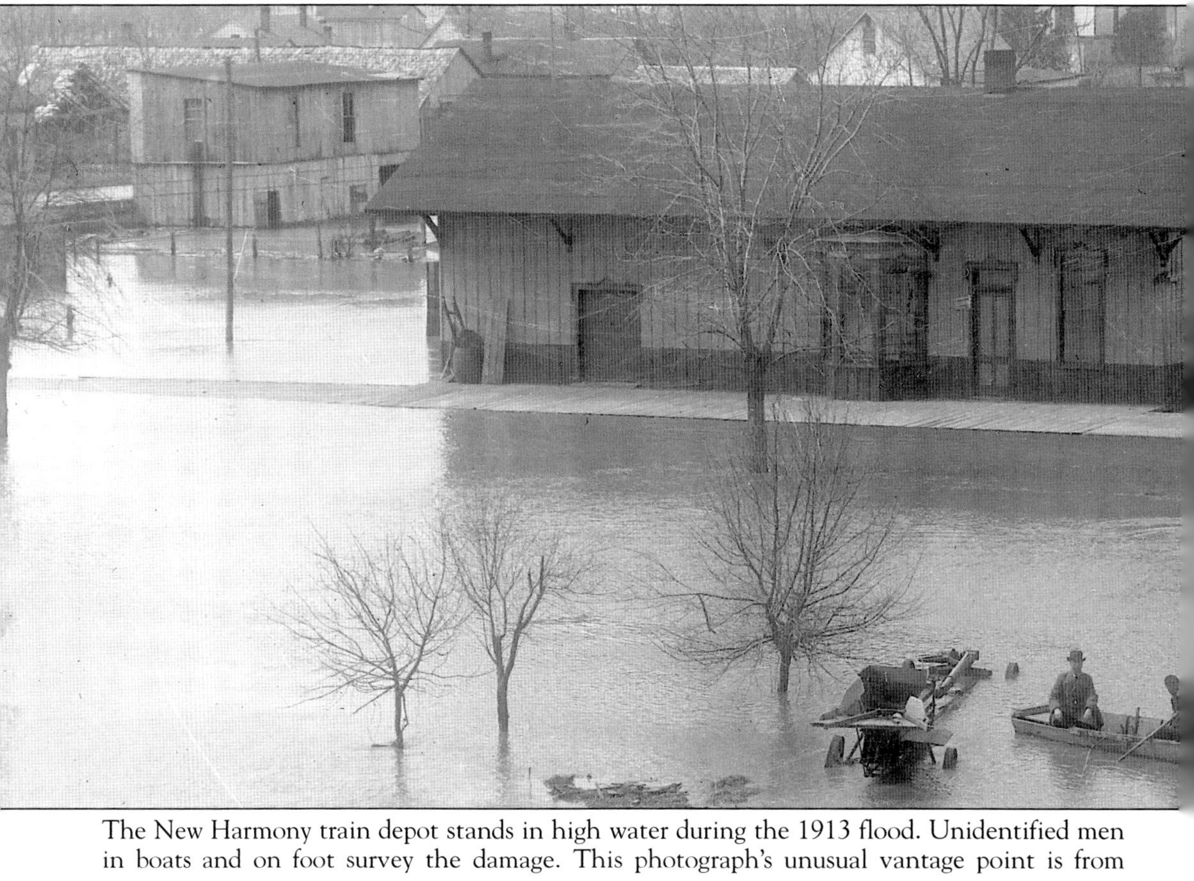

The New Harmony train depot stands in high water during the 1913 flood. Unidentified men in boats and on foot survey the damage. This photograph's unusual vantage point is from

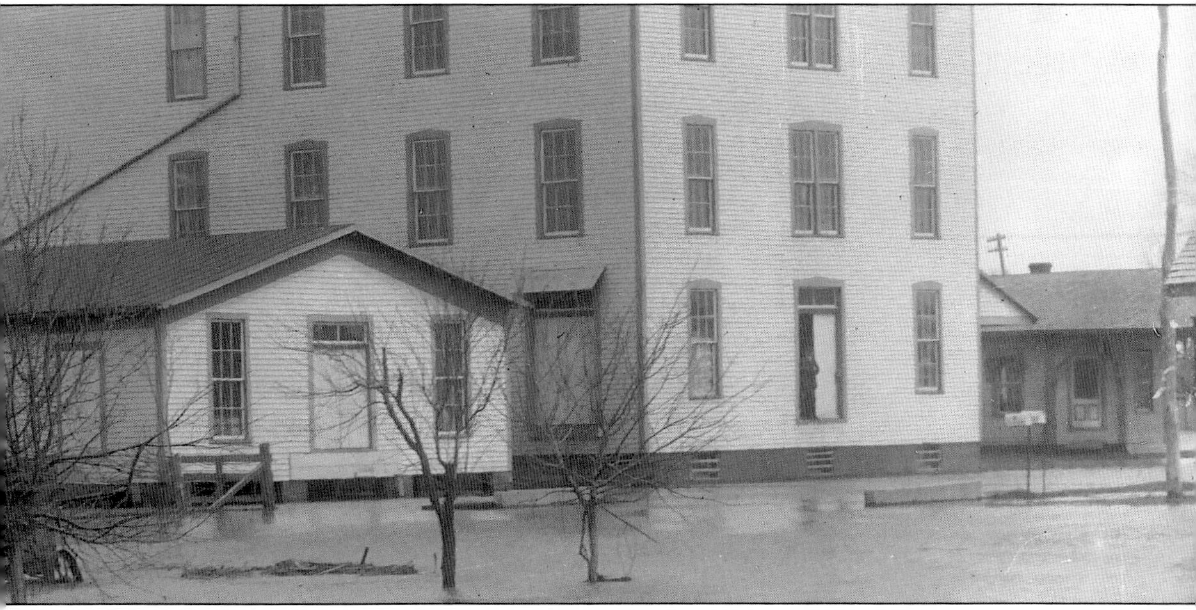

in the mill's west-facing lower door. (Photographer: William Frederick Lichtenberger.)

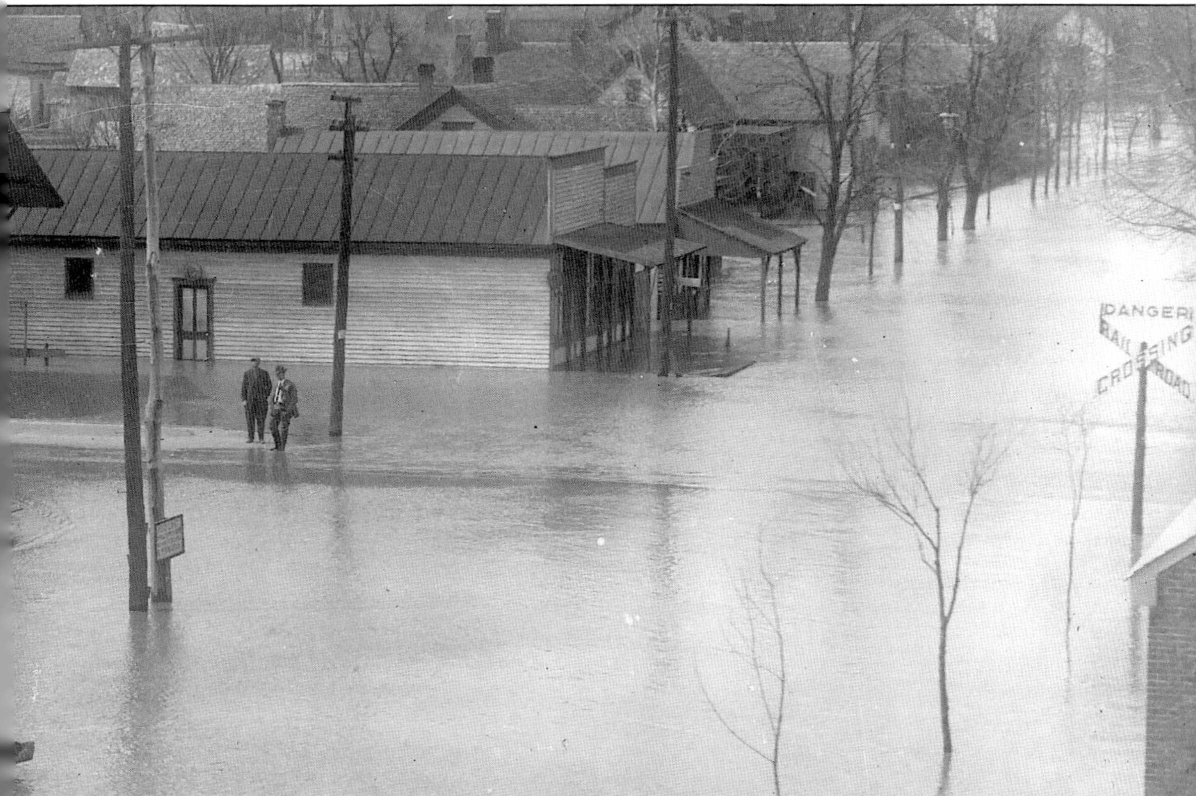

the upper stories of the Corbin Milling Company offices. (Photographer: William Frederick Lichtenberger.)

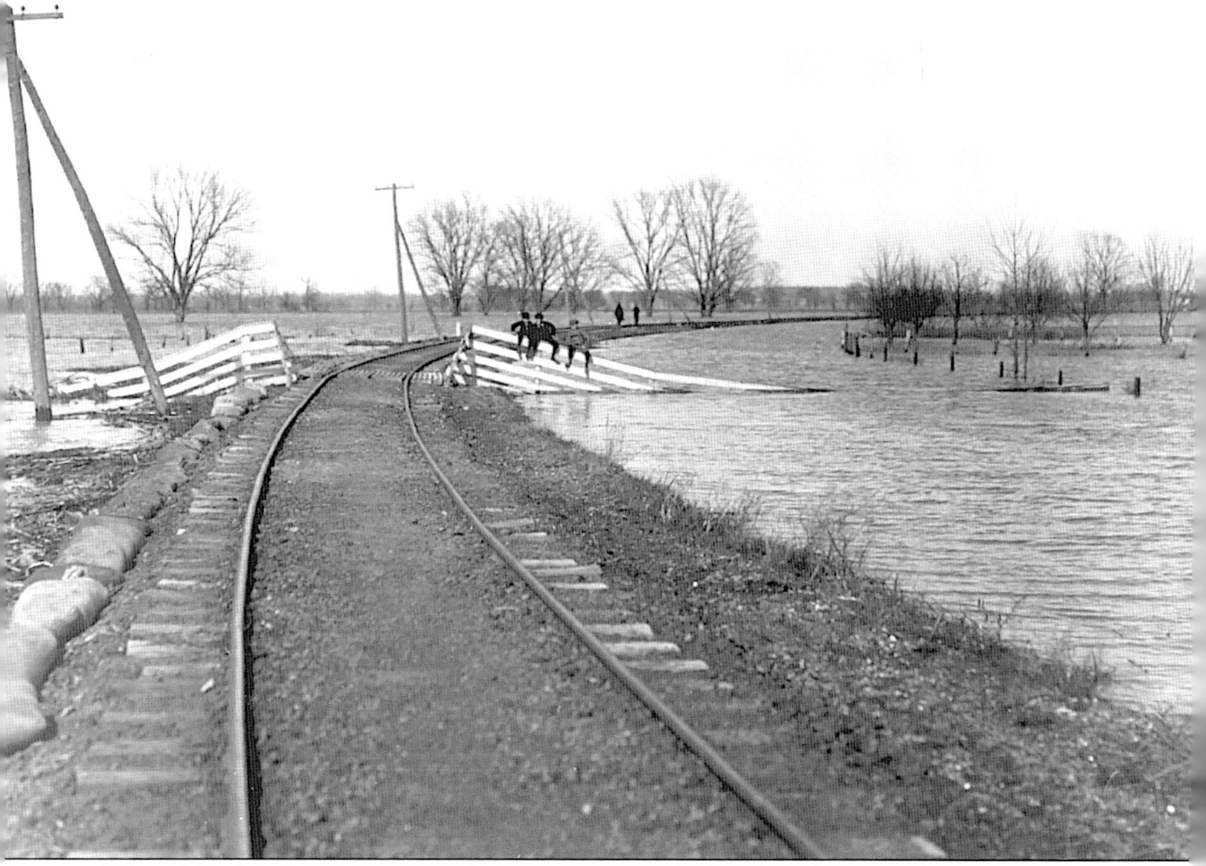

This 1904 photograph shows high water along the railroad tracks somewhere outside of the New Harmony town limits. Unidentified children pose on the fence at right. (Photographer: William Frederick Lichtenberger.)

Six

Centennial

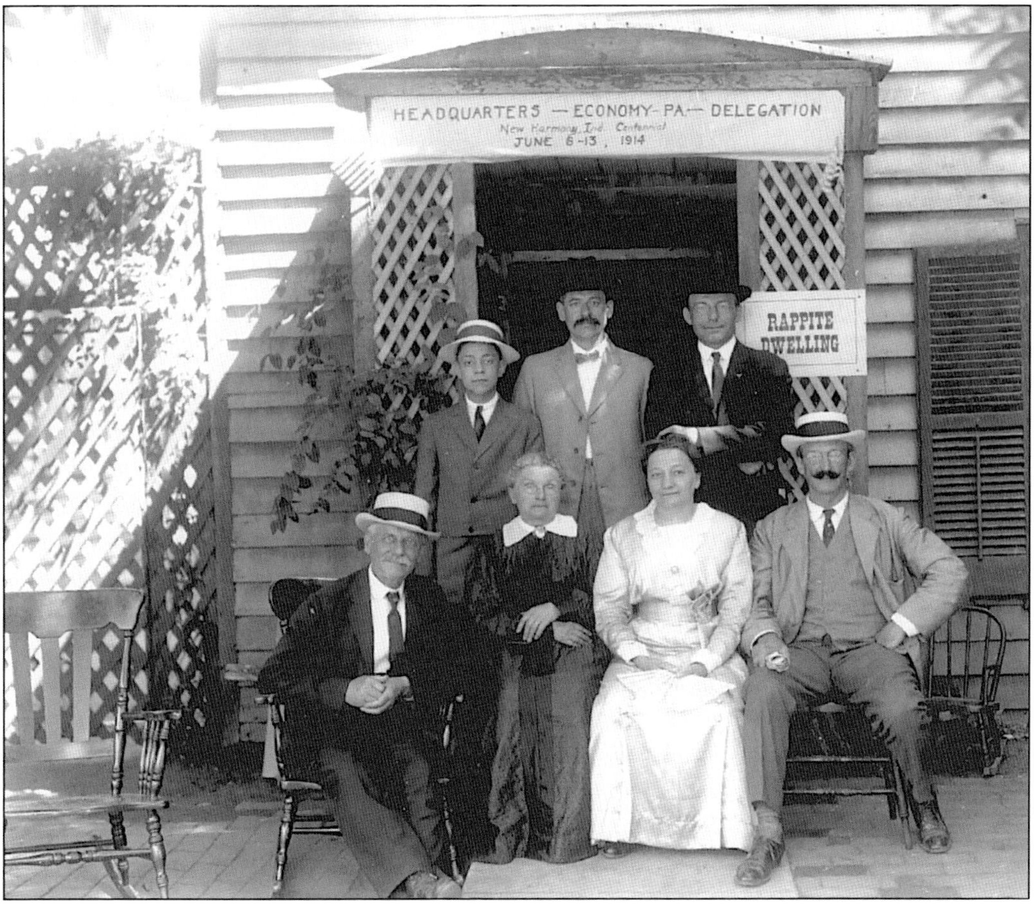

This group of unidentified individuals represents Old Economy, the final community of the Harmony Society, located in Ambridge, Pennsylvania. They are assembled outside an unknown "Rappite"—Harmonist—building in New Harmony, and are invited guests at the 1914 Centennial. When compared with other portraits, it seems likely that John and Susanna Duss, the last trustees of the Harmony Society, are seated in the front row, at right.

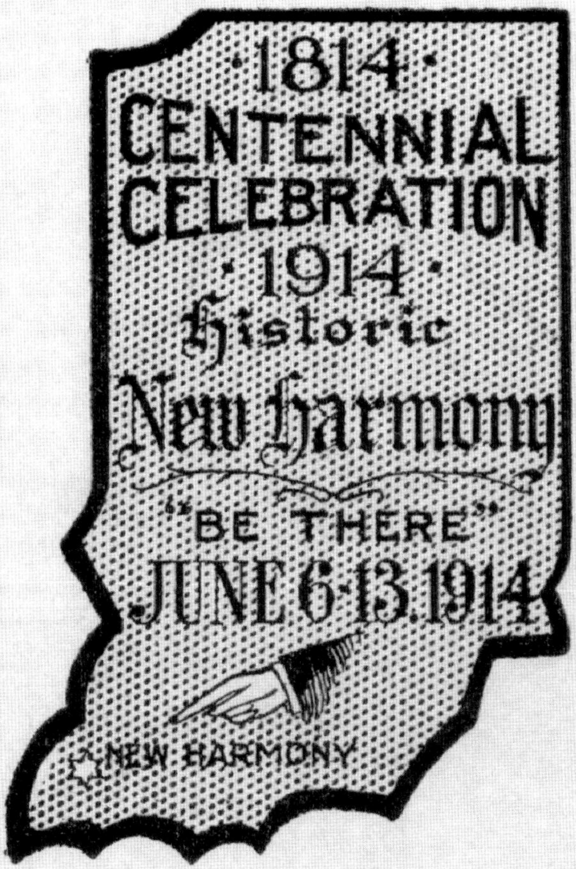

This booklet, prepared for the 1914 New Harmony Centennial celebration, was available to those who attended the week-long event and is a remarkable record of the effort that went

Program

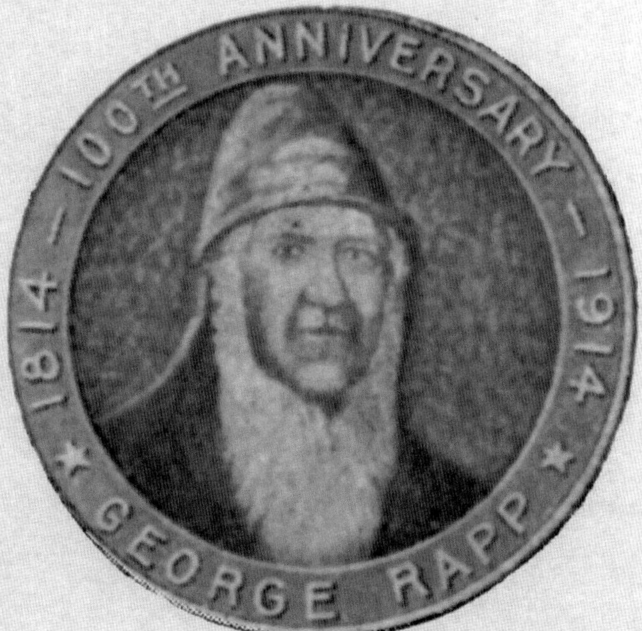

of the

Centennial Celebration

at

NEW HARMONY, IND.

into the celebration.

OFFICERS OF THE COMMISSION

HORACE P. OWEN .... President

LAURA CORBIN MONICAL .... Vice President

CLARENCE P. WOLFE .... Treasurer

GEORGE C. TAYLOR .... Secretary

EXECUTIVE COMMITTEE

Frank R. Lawless, Chairman

A. Clarence Thomas
Homer Lichtenberger
Arthur E. Fretageot
Clarence P. Wolfe
George C. Taylor

JOEL W. HIATT
Chairman of Reception Committee

ROBERT R. RIBEYRE
Chairman of Finance Committee

J. L. CRABB
Chairman of Transportation Committee

COURTLAND G. CORBIN
Chairman of Publicity Committee

THOMAS MUMFORD
Chairman of Invitation Committee

MOLLIE WILEY FORD
Chairman of Accommodation Committee

FRED LICHTENBERGER
Chairman of Decoration Committee

This listing (and those on pages 105-116) are from a program for the centennial celebration held in 1914.

TO THE PUBLIC

This, the year **1914**, is the One Hundredth Anniversary of the founding of the town of New Harmony, Indiana, by the Harmonists or Rappites under the leadership of George Rapp.

Cognizance was taken of the approaching event by the Board of Trustees of the town early in **1913** in the creation of a Centennial Commission, consisting of the members of the Board of Trustees, the Trustees of the Working Men's Institute, and ten citizens of the town to be appointed by the President of the Board of Trustees, five of whom must be women recommended by the Woman's Library Club.

The purpose of this Commission was to devise and execute plans for a Centennial Celebration to be held in the town some time during the year **1914**, commemorating the event.

This Commission through its officers and committees decided early in **1913** to hold the celebration for a period of eight days and selected June **6**th to **13**th, **1914** as the date.

It was also decided by the commission that the celebration should be one of a very high-class nature, such as would reflect credit upon the community, the state and nation.

We have here a community with a reason for a Centennial Celebration and one with ample material for making the event of state wide and even national and international interest.

No town or city in the United States boasts a history of greater romantic or sociological interest.

A pride in the preservation of historical objects and records has been developed here and the community is rich in historical associations.

The Commission has tried to eliminate all objectionable features and to secure material for the celebration that will please, educate and be uplifting.

After much thought and deliberation on the part of every one connected with the coming celebration, we herein present the program for the eight days of the celebration, and trust it may meet the approval of the public.

We trust that the celebration will not only be a fitting end to New Harmony's century, but also a proper introduction to the still greater century which is to follow.

In conclusion, the Centennial Commission, on behalf of the citizens of New Harmony, extends a most cordial invitation to all to lay aside their duties and be with us during the coming celebration.

The Centennial Commission

ANNOUNCEMENTS

Group Eight of the Indiana Banker's Association will meet here on Wednesday, June **10, 1914.**

The Republican Editorial Association of Indiana will be here Saturday, June **13, 1914.**

The District Meeting of the Knights of Pythias of the Twentieth District will be held here on Fraternal Day, June **11, 1914.**

The Grand Sire and the Grand Lodge Officers, accompanied by the entire Field Staff and two cantons of the Patriarch Militant of the Independent Order of Odd Fellows will be here on Fraternal Day.

The Grand Lodge Officers of the Knights of Pythias of Indiana and two companies of the Uniform Rank will be here on Fraternal Day.

The famous Goodman Fourth Infantry Band of Decatur, Ill. under the leadership of Prof. Robert Walters will furnish music during the entire eight days.

In connection with the regular service, the Illinois Central Railroad will run a Special Train daily, leaving Evansville at **9:00** A. M., returning will leave New Harmony at **10:30** P. M., making all stops, New Harmony to Evansville.

Ample accommodation will be provided for the comfort and convenience of visitors.

Program for

"RAPP DAY"

At the Centennial Celebration

SATURDAY, JUNE 6, 1914

MARTIN T. GOLDEN, Chairman

3:00 A. M.—The Rappite Morning Call.

4:00 A. M.—Booming of Cannon, Ringing of Bells and Blowing of Whistles.

10:00 A. M.—Parade.

AT THE PLAZA

10:30 A. M.—Introductory remarks—Mrs. Laura Corbin Monical, Vice President of Commission.

10:45 A. M.—Address of Welcome—Geo. C. Taylor, Secretary of Commission.

11:00 A. M.—Response—Col. Geo. B. Lockwood, of Muncie, Indiana.

AT THE PLAZA

1:30 P. M.—Concert by the Goodman Band and German Allied Societies.

2:00 P. M.—Address—The German Americans—Benjamin Bosse, Mayor of Evansville, Indiana.

2:30 P. M.—Address—George Rapp and Associates—John S. Duss, of New Smyrna, Fla.

AT THE PLAZA

7:30 P. M.—Concert by the Goodman Band.

8:00 P. M.—Concert by the German Allied Societies, of Evansville, Ind.

Program for

"DEVOTIONAL DAY"

At the Centennial Celebration

SUNDAY, JUNE 7, 1914

A. E. FRETAGEOT, Chairman

9:30 A. M.—Ringing of Church Bells.

10:30 A. M.—Services in the various Churches.

AT THE PLAZA

2:00 P. M.—Sacred Music by the Goodman Band.

Invocation—Rev. G. B. Walls, of the Johnson M. E. Church.

Vocal Solo—C. Edwyn Jordon, of New York City.

Address—Dr. Ferdinand C. Iglehart, of New York City.

Music.

Benediction—Rev. L. E. Birchby, of St. Stephens Episcopal Church.

AT THE PLAZA

8:00 P. M.—Sacred Concert.

Program for

"OWEN DAY"

At the Centennial Celebration

MONDAY, JUNE 8, 1914

CLARENCE P. WOLFE, Chairman

AT THE PLAZA

9:30 A. M.—Concert by the Goodman Band.

AT THE AUDITORIUM

10:30 A. M.—Reception to Honorable William Howard Taft.

AT THE PLAZA

1:30 P. M.—Concert by the Goodman Band.

2:30 P. M.—Address—Hon. William Howard Taft.

AT THE PLAZA

8:00 P. M.—Concert—Riheldaffer—Konecny Concert Company.

Program for

"WOMAN'S DAY"

At the Centennial Celebration

TUESDAY, JUNE 9, 1914

MISS M. E. FAUNTLEROY, Chairman

AT THE PLAZA

9:00 A. M.—Concert by the Goodman Band.

9:00 A. M.—Auto ride, visiting places of interest.

AT THE AUDITORIUM

10:00 A. M.—Greeting—Miss M. E. Fauntleroy, Chairman.

10:10 A. M.—Vocal Solo—Auld Lang Syne.

10:20 A. M.—A Message from the Woman's Library Club —Mrs. Mary Donald, President of the Woman's Library Club.

10:30 A. M.—Roll Call—Responses—Quotations from our old people.

10:40 A. M.—"The Pioneer Mother"—Charity Dye.

10:50 A. M.—"The Rappite Women"—John S. Duss.

11:00 A. M.—"Constance Owen Fauntleroy"—Ellinor Runcie.

11:10 A. M.—"The Minerva Club"—Mrs. Rachel Fauntleroy, a charter member of the club.

11:30 A. M.—"Club Life"—Virginia Twigg.

11:40 A. M.—"State and National Club Federation"— Mrs. Demarchus Brown.

11:50 A. M.—Vocal Solo—Eugene Eagleson.

"WOMAN'S DAY"—Continued

AT THE AUDITORIUM

2:00 P. M.—Music—Piano Solo—Mrs. Helen Corbin Heinl.

2:10 P. M.—"Origin of the Tri Kappa Sorority"—Mrs. C. A. Greathouse.

2:20 P. M.—"Indiana Homes"—Mrs. Albion Fellows Bacon.

2:30 P. M.—"Local and State D. A. R."—Mrs. Sarah Dinwiddie, Vice-President General N. S. D. A. R.

2:40 P. M.—"National D. A. R."—Mrs. James M. Fowler, Ex-Vice President General N. S. D. A. R.

2:50 P. M.—"Address"—Miss Fola LaFollette.

RECEPTIONS

4:00 P. M.—Public Reception at the Library Building.

4:30 P. M.—Tri Kappa Reception at the home of Mrs. Robert Ribeyre.

4:30 P. M.—Reception at the "Old Fauntleroy Home", the birthplace of the first Woman's Club in America.

AT THE PLAZA

7:30 P. M.—Concert by the Goodman Band.

8:00 P. M.—Address—Hon. Charles Warren Fairbanks.

AT THE ASSEMBLY ROOM

9:00 P. M.—Old Fashioned Ball under the auspices of the New Harmony Chapter of the D. A. R.

Program for

"INDIANA DAY"

At the Centennial Celebration

WEDNESDAY, JUNE 10, 1914

GEO. C. TAYLOR, CHAIRMAN

10:00 A. M.—Concert by the Goodman Band on the Plaza.

10:00 A. M.—Reception of visitors at the Auditorium.

11:00 A. M.—Auto Ride over the city, visiting places of historical interest.

AT THE PLAZA

1:30 P. M.—Concert by the Goodman Band.

2:00 P. M.—Address—Hon. Samuel M. Ralston, Governor of Indiana.

3:30 P. M.—Address—Hon. John W. Kern, Junior Senator from Indiana.

AT THE PLAZA

7:30 P. M.—Concert by the Goodman Band.

8:00 P. M.—Address—Hon. Benjamin F. Shively, Senior Senator from Indiana.

Group Eight of the Indiana Banker's Association will meet here on this day.

Program for

"FRATERNAL DAY"

At the Centennial Celebration

THURSDAY, JUNE 11, 1914

HENRY BROWN, Chairman

9:30 A. M.—Reception to visitors at the various lodge rooms.

10:30 A. M.—Fraternal Parade.

AT THE PLAZA

1:30 P. M.—Band Concert and Drill.

1. By the Uniform Rank of the Knights of Pythias.
2. By the Patriarch Militant of the I. O. O. F.

2:00 P. M.—Address—By a representative of the Modern Woodmen of America.

2:30 P. M.—Address—W. N. Nauer, Grand Master, representing the I. O. O. F.

3:00 P. M.—Address—John M. Lewis, Grand Chancellor, representing the Knights of Pythias.

3:30 P. M.—Address—C. A. Keller, Grand Sire of the I. O. O. F.

AT THE PLAZA

7:30 P. M.—Band Concert.

8:00 P. M.—Address—Hon. James E. Watson, of Rushville, Ind.

Note:—The District Meeting of the Knights of Pythias will be held here on the afternoon of this day.

Program for

"POSEY COUNTY DAY"

At the Centennial Celebration

FRIDAY, JUNE 12, 1914

CAPT. ALFRED RIBEYRE, Chairman

10:30 A. M.—AUTO FLORAL PARADE AND BAND TOURNAMENT.

First Price for best decorated auto . . $50.00
Second Prize for best decorated auto . 25.00
Third Prize for best decorated auto . . 15.00
Fourth Prize for best decorated auto . 10.00
Competition open to the world.
Entrance Free.

1:30 P. M.—BAND TOURNAMENT. Ribeyre Prize.

First Price . . . . $50.00 in Gold.
Second Prize . . . . 25.00 in Gold.
Third Prize . . . . 15.00 in Gold.
Fourth Prize . . . . 10.00 in Gold.

The prizes in the Band Tournament are SPECIAL PRIZES given by Capt. Alfred Ribeyre to bands of Posey County.

Not less than four bands to compete for the above prizes.

"POSEY COUNTY DAY"—Continued

HORSE SHOW PROGRAM

FROM 2:00 P. M. to 5:00 P. M.

2:00 P. M.	—Ring 1-Best Draft Stallion.....	$15.00	$10.00
2:20 P. M.	—Ring 2-Best Coach Stallion....	15.00	10.00
2:40 P. M.	—Ring 3-Best General Purpose Stallion..............	15.00	10.00
3:00 P. M.	—Ring 4-Best Light Harness Stal.	15.00	10.00
3:20 P. M.	—Ring 5-Best Stallion owned in Posey County............	15.00	10.00
3:40 P. M.	—Ring 6-Best Draft Team......	15.00	10.00
4:00 P. M.	—Ring 7-Best Match Team.....	15.00	10.00
4:20 P. M.	—Ring 8-Best Lady Driver.....	15.00	10.00
4:40 P. M.	—Ring 9-Best Speed Buggy mare or gelding (Trot).........	15.00	10.00
5:00 P. M.	—Ring 10-Best Speed Buggy mare or gelding (Pace)........	15.00	10.00

No entrance Fee. In rings without competition, second premium only will be paid. Competition open to the world except in Ring Five (5) which is confined to horses owned in Posey County.

7:30 P. M.—Band Concert at the Plaza by the Goodman and Visiting Bands.

8:00 P. M.—Awarding Prizes to the winners in the Auto Floral Parade.

8:15 P. M.—Awarding Prizes to the winners in the Band Tournament.

8:30 P. M.—Address—"Posey County"—Major G. V. Menzies of Mt. Vernon, Ind.

Note:—All autos and bands for the parade will assemble at Murphy Park at 10:00 A. M. and will be assigned their places in the parade.

"CHILDREN'S DAY"

At the Centennial Celebration

SATURDAY, JUNE 13, 1914

PROF. W. V. MANGRUM, Chairman

10:00 A. M.—Children will assemble at the School Building and form in procession and march to Murphy Park.

AT MURPHY PARK

10:30 A. M.—Children Play Festival.

2:00 P. M.—At Murphy Park.

1. Folk Dances.
2. May Pole Dance.

AT THE PLAZA

"AT EARLY CANDLE LIGHT"—Historical Pageant of New Harmony, by the School children of New Harmony and their friends, showing the Pre-Rappite, Rappite and Owenite Periods.

Note:—Miss Charity Dye of Indianapolis is the writer of the Pageant, Mrs. Mary H. Flanner of Indianapolis is the director and Mrs. Nora C. Fretageot of New Harmony is the Historian.

This will be given as the grand finale number of the Centennial.

The Republican Editorial Association of Indiana will meet here on this day.

A FEW FACTS ABOUT NEW HARMONY

Section Thirty-six, Township Four South, Range Fourteen West, in which is situated New Harmony was entered by George Rapp and Associates May 9, 1814.

Patent granted by James Madison, President of U. S. to George Rapp and Associates, for same section August 16, 1815.

Town founded by George Rapp and Associates in 1814.

Deeded to Robert Owen by George Rapp and Associates, numbering 501 persons, December 10, 1825.

The first Woman's Club, "The Minerva" was organized here in 1859 by Miss Constance Owen Fauntleroy.

The first kindergarten was organized here in 1826.

The first free school in America was established here in 1826.

The first co-educational school was established here in 1826.

Manual training was early recognized as an important factor in the educational system.

Prohibition by administrative government was first enforced here.

The right of woman to take part in local legislative government was first asserted here by Frances Wright.

Though these "facts" have not been historically researched and verified, the pride engendered in the community's history is noteworthy.

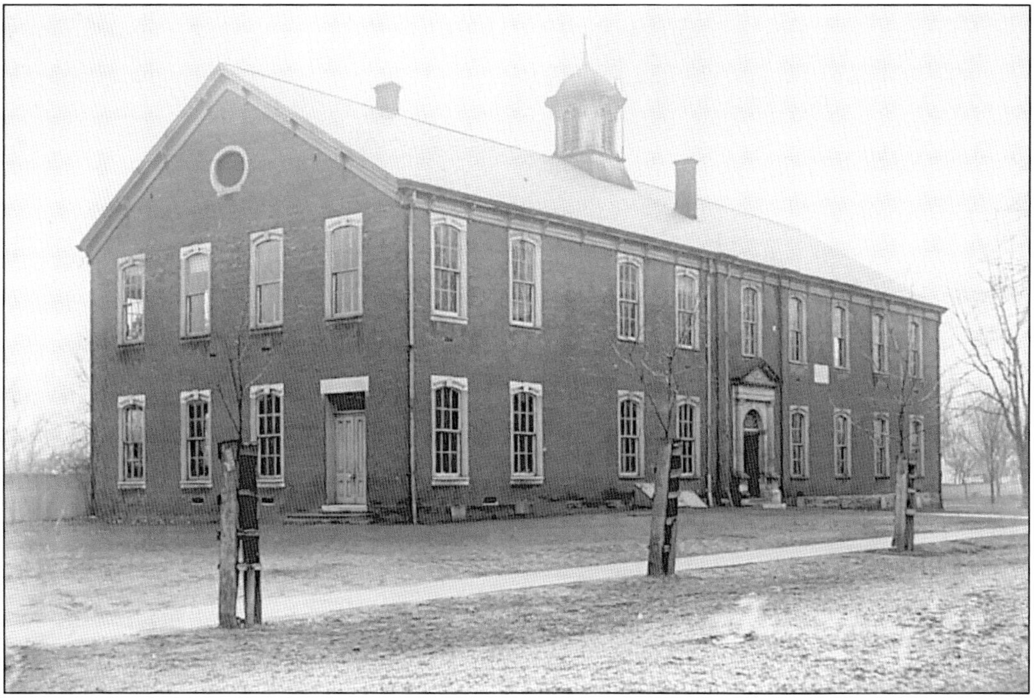

The old New Harmony School is shown from its east side in this January 13, 1907 photograph. (Photographer: Homer Fauntleroy.)

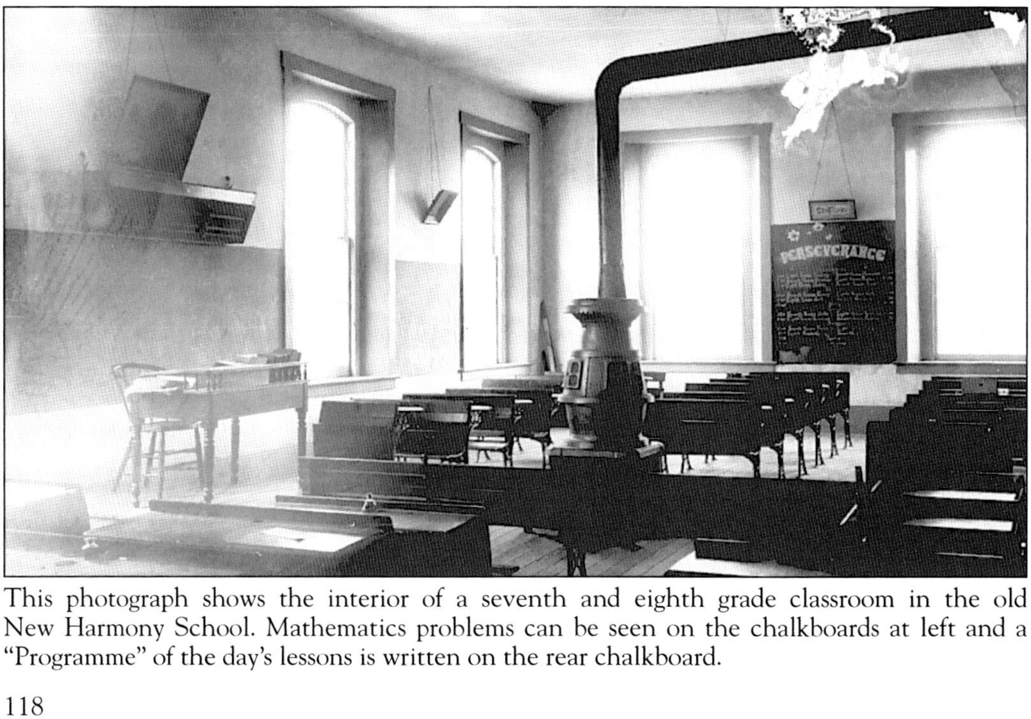

This photograph shows the interior of a seventh and eighth grade classroom in the old New Harmony School. Mathematics problems can be seen on the chalkboards at left and a "Programme" of the day's lessons is written on the rear chalkboard.

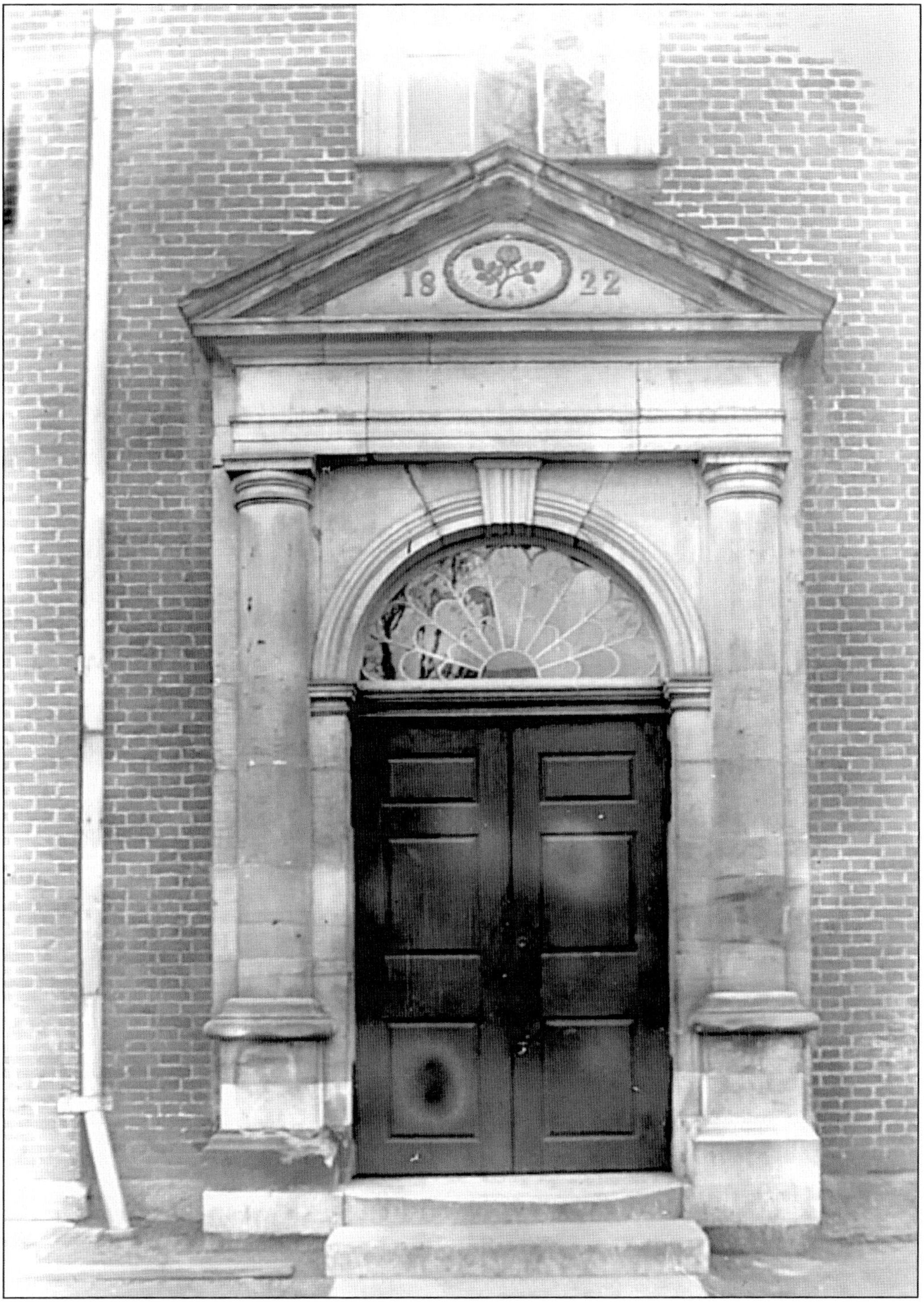

The Harmonist Church door, which was incorporated into the north elevation of the New Harmony School building, is shown in a photograph from April 5, 1903. (Photographer: Homer Fauntleroy.)

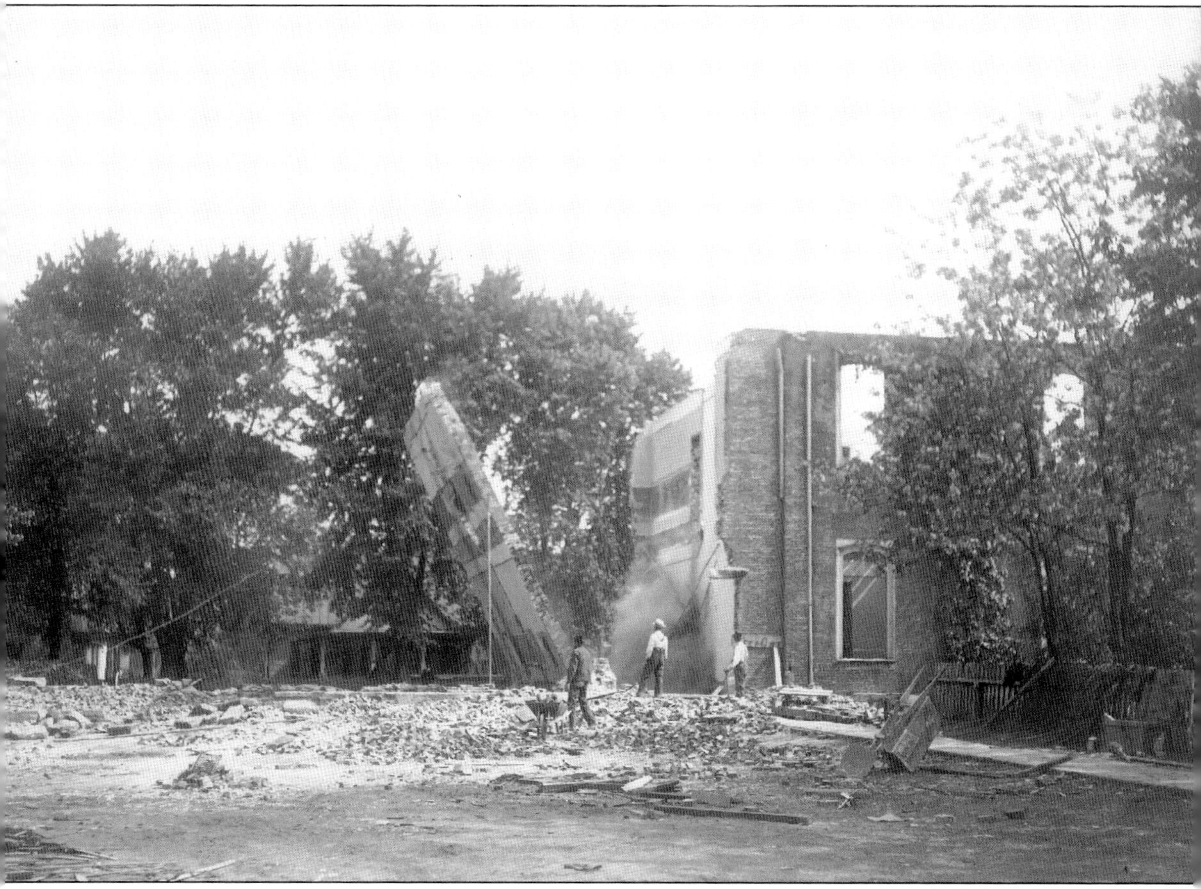

This 1913 photograph shows the demolition of the old New Harmony School building, which was undertaken to make way for the new school building. This new building was erected in time for the 1914 Centennial celebration, and incorporated the Harmonist Church door into the west side of the building. (Photographer: Homer Fauntleroy.)

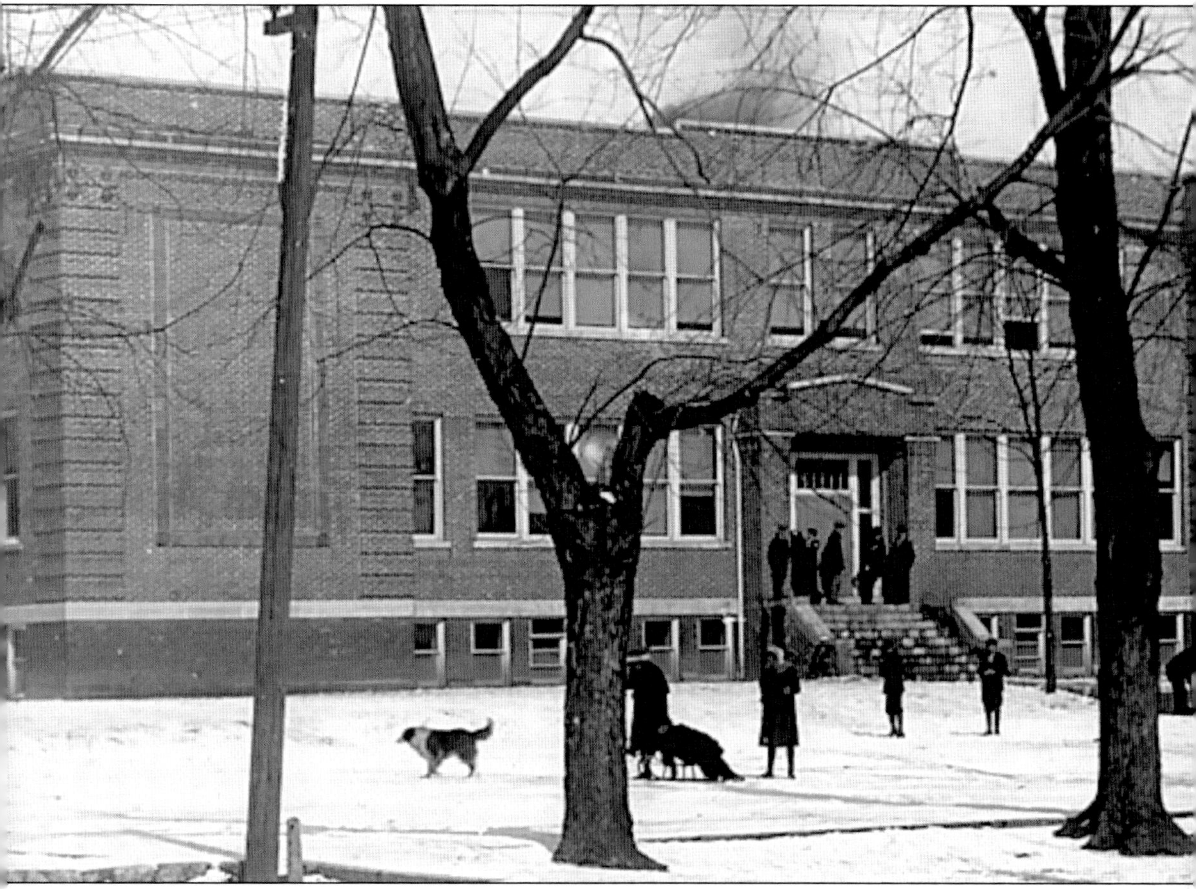

The new New Harmony school building is pictured, probably at recess time.

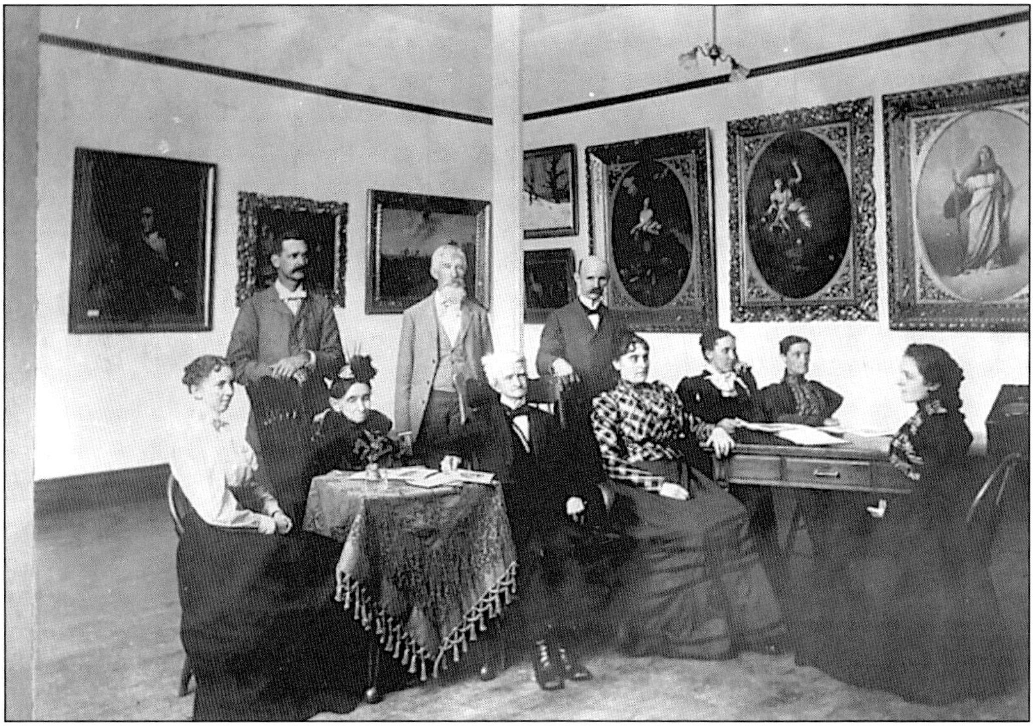

This October 1898 photograph highlights a gathering of the members of the Workingmen's Institute. Dr. and Mrs. Edward Murphy, aged 85 and 86 respectively, are seated at the table with the fringed tablecloth. Standing, from left to right, are Henry Hundson, William Ford, and Homer Lichtenberger. The ladies pictured are, from left to right, as follows: Annie B. Ford, Marcia Corbin, Jen Twigg, Mrs. William Robb, and Miss Maud Miller, librarian.

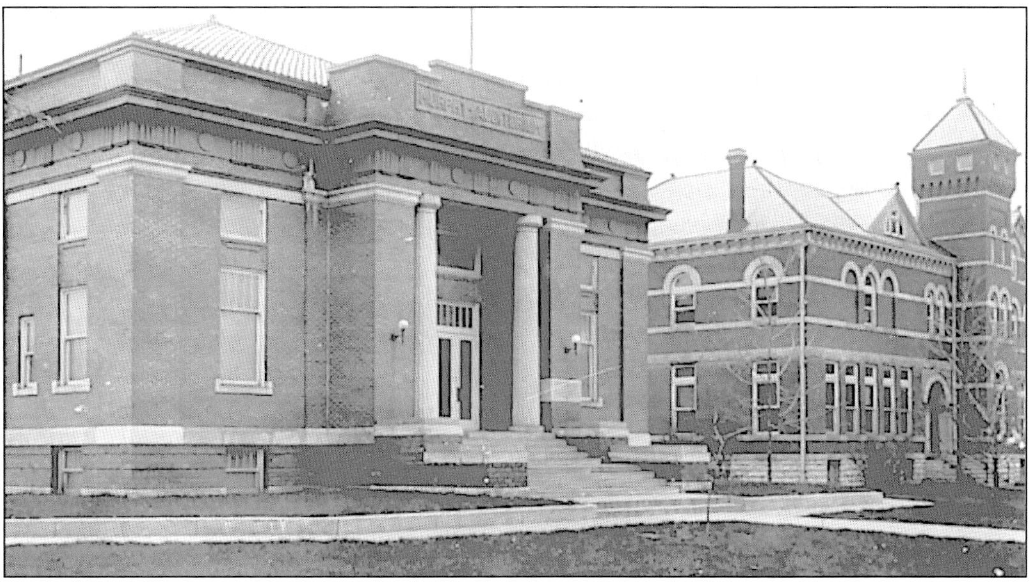

Here the Murphy Auditorium and Workingmen's Institute stand side by side. A clue to the age of this photograph can be found in the small size of the trees that are planted in front of these buildings. Murphy Auditorium was constructed in 1913 and the WMI in 1894.

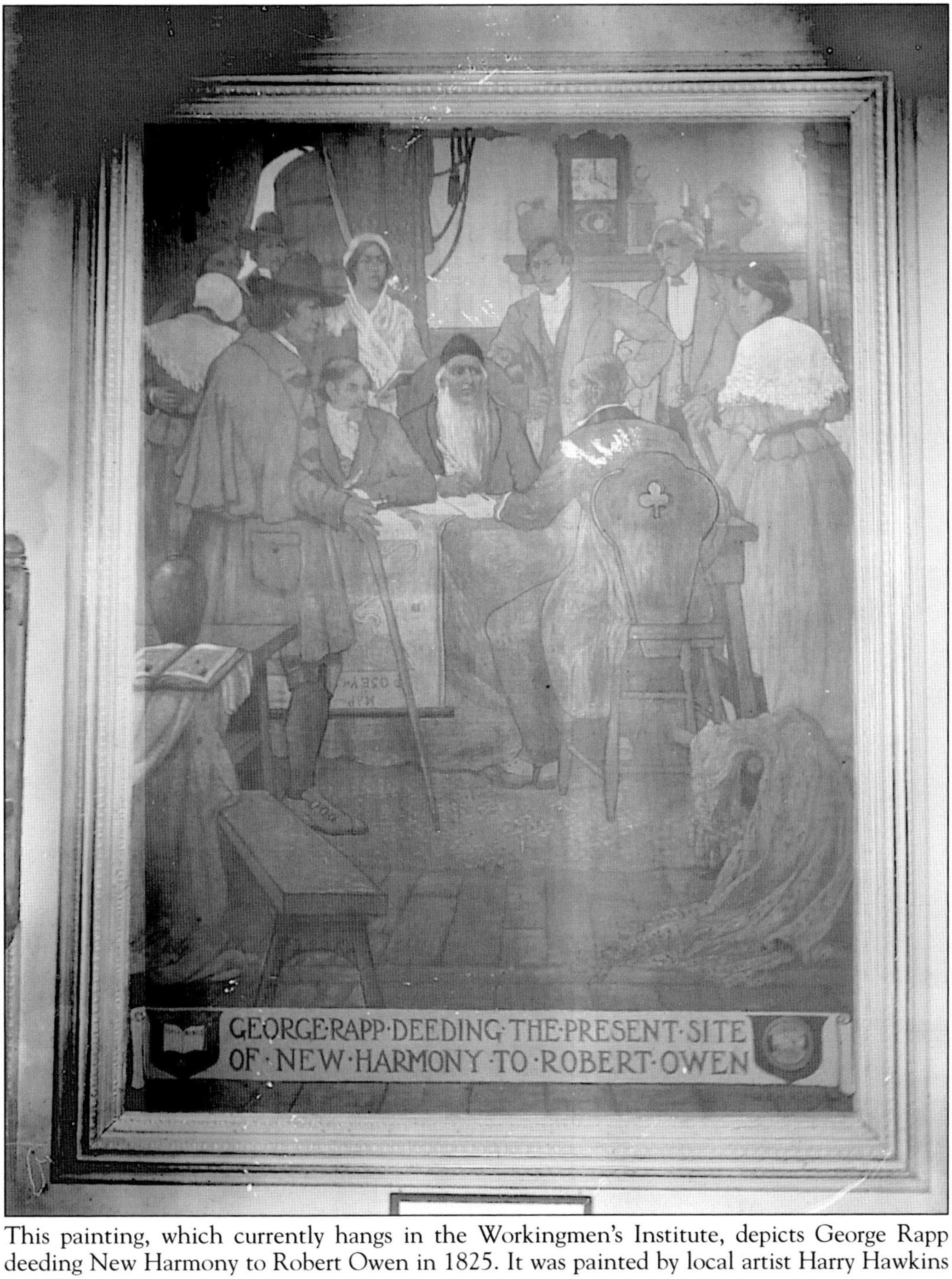

This painting, which currently hangs in the Workingmen's Institute, depicts George Rapp deeding New Harmony to Robert Owen in 1825. It was painted by local artist Harry Hawkins in 1909.

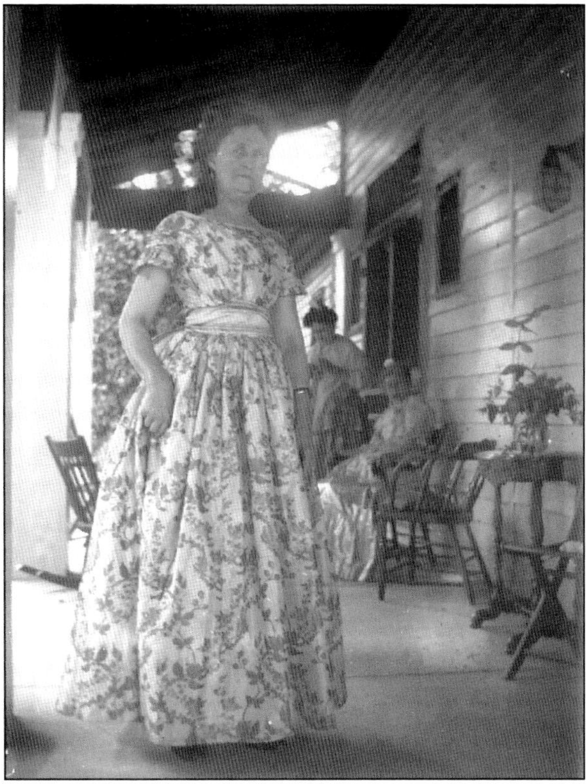

New Harmony resident Helen Chadwick poses on the porch of the Fauntleroy Home during the week of the New Harmony Centennial, June 6-13, 1914.

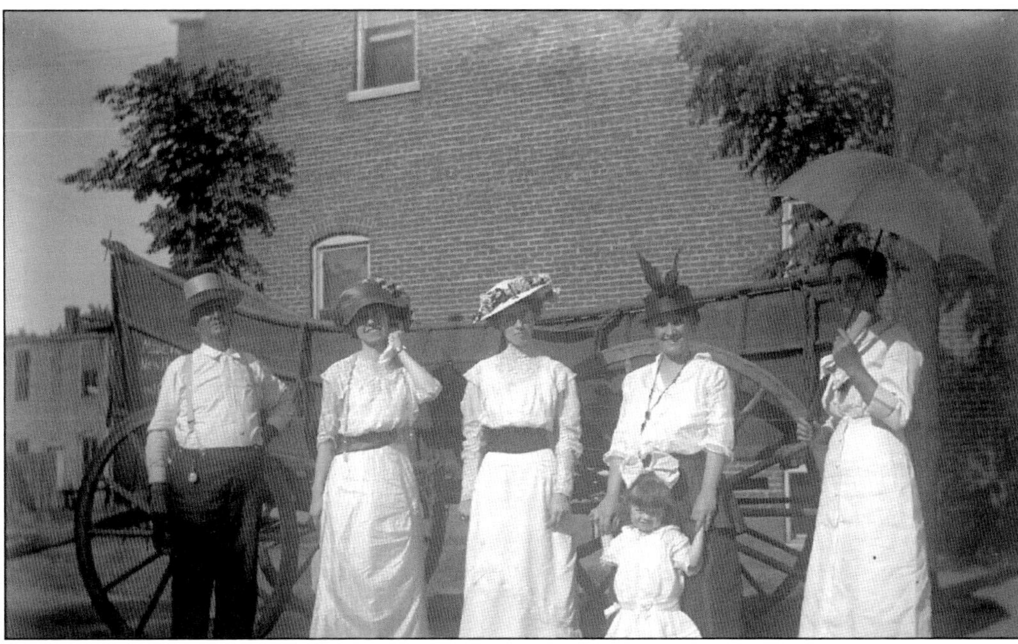

This photograph shows the Harmonist wagon in the streets of New Harmony sometime during the 1914 Centennial celebration. Pictured, from left to right, are William Wheatcroft, Miss Ziliak, Mary Donald, Emma and Elizabeth Freret, and Maud Fauntleroy. (Photographer: Homer Fauntleroy.)

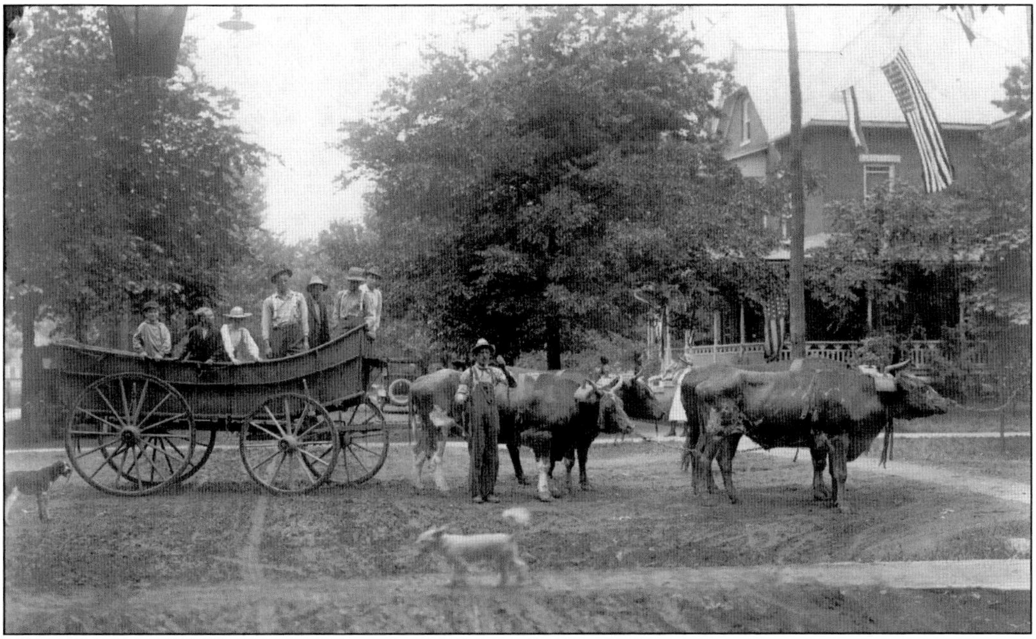

The Harmonist wagon is pictured at the intersection of Church and West Streets sometime during the 1914 Centennial. The New Harmony residents surrounding the wagon are unidentified. The Chadwick House is visible in right background. (Photo courtesy of the Mumford Family Collection.)

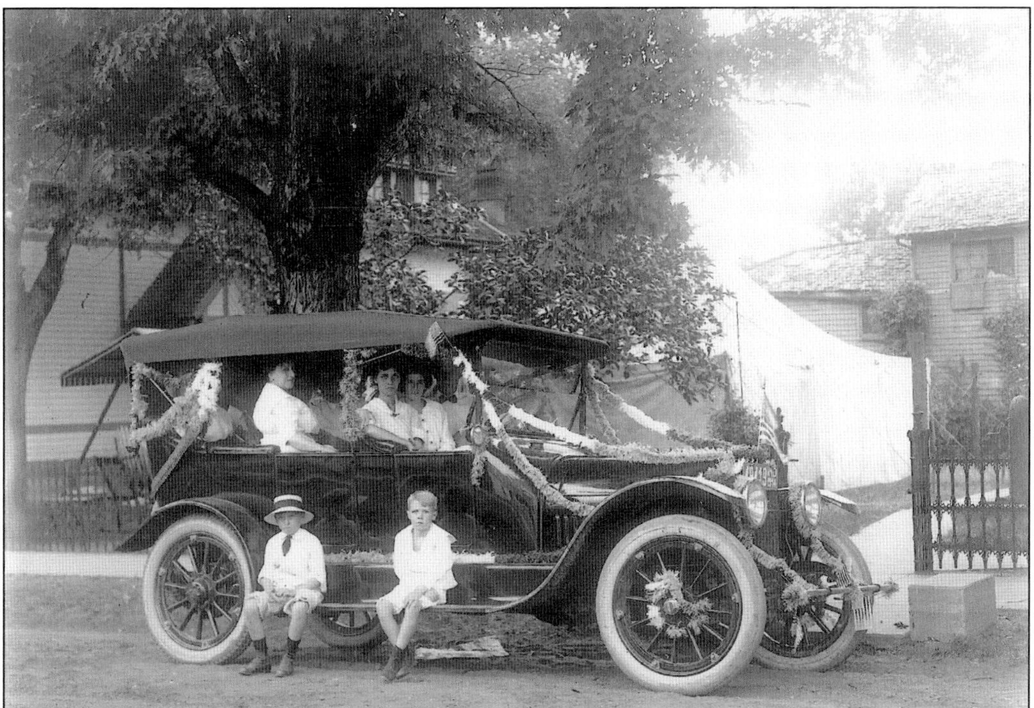

New Harmony resident Emma Freret (in the back seat) poses with family and friends in an automobile decorated in a patriotic fashion sometime during the 1914 Centennial, June 6-13.

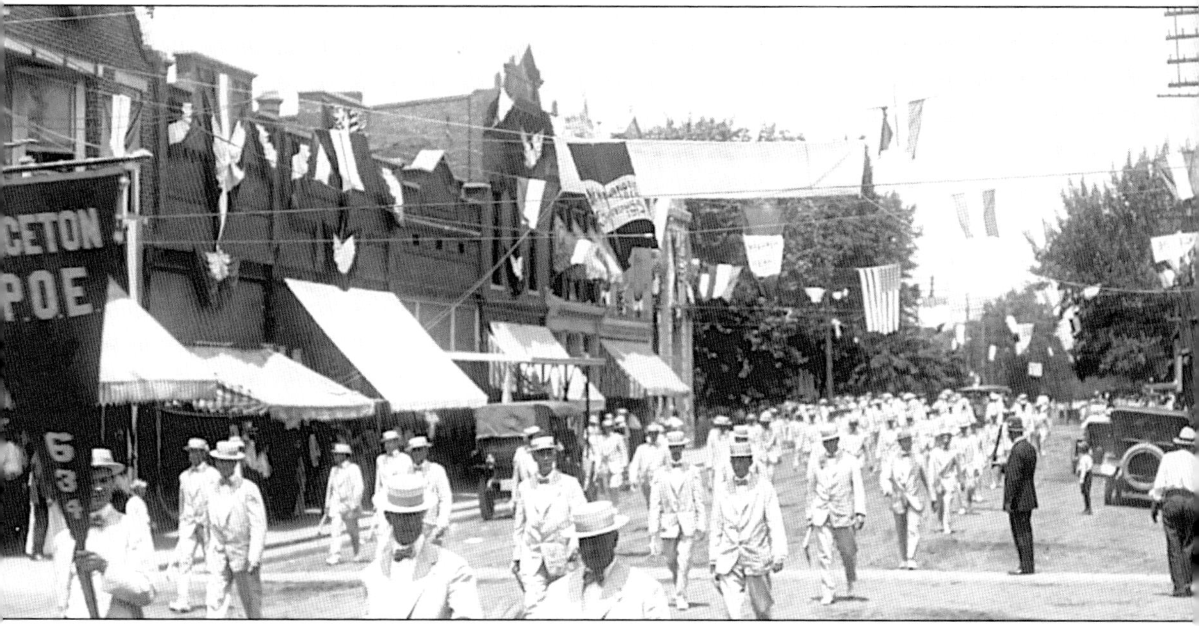

The Princeton Benevolent and Protective Order of Elks Post #634 marches south past Monitor Corner (on left side of photograph) on Main Street during New Harmony's Centennial celebration. (Photographer: William Frederick Lichtenberger.)

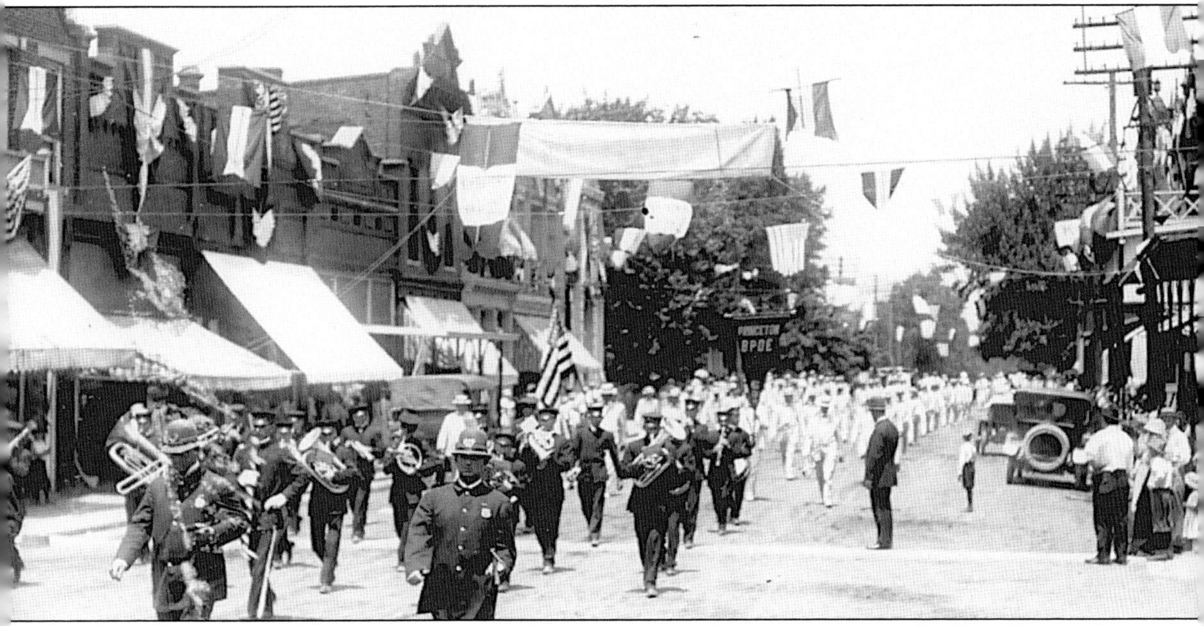

A marching band proceeds south on Main Street past Monitor Corner (and in front of the Princeton B.P.O.E. #634) during the 1914 New Harmony Centennial celebration. (Photographer: William Frederick Lichtenberger.)

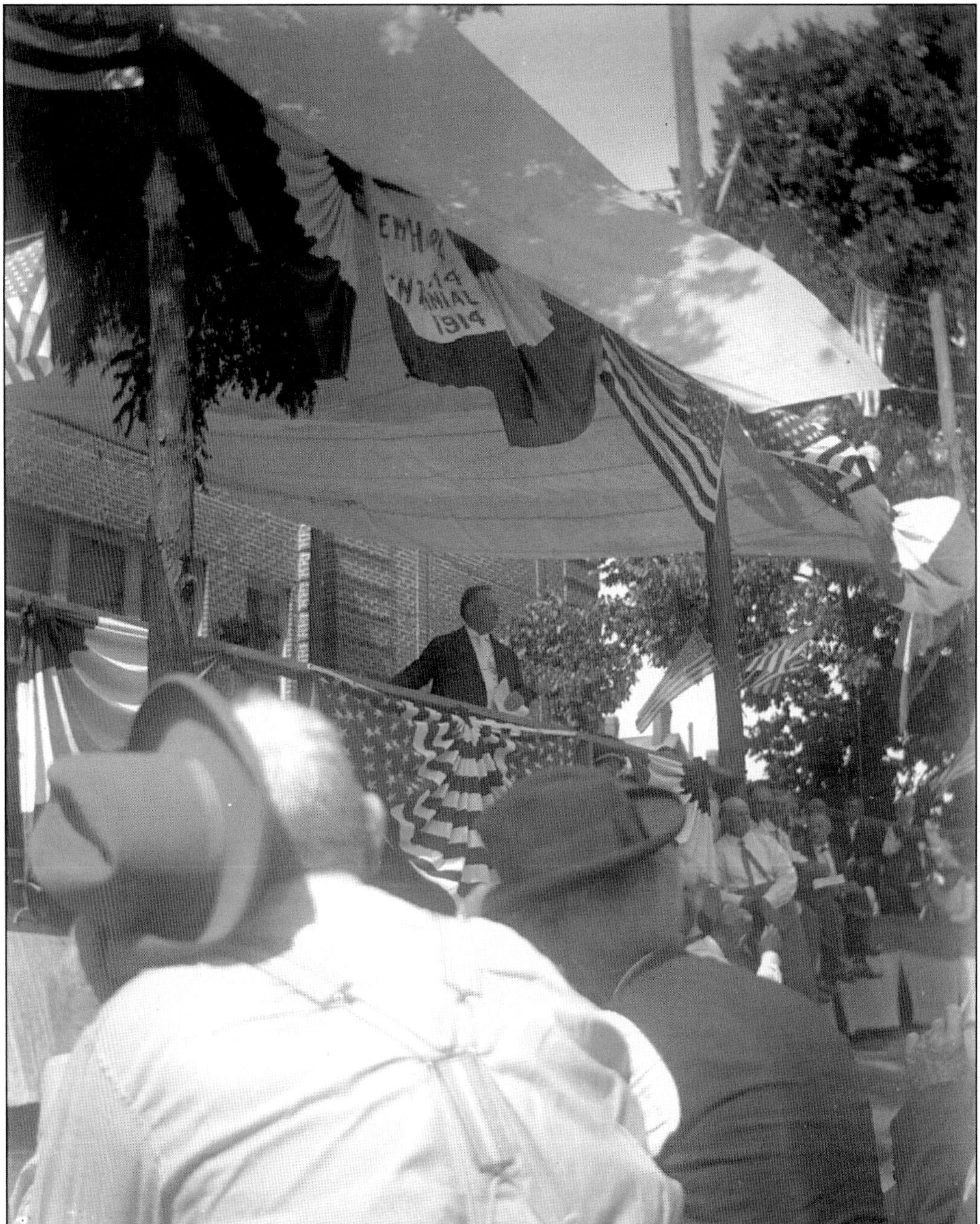

Former President William Howard Taft addresses the assembled crowd during the 1914 Centennial.